TRUE CRIME

Serial Killers

BY
THE EDITORS OF
TIME-LIFE BOOKS
Alexandria, Virginia

Serial Killers

'The Nature of the Beast

There is no such thing as a profile of serial killers—no single description that covers in all cases who they are and why they kill. The behavioral scientists who study them define them narrowly as killers who, over a period of time, slay three or more victims, compelled by some inner drive that finds release only in killing. But, the experts say, there are as many kinds of compulsions as there are motives for killing, and so there are as many kinds of serial killers as there are motives.

Nevertheless, there are some general truths about these killers. The overwhelming majority are white, male, and of at least average intelligence. And they usually fall into two categories: psychotics and psychopaths.

Psychotics—a minority among serial killers—are insane. They fail to perceive reality correctly. They hear voices or see visions, or sometimes both, and murder is a symptom of their madness. David Berkowitz, the infamous Son of Sam murderer, who terrorized New York City in the 1970s, was such a killer. Most serial killers, however, are not insane. For every psychotic, there are perhaps nine psychopaths.

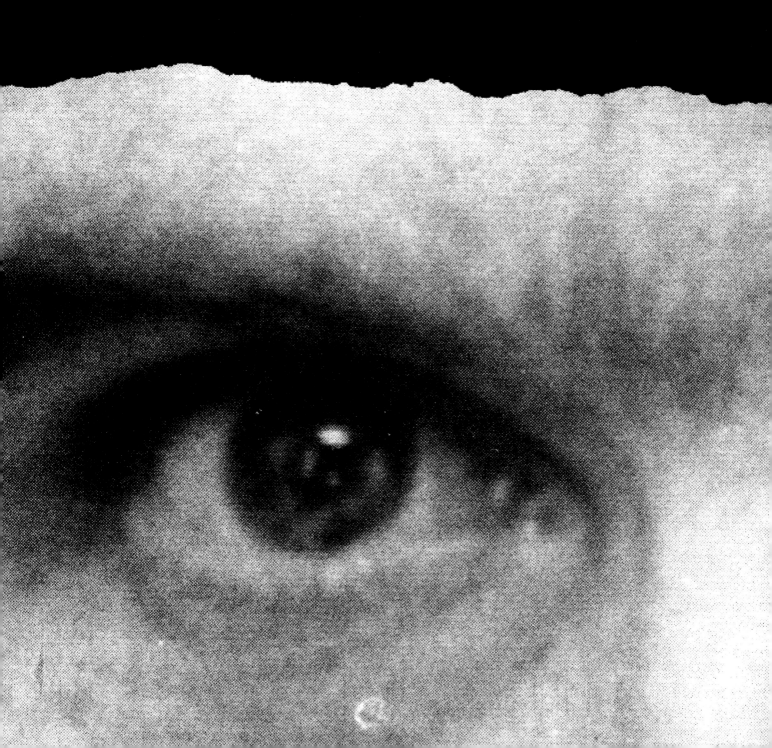

Psychopaths—also called sociopaths or antisocial personalities—do not suffer from a mental illness but from a character flaw. They are in touch with reality. They know right from wrong, and they know killing is wrong. But they don't care. Psychopaths lack a vital component of the human personality that most other people take for granted—conscience. Either they have no conscience, or their conscience is too weak to inhibit the violence they commit. Psychopaths kill without guilt and without remorse.

No one knows for certain what creates a psychopathic killer. Some theories stress genetics—an inborn predisposition to kill. Others favor an environmental explanation—factors in an individual's upbringing that make him a killer. Many experts believe the truth lies in a combination of genetics and environment.

Perhaps the psychopathic serial killer's most frightening quality is his ability to live unnoticed among his fellow humans. He seems normal. He may even be intelligent and charming. Ted Bundy, who killed countless young women, was this sort of psychopath. But beneath the surface, two traits are almost always present in psychopathic killers: sexual abnormality and a consuming need for power. Killing satisfies them sexually, and it satisfies their need for control—the ultimate control over life and death. Simply put, killing gives them pleasure. They kill, the experts say, because they want to. They kill because they like it.

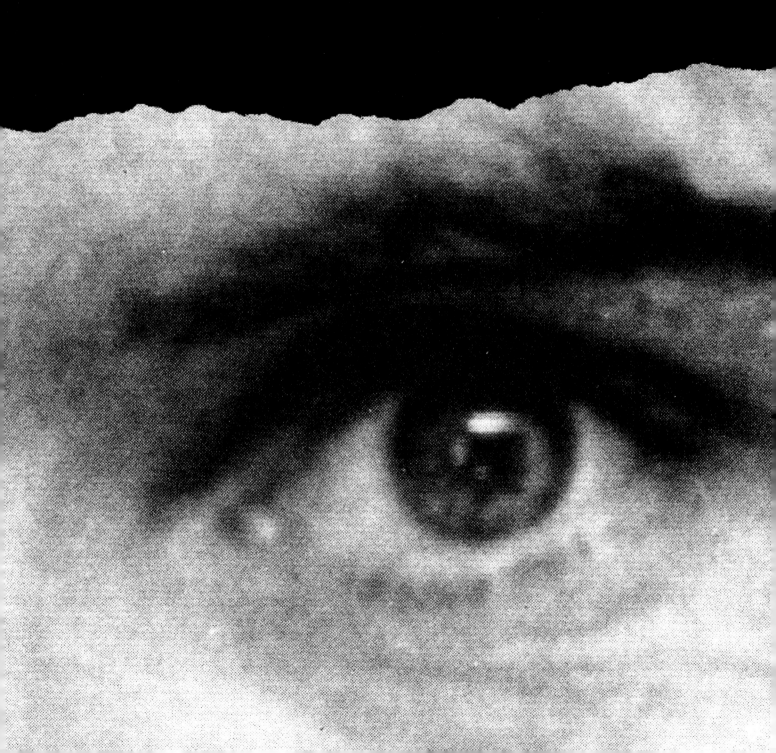

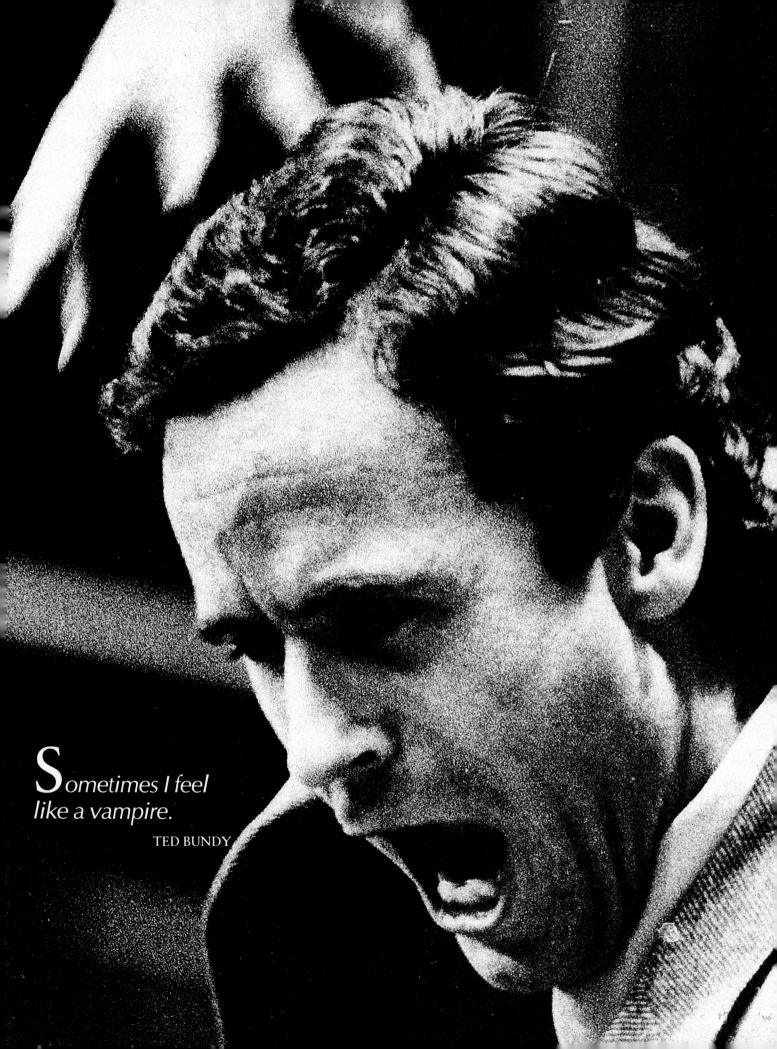

Sometimes I feel
like a vampire.
TED BUNDY

1

Lady-Killer

Carol DaRonch was beautiful, blessed with the willowy, well-bred good looks that suggest refinement, good family, careful tending. Her face was doe-eyed and delicate, framed by long, dark hair parted in the middle. At 18 she was, perhaps, still too young to know that beauty can confer a certain privilege and power: People who knew her said she was quiet, even shy—and maybe a little naive. Less than a year past high-school graduation, she was working as a telephone operator and still living with her parents.

On the Friday evening of November 8, 1974, she left the family home in Murray, Utah, and drove to a local mall to shop. She was browsing in a bookstore when she looked up from a novel to see a man close to her, staring at her. Startled, she quickly recovered and assessed his appearance. Almost any girl would have done the same; he was quite handsome, with wavy brown hair, deep-set blue eyes, chiseled nose, sensitive mouth beneath a modest mustache. He was young, probably in his twenties, and his sports jacket and slacks fit nicely on his slim, six-foot frame. He introduced himself as a policeman and asked DaRonch where she'd parked her car. She told him, and he nodded as though satisfied. He said that someone had been spotted trying to break into it with a coat hanger. "Would you mind coming with me," he asked, "so we can check to see if anything has been stolen?"

The story was not, of course, very plausible. How could anyone have matched one particular mall patron to a car out in the parking lot? But Carol DaRonch, a well-brought-up young lady, respected authority. And this particular policeman was so polite and self-assured. She followed him out of the mall.

He kept up a steady flow of conversation. There was nothing to worry about, he told her. The would-be thief was already in custody. DaRonch would have to identify him. (Identify him? She'd been in the mall. She wouldn't have seen him.) They reached the car, which looked all right to Carol. She unlocked the door and checked inside. "It's all here," she said. "There's nothing missing." The man told

her to open the passenger door so he could check for himself. (Why? How would he know if anything was missing? Something was wrong here.)

DaRonch asked to see some identification, but the man waved off the request with a chuckle, leaving her feeling a little foolish. He was talking faster now. Insisting that they'd have to check in with his partner, he steered her back toward the mall. "They must have gone back to our substation," he said. "We'll meet them there and identify him." DaRonch objected; she couldn't possibly identify a thief she'd never seen. Once again, she asked to see some ID. He took out his wallet and flashed a small gold badge. "Officer Roseland," he said. "Murray Police Department."

Officer Roseland took her back through the mall and out another exit, supposedly steering her toward a police substation on the premises. He stopped at a door marked only "139." It was locked. Scarcely missing a beat, Roseland said DaRonch should go with him to police headquarters to file a complaint. (Complaint about what?) Increasingly uneasy, she nevertheless let him lead her to his car, a battered, light-colored Volkswagen bug. Opening the door, he asked her to get in. She did. And as soon as the door slammed shut, she knew she'd made a desperate mistake.

The VW shot out of the parking lot, heading in the opposite direction from the police station. Officer Roseland was breathing hard now, almost panting, and she caught a strong scent of alcohol on his breath. She considered jumping out, but already the car was going too fast. The driver scared her, but so did the speed. The car screeched to a stop in front of a grade school, hitting the curb so hard that it bounced up onto the sidewalk. Roseland turned in his seat. He seemed actually, physically, changed. His eyes were wild, his face congested with rage. In that instant, Carol DaRonch knew with cold certainty that she was going to have to fight or die.

He lunged at her, holding a set of handcuffs. She fell back and clawed at the door handle, loosening the catch, but somehow he managed to clamp one of the cuffs onto her right wrist. She fought with all her strength, ripping a fingernail as she tore at his face. The little car rocked with the struggle. Screaming, DaRonch twisted and kicked as the other cuff slapped against her wrist. But mercifully, in the violence of the fight, it failed to catch. Her attacker's handsome face was now ugly and twisted with fury. He snatched up a small gun and held it to her head. "If you don't stop screaming," he growled, "I'll blow your brains out."

And then, another seeming act of God: The passenger door popped open. DaRonch tumbled out onto the wet ground, scrabbling for freedom. But he was still there. He'd fallen out with her, dropping the gun in his effort to hang onto her. Now he grabbed back inside the car for a tire iron. She saw him raise the heavy bar high over his head, and she knew that it could very well be the last thing she'd ever see. She raised her arms, bracing for the blow, and somehow

managed to catch and deflect it as the bar came crashing down. Aiming a desperate kick at the man's crotch, she broke free and lurched into the street.

Wilbur and Mary Walsh were driving cautiously along the rain-slick road when their headlights caught a young woman stumbling toward them. Her hair and clothes were wild; she was wearing only one shoe. Slamming on his brakes, Walsh skidded to a stop, swerving to avoid hitting her. Carol DaRonch threw herself against the car and flung open the passenger-side door. "He was going to kill me," she sobbed, collapsing across Mary Walsh's lap. "He said he was going to kill me if I didn't stop screaming." A few yards away, a light-colored Volkswagen made a U-turn and disappeared into the night.

Carol DaRonch was safe, but still terrified. She would be

The parking lot of the Fashion Place Mall in Murray, Utah *(background)*, was the scene of the abduction of Carol DaRonch *(above)* by Ted Bundy on November 8, 1974. Bundy posed as a policeman to lure DaRonch into his battered Volkswagen *(left)* from which she had to fight her way to freedom.

terrified for years. It would be some time, in fact, before she could bring herself to go out alone, even in broad daylight. But for all that, she was lucky. She escaped. She lived. At least three dozen other women—maybe many more—met up with "Officer Roseland," and they were not so lucky. Officer Roseland's real name was Ted Bundy.

Over the course of his 42 years, Theodore Robert Bundy would have many names and wear many masks. To his mother he was the ideal son. To political friends he was a bright young man on the way up, a rising star in the legal profession—a future governor, maybe, a future senator. To his girlfriends—and there were many—he was a dream come true: tender lover, attentive companion, romantic suitor, the sort who sent flowers and love poems.

Men envied his looks and charm and easy grace. "If there was any flaw in him," a male acquaintance once said, "it was that he was almost too perfect." The description would have greatly pleased Bundy, who struggled hard to craft this image of perfection. But the truth was something very different. His image was a well-wrought lie, so finely fashioned that sometimes even he was fooled. He thought he was a genius, and he was, in fact, quite bright. But he was not smart enough, finally, to elude either the law or his own inner demons. He adopted the pose of connoisseur of the good life—choice food, fine wines, fashionable clothes. But the money that bought them was stolen, and the aura of good breeding that he affected was hard-won and tissue-thin. Even his celebrated charm was no more than a charade, a parlor trick, a useful disguise: Ted in the role of lover of women was the emptiest pose of all.

By all evidence, what he really felt for women was a vast

and bottomless rage. Ted in his mask attracted them, even enchanted them. The real Ted stalked them and abducted them, raped them, tortured them, beat them, strangled them—even tore their flesh with his teeth, like a wild beast. He desecrated their bodies, often dismembered them, sometimes discarded them for other animals—four-legged ones—to finish off. His last victim—a 12-year-old child—he left to rot in a garbage-strewn hog shed. Charming Ted.

A federal lawman, an expert on serial killers, came to know Bundy well and said this of him: "When you look at it, Ted Bundy is a terrible killer, perhaps the most despicable killing machine that modern America has ever known." To the very end, Bundy seemed to view his crimes with a sort of detached fascination, as though marveling at his own evil guile and at the magnitude of pain he was able to inflict. There is no convincing sign that he ever felt remorse. The only death he ever wept for was his own.

Ted Bundy's mother, Louise Cowell, was 21 years old in 1946 when she got pregnant. The identity of the father—contributor of one-half of Ted Bundy's genetic legacy—would remain a mystery. Cowell would later describe him only as a member of the armed forces, a man she dated a few times. In the postwar era of Ted's conception, having an illegitimate child was scandalous—a potentially life-wrecking experience for a young woman—and Cowell, the product of a strict Methodist background, could barely find the courage to tell her parents about her condition. Abortion, even had it been legal, was morally out of the question for the Cowells, so Louise left Philadelphia to enter the Elizabeth Lund Home for Unwed Mothers in Burlington, Vermont. Just over two months later, on November 24, 1946, she gave birth to a son, Theodore Robert Cowell.

Shortly after the baby's birth, the young mother traveled home, leaving her son with strangers while she and her parents debated whether to put him up for adoption. After about two months, the family elected to keep the boy, and Louise returned to Vermont and carried him home.

It was a rather peculiar home. In a transparent attempt to silence any whispers about the baby, Louise's parents, Sam and Eleanor, let it be known that he was their own adopted son. Ted, it seemed, always knew that Louise was his mother, but for public consumption she was his older sister. Few were fooled by the family fiction. "I knew it had to be Louise's baby," recalls Virginia Bristol, one of Sam Cowell's

sisters, "but they wanted to cover up. All we ever got was evasions." Julia Cowell Sunday, Louise's younger sister, says the baby's origin remained a taboo subject, even within the immediate family. "It was never spoken of," she remembers. That was not especially unusual. Much in the Cowell family was never spoken of.

Ted came to adore Sam Cowell—or so Bundy always said, recalling with rosy nostalgia happy boyhood camping and fishing trips with his grandfather. Louise Bundy would affirm this sunny portrait, vowing that her amiable father—a "very loving and intelligent" man—doted on the boy. But Sam Cowell the genial patriarch was not the Sam Cowell that other family members recall. By some accounts, the old man was an ill-tempered tyrant. He was a landscape gardener, a perfectionist in his craft, but apt to be more patient with plants than with people. Some of the Cowell kin avow that he dispensed verbal abuse liberally and, toward his wife, occasional physical abuse as well. A declared racist, and intolerant in general, Sam Cowell could not abide anyone who failed to measure up to his exacting standards. His harshness extended even to animals; dogs that came near him got a swift kick, cats were swung by the tail.

Cowell's wife, Eleanor, suffered frequent bouts of depression, episodes bad enough to lead eventually to electroshock treatments. In time, she developed an irrational fear of open spaces, and she never left her house.

As for young Ted, already there were indications that he was not a typical child. When his Aunt Julia was 15 years old, she awoke on more than one morning to find her nephew stealthily lifting her blanket and slipping butcher knives into the bed beside her. "He just stood there and grinned," Julia Cowell Sunday later recounted. "I shooed him out of the room and took the implements back down to the kitchen and told my mother about it. I remember thinking at the time that I was the only one who thought it was strange. Nobody did anything." Ted was then three years old.

As he grew, the truth of his parentage became harder to hide, and Louise feared that the secret might leak out and make the boy's life miserable. In 1950 she moved Ted 3,000 miles away to Tacoma, Washington, where some obliging Cowell relatives took the pair in. Hoping to pass as a widow or divorcée, Louise changed her name, and Ted's, from Cowell to Nelson. Such a common name, she reasoned, would afford the child a measure of anonymity as he started school. She found work as a secretary and attended a Methodist church, where she met a kindly hospital cook named John Culpepper Bundy. She married him on May 19, 1951. Ted went to the wedding, and in the course of one day acquired both a stepfather and a third new name: Theodore Robert Bundy. The boy was not yet five years old.

When he began grade school, Ted's intelligence became apparent. Scattered among his good grades, however, were concerned notes from teachers: Ted, they warned, needed to learn to control his violent temper. Friends remember that the boy generally avoided confrontations, but when provoked, he could explode with frightening ferocity.

Still, on the surface, the future killer's childhood and early adolescence seemed in many ways a study in normalcy. Maintaining a low profile during junior high and high school, he kept his grades up, was active in the Boy Scouts, went to church with his parents. "He was attractive, and well dressed, exceptionally well mannered," recalls a female classmate. "I know he must have dated, but I can't ever remember seeing him with a date. He was kind of shy—almost introverted." In fact, Ted had only one date in his high-school years. In a sociosexual sense, he seemed to lag behind most of his peers. He tried to keep up with the usual locker-room boasts, but the effort was hollow. Much of the talk he didn't even understand.

Boy Scout boyhood, teenage awkwardness—all part of the typical youth of an all-American male. But beneath the unremarkable facade, something dark was taking on shape and substance. By the time he finished high school, Bundy was sneaking out of his house at night and peering into windows to watch women as they undressed. Sometimes he took the voyeurism a step further, disabling a woman's car to render her less mobile, and thus more vulnerable. He found such escapades sexually thrilling, the greatest adjunct to the compulsive masturbation that he practiced. And sex was not the only taste that he learned early to indulge in dubious ways. The young Bundy thought nothing of shoplifting ski equipment and expensive clothes—items far beyond his family's slender means. He would tell his mother these things were gifts from the department store where he worked part-time. At least twice, juvenile authorities picked him up on suspicion of auto theft and burglary.

The need to acquire things, to take what he could not afford, became a Bundy hallmark. Louise Bundy had always been acutely status conscious, perhaps because of her father's intolerance, aggravated by her youthful fall from

If you don't stop screaming I'll blow your brains out.

grace. In her son, social distinctions would take the form of a chasm yawning between his origins and his aspirations. The working class—the social niche where Johnnie Bundy fit comfortably, and to which Louise Bundy adapted—was nowhere near good enough for Ted. He needed to possess expensive things, just as he would soon need to possess unto death bright, pretty young women. To have such things was to have power. From early in his youth, power was a hunger, constant and keenly felt. To feed it, he began creating an elaborate fiction of the Ted he wanted to be: suave and stylish Ted, wealthy and successful Ted, brilliant and accomplished Ted, famous celebrity Ted. Lady-killer Ted.

One of reality's major intrusions on this fiction was the matter of his birth. It remains unclear exactly when Bundy realized that he was illegitimate. But according to a story that he would later tell a girlfriend, he was about 10 or 12 when one of his cousins called him a bastard and showed him the birth certificate that proved it. He would say, in later years, that the subject was insignificant. "I can't understand why everyone wants to make such a big deal out of that," he once remarked. "I don't consider it to be important." At the time, however, he appeared to care very much. When a friend tried to console him, Bundy's response was bitter. "It's not you that's a bastard," he snapped. It seemed that he could never quite forgive his mother for this barrier to his own potential status. "She never even had the decency to tell me herself," Bundy once said. Nor could he forgive Johnnie Bundy for what Ted saw as unrefined intellect and lower-class taste. Once, as a youth, Ted even went so far as to ask a well-educated, well-to-do relative to adopt him. "When I heard that," recounts his Aunt Julia, "I knew something was terribly, terribly wrong."

The All-American Boy

There's a common myth that killers are invariably shaped by brutal or deprived childhoods. Yet the snapshots on these three pages seem to show that young Ted Bundy was loved very much. The pictures are almost emblematic of the all-American middle-class boyhood. They would be at home in the albums of millions of families.

Scenes from the Bundy family album shown clockwise from top left on this page begin with Ted as a toddler, sniffing an iris at his grandfather Sam Cowell's Philadelphia home in 1948. Not quite two years later, he poses proudly with his sled and snowman. In the fall of 1950, cowboy-clad Ted displays his two favorite sets of wheels, a tricycle and a red wagon. A few months earlier, he vacations at a New Jersey beach with his much-adored grandfather and his mother.

By December of 1953, Ted is tall enough to help decorate the family Christmas tree in the house in Tacoma, Washington, where he and his mother, Louise, live with Ted's stepfather, Johnnie Bundy, and half sister Linda.

Johnnie Bundy and Ted roast hot dogs in front of the family fireplace in 1953.

Ted proudly shows off his catch of the day after a fishing excursion to Port Defiance with his grandfather during a family visit in 1954.

Fifteen-year-old Ted used the earnings from his newspaper route to buy this boat, which he rows in 1962 on Crescent Lake near the family's A-frame vacation home.

The Bundy family picture taken at Christmas 1960 shows, left to right, Sandra, Glenn, Louise, Linda, and Ted. Ted's younger half brother, Richard, would be born in 1961.

Ted dons a cap and gown for his 1965 graduation from Wilson High School, where he consistently maintained a B average.

Something was, indeed, wrong, and Ted Bundy knew it himself. In junior high he was generally regarded as sociable enough, exceptionally bright, the wielder of a precocious wit. But somewhere in his teens he began to realize that he wasn't like other people. "In my early schooling, it seemed like there was no problem in learning what the appropriate social behaviors were," he would one day tell an interviewer. "It just seemed like I hit a wall in high school." The wall, apparently no great barrier for his peers, was built of a lack of instinctive understanding for other people. "I didn't know what made things tick," Bundy would recall. "I didn't know what underlay social interactions."

But social interactions were merely the tip of the problem. There was a deeper flaw involving a failure to develop even the most rudimentary feeling for people, an inability to even comprehend them as fellow creatures. Young Bundy was smart enough to sense that while others lived in a world of people, he lived in a world of objects, things to be used or acquired or discarded—but not loved, not felt for in any substantial way. He was trapped in an emotional infancy where his own needs and wants were all that mattered: More, they were all that existed. In short, Ted Bundy was a budding psychopath. Somewhere along the line, he failed to develop a capacity for caring, and with it, a conscience. Perhaps he was even born without one—a possibility that he himself considered. "Maybe," he once said of his basic flaw, "it's something that was programmed by some kind of genetic thing."

Whatever his inner lacks and conflicts, the young Bundy managed to function in the everyday world. If he could not feel normal emotions or understand them, he could study and mimic them, aided by his considerable intelligence. He continued to do well academically. In 1965 he graduated from high school and was awarded a scholarship to the University of Puget Sound in Tacoma. Soon he transferred to the University of Washington. And there he met a coed named Leslie Holland.*

The daughter of a wealthy San Francisco family, Holland was a thoroughbred beauty who seemed the sum and embodiment of all Bundy's aspirations. To the crippled extent that he could love another human being, he loved her—or loved in her the things that filled his own wants and needs. He loved her tall, slender body and her long, dark hair, her money, her sophistication, her casually perfect style. He loved, hopelessly, her very unattainability; for while the two often dated, the relationship was for Leslie a pastime, not a passion. "She and I had about as much in common as Sears and Roebuck's has with Saks," Bundy would later say. Nevertheless, he did everything he could to please her, following her around like an eager puppy, tagging along on ski trips, even trailing in her wake to Stanford University in 1967.

But for Holland, Ted's boyish charm soon seemed no more than tiresome childishness, and she broke with him in the late summer of 1967. Bundy left Stanford and returned to the University of Washington, but he was so devastated that his academic work suffered and he dropped out. Then began a strange cross-country odyssey that took him to California, Colorado, and back East to visit his grandparents. It was a time he would remember as a painful, groping period when he tried to recover the sense of himself that Holland's rejection had stripped away. But in the fall of 1968 he rallied, mounting an obsessive campaign to win her back. The effort involved transforming his outward self to match the suave and charming fictional self that lived inside his mind, the sophisticated Ted that the Leslie Hollands of this world would find desirable. He polished his manners, took greater care with his appearance, and began building the sort of résumé that Holland might admire.

Politics was his chosen road toward status. He became active in the Washington State Republican party. The tasks he took on were menial, but he met people, made contacts. Not a few highly placed officials were impressed with his intelligence, his looks, his steady conservative views, his willingness to serve. Bundy the boyhood thief became the model citizen, squarely on the side of law and order. Once, after running down a purse snatcher, he won a commendation from the Seattle Police Department. In 1970, during a visit to a lake, he dashed into the water to save a drowning toddler. By 1971 he was reenrolled in the University of Washington and earning pocket money working for a suicide hot line, helping to calm and comfort distraught callers until help could be dispatched. A coworker for the hot line was writer Ann Rule, who would later author a best-selling book about Bundy. Rule remembers her young colleague as patient and professional. "If, as many people believe today, Ted Bundy took lives, he also saved lives," she insists. "I know he did, because I was there when he did it."

On the whole, Bundy's path was winding steadily upward, but it was not always smooth. In the fall of 1968, he found himself unemployed after the Republican candidate

* Denotes pseudonym, used at the request of people who want their privacy protected.

Among Bundy's early victims were Lynda Ann Healy, abducted and killed early in 1974; Georgann Hawkins, slain after she stopped to help Bundy, who was faking an injury, in June 1974; and Kathy Parks, kidnapped in Oregon and murdered in Washington in May 1974.

LYNDA ANN HEALY

GEORGANN HAWKINS

he was working for lost an election. Bundy went back East again in 1969, staying with his grandparents while attending Temple University for a few months. But the life didn't suit him. He had trouble concentrating on school, and in the summer of 1969, he went back home. After much floundering, he graduated from the University of Washington in 1972 with a respectable academic record and a degree in psychology. He applied to several law schools, but his entrance test scores were lackluster and he was rejected. In 1973 he applied again, this time to the law school of the University of Utah. Washington governor Dan Evans signed a glowing recommendation for the engaging young Republican, and Bundy was accepted. As things turned out, he would not enroll at Utah until the fall of 1974. In the meantime, he opted to stay in Washington, where he had a lucrative political job, and to study law at night at the University of Puget Sound.

His 1973 application to Utah contained an especially telling passage. "I apply to law school," Bundy wrote, "because this institution will give me the tools to become a more effective actor in the social role I have defined for myself." By then, he was already an "effective actor" when it came to attracting women, though his relationships were riddled with lies. In a sense, his romances were simply practice: He still meant to win back Leslie Holland. At last, in the summer of 1973, he felt ready to confront her. Now 26, Bundy had become the very image of attractive eligibility. While on a business trip to California on behalf of the Washington Republicans, he took Holland to dinner and dazzled her with his newfound social graces. She agreed to visit him in Seattle, and the courtship resumed in earnest. Before long, the two were engaged.

And having reinvented himself to win his ladylove, Bundy dropped her, early in 1974, without so much as a good-bye. When Holland called for an explanation, he simply hung up the phone. "I just wanted to prove to myself that I could have married her," he would later explain.

By then the killing had already begun.

On the night of January 4, 1974, 18-year-old Maggie Reed* went to sleep as usual in the basement room she rented in a large house near the University of Washington. When she didn't show up for breakfast the next morning, her housemates, all young men, merely assumed that she was sleeping late. But by midmorning, they were worried. A knock at her door got no response. They pushed open the door and stepped inside.

Reed lay unconscious on the bed, her face and hair covered with dried blood. A metal rod was missing from her bedframe. Gingerly, her friends pulled back the thin sheet that covered her and saw to their horror what had happened to the rod: It had been viciously jammed into the young woman's vagina. Blood and viscera flowed around it, gathering in a dark pool on the mattress. Maggie Reed would spend several months in a coma, but she would survive, and mercifully, she would not remember the attack.

Lynda Ann Healy would not survive. Like Maggie Reed, the 21-year-old psychology student lived in the basement room of a house near the university. An attractive, dark-haired young woman, Healy had a pleasant voice that won her a part-time job reading ski reports on the air. Because her work required her to wake up at 5:30 each morning, she kept fairly regular habits and went to bed early almost every night. The night of Thursday, January 31, was no exception. But the next day, she never arrived at work, or at her classes later in the day. On Friday evening, her parents called the police. Detectives Wayne Dorman and Ted Fonis of the Seattle Police Homicide Unit soon arrived at Healy's house and were shown to her room. The officers pulled back the spread on her neatly made bed. A thick crust of dried blood covered the pillow, and a large stain had soaked through the sheets into the mattress. The pillowcase was missing. After a quick search, Dorman and Fonis discovered Healy's nightgown stuffed into the back of a closet, the neckline stiff with dried blood. A backpack and the clothes she'd worn the night before were all missing.

KATHY PARKS

Six weeks after Healy's disappearance, 19-year-old Donna Gail Manson left her dormitory at Evergreen State College to attend a jazz concert. She never arrived. The following month, Susan Elaine Rancourt, a freshman biology major at Central Washington State College, disappeared on her way to a campus movie. Three more young women—Kathy Parks, Brenda Ball, and Georgann Hawkins—would vanish over the course of the next two months. All the women were Washington residents except for Kathy Parks, who was abducted in Oregon and killed in Washington.

It would be some time before police would establish a pattern. There would be scattered reports about a stranger being on campus around the times of the abductions, an awkward stranger with an injured arm, or on crutches, who asked various coeds to help him carry his books. But these accounts were not pieced together, largely because Ted Bundy, who had killed six women in as many months, carefully covered his tracks. He knew that a cluster of murders in one location would concentrate police efforts, so he crisscrossed wide swaths of territory in his VW, homing in on the college campuses that were his natural hunting ground. Colleges were where the vulnerable women were—the young, pretty, bright ones. Society's cream. Bundy chose his victims carefully, sometimes following them for some time before striking. All of them were intelligent. All were attractive, some even beautiful. Most had long hair, parted in the middle. They tended to look like each other. They tended to look like Leslie Holland.

Incredibly, even while he killed at night, Ted Bundy maintained his daytime mask of normalcy. For more than four years he had carried on a relationship with a secretary named Beth Archer,* a woman a few years older than he. They'd met in a bar where Bundy introduced himself as a law student and boasted that he was writing a book about Vietnam. In fact, he had not yet entered law school and was working as a legal messenger. But Archer was im-pressed. By the end of the evening, she would later recall, "I was already planning the wedding and naming the kids."

Beth Archer, recovering from a painful divorce, had reason to be suspicious of men, yet she was entranced by Ted Bundy. She was sure he was destined for success, and she often lent him money to help him make ends meet in the meantime. She was happy to do it: In many ways, he was her ideal man. He was usually loving and attentive. He marked every anniversary of their first meeting with a single red rose. He was devoted to Archer's young daughter, Annie.* He had clean habits: He lived near the University of Washington in a boardinghouse room where "he kept everything orderly and spotless," according to Archer, and he seemed to be the gentlest of souls. His landlady recalls that he once stopped her from swatting an insect. "Don't kill it!" he cried, chasing the pest out a window. Ted Bundy, it appeared, was a man who wouldn't hurt a fly.

Even from their earliest days together, however, Archer sensed that Bundy was not quite what he seemed. He could be moody and evasive, and she learned to fear his violent temper. He disappeared for days at a time, mumbling vague explanations when he returned. She knew, too, that he cheated on her with other women, though he denied it when confronted. In fact, Bundy's philandering was more serious than she could have dreamed. Archer did not know that for a brief period in 1973, as she and Bundy were discussing marriage, he was also engaged to Leslie Holland.

For Bundy, it was a heady experience, having such power over two women at once. Evidently, however, it was not thrilling enough.

Sunday, July 14, 1974, was a bright, clear day in Seattle, with temperatures climbing toward the 90s. At Lake Sammamish State Park, 12 miles east of the city, more than 40,000 picnickers and sunbathers turned out to enjoy the weather. About noon, a 22-year-old office worker named Janice Graham was standing near the park bandstand, waiting for her husband and parents to arrive. A man approached her. He was wearing jeans and a white T-shirt. She placed his age at about 24 or 25.

"Say, could you help me a minute?" he asked.

The young woman looked down and saw that his left arm was encased in a plaster cast. He held it close against his body, suspended in a beige sling. "Sure," she answered. "What do you need?"

Some 40,000 people packed the beach at Lake Sammamish *(above)* on July 14, 1974, the day Bundy kidnapped two young women from the crowd. Witnesses who saw him with both victims helped police prepare a composite drawing *(left)* of the mysterious "Ted."

He needed help, he explained, to load a sailboat onto his car. He couldn't manage it alone with his injured arm. Graham looked him over carefully. He seemed polite, apologetic about disturbing her—and also a little nervous. His anxious chatter never stopped. He'd hurt his arm playing racquetball, he said. Had she ever played? What about this great weather? How about this big crowd? Harmless enough, Graham concluded. She agreed to lend him a hand, and she walked with him toward the parking lot. He led her to a Volkswagen bug. There was no sign of a sailboat.

"Oh, I forgot to tell you," the man said. "It's up at my folks' house—just up the hill." He waved her toward the passenger door. She hesitated. "I really can't go with you,"

JANICE OTT

DENISE NASLUND

Janice Ott and Denise Naslund were the two victims kidnapped by Bundy at Lake Sammamish on July 14, 1974.

she said. "I have to meet my husband and folks. What time is it?" He glanced at his watch and told her it was about 12:20. Graham hesitated a second longer, then said she was sorry but she really couldn't help him. She was running late. The handsome stranger gave her a friendly smile. "That's OK," he said. A few minutes later, as she stood eating a snow cone in the shade of a concession stand, she saw the man again, heading toward the parking lot. At his side was another young woman. This guy, Graham thought, is a pretty fast worker.

Later, a badly rattled Janice Graham would tell police that she nearly changed her mind and climbed into the car. "He was very polite at all times," she said. "Very sincere. Easy to talk to. He was really friendly, and he had a nice smile." A fatal charm, so to speak.

By coincidence, the woman who did decide to help Bundy that day was also named Janice. Janice Ott was a 23-year-old probation-office worker, a slender, attractive woman barely five feet tall. She had striking gray-green eyes and blond hair that reached almost to her waist. She was married, but her husband was hundreds of miles away, finishing some schooling. In a recent letter to him, she'd bemoaned their long separation. "Someone could expire before you ever got wind of it," she wrote.

Shortly after noon, Ott found a spot on the crowded beach and spread out her blanket. Peeling off the shorts and blouse she wore over her black bikini, she sat down and began rubbing cocoa butter onto her skin. She'd barely stretched out to sun herself when she felt a shadow fall across her face. A tall man hovered over her. He had one arm in a sling.

Picnickers nearby would overhear several minutes of conversation between the two—something about a sailboat, and a broken arm. The man, several witnesses said, gave his name as Ted. The chat ended with Ott standing up, slipping on her shorts and blouse, and following the stranger toward the parking lot. That was the last time anyone saw her alive.

But Ted was not yet done for the day.

Denise Naslund arrived at Lake Sammamish in the early afternoon, along with her boyfriend, Kenny Little, and an-other couple. A dark-haired 18-year-old, Naslund worked as a secretary while she was studying to become a computer programmer. Pretty and slim, she fussed a lot over her appearance. That day, she was wearing a pair of blue cutoff shorts and a blue halter top. She had also thoughtfully painted her fingernails blue—her boyfriend's favorite color. In midafternoon the two couples roasted hot dogs at a picnic site. What with the heat and the food, they eventually fell asleep. At 4:30 p.m., Naslund awoke from her nap on the beach and strolled off toward the rest rooms, leaving her purse, her car keys, and her sandals behind. She never returned.

The evening of the day that Janice Ott and Denise Naslund disappeared, Bundy took Beth Archer to dinner at a Seattle bowling alley renowned for its huge hamburgers. He ate two, then suggested that they go for ice cream. He was, he said, starving.

The attacks at Lake Sammamish signaled a grotesque high point: Ted Bundy at his killing best. Not nighttime assaults, spaced weeks apart, but the abduction of two young women in one day, in broad daylight, amid thousands of people. And he hadn't crudely grabbed his victims; he had lured them with charm and guile. He was no common killer, or so he surely thought: Ted Bundy killed with class. And with daring. He'd even had the nerve to identify himself, although at the time no one believed that Ted was the attacker's real name. Lake Sammamish marked the apex of Bundy's lethal power game. Before long, it would begin to unravel.

The abductions at the lake fell under the jurisdiction of the King County Major Crimes Unit. Detective Robert Keppel, the newest man in the unit, was among the first to connect the disappearances of Janice Ott and Denise Naslund to the six earlier cases scattered across the state. Now that Ted had allowed himself to be seen, Keppel and his colleagues had something to go on. Police sketches were widely circulated. Several witnesses underwent hypnosis in an effort to sharpen their recall of events. Police divers probed the depths of Lake Sammamish, and search teams combed the 400-acre park. They found nothing.

Public interest in the case soon verged on hysteria, fueled by an avalanche of news and speculation in the Seattle media. Everyone, it seemed, had a theory about the mysterious Ted: A police hot line registered more than 3,000 telephone calls. Wild rumors flew: one of the victims had been decapitated, according to one story; another's bones had been boiled. One woman became frantic when her car broke down near Lake Sammamish. "God I'm glad to see you!" she cried when a police cruiser reached her. "Here I am stranded in Ted's country!"

At the time of the Naslund-Ott abductions, Bundy had been working for two months at the Washington State Department of Emergency Services in Olympia. When the Lake Sammamish story broke, some of his coworkers, especially a young woman named Carole Ann Boone, teased him about his resemblance to the Ted in the police sketches. Bundy bore it with good humor.

To some, however, it wasn't a joke. At least four people would suggest Ted Bundy's name to the police as a possible suspect. One was his girlfriend, Beth Archer. Archer had wrestled with her suspicions for days before making the call. On the one hand, it seemed inconceivable that the man she loved could be a killer. But certain coincidences couldn't be ignored. Bundy did bear a likeness to the newspapers' descriptions of the suspect, and his car was similar to the one that witnesses described. One thing in particular nagged at her. Months earlier, while snooping through her lover's desk drawers in search of evidence of infidelities, she'd discovered a supply of plaster of paris, the sort used by hospitals to make casts. When she asked about it, Bundy casually dismissed the matter. You never know, he said, when you might break a leg.

The call, once Archer made it, proved anticlimactic. It caused no immediate problems for her lover; in fact, it drew hardly any response. Bundy's name was one of thousands submitted to police that summer, and not a particularly promising one. He'd broken no laws, and his public persona did not dovetail with any known serial-killer profile. In all, police would check out more than 2,000 potential suspects, and close to 900 Volkswagens. Ted Bundy, whose conduct seemed above reproach, was easily overlooked.

Despite all the private suspicions and public outcry, there was, as yet, no hard evidence of murder in the Ted case. Police had managed to link one brutal assault against a young woman, and eight disappearances. Certainly, authorities suspected that they might be dealing with a murderous psychopath. But what they did not have was the final confirmation—the bodies.

That changed on September 7, 1974. It was the first day of grouse season, and hunter Elzie Hammons set out with a friend that morning to try his luck on a hillside near Issaquah, about four miles from Lake Sammamish. As Hammons walked along a weed-choked road that had once been used for logging, he looked down and stopped dead in his tracks. Lying across the road was a skeleton, its discolored bones still partially strung together by dried sinews. Nearby was a skull, obviously human.

By noon, a team led by Detective Bob Keppel of the King County police had cordoned off the hillside and begun a search. Their grisly yield would be one skull, the lower jaw of another, a rib cage, a spinal column, five thigh bones, assorted smaller bones, and eight hanks of hair—some red-blonde, some dark. These pitiable leavings were all that remained of Janice Ott, Denise Naslund, and a third victim who could not be positively identified but who was believed to be Georgann Hawkins. It appeared that the bodies had been dumped farther up the hillside and later dragged by animals. The bones had been gnawed by coyotes and rodents, and maybe bears.

On March 1, 1975, two forestry students found a skull on the lower reaches of Taylor Mountain, 10 miles east of Issaquah. Keppel led a team of 200 officers and volunteers in scouring the entire side of the mountain. It turned out to be another dumping ground. Over the course of eight days, searchers recovered the remains of Brenda Ball, Susan Rancourt, Kathy Parks, and Lynda Healy. At this site, even less was left of the victims; they had been dead longer than those at Issaquah. Lynda Healy was identified on the basis of a single tooth.

On October 12, 1974, a deer hunter hiking along a path a few miles south of Olympia found a human skull, with the long hair still attached. A subsequent police search turned up hair, bones, and teeth—remains indicating that two victims had been dumped at the site. One of them was never identified. The other was Carol Valenzuela, 20, who had disappeared from Vancouver, Washington, on August 2, 1974.

Investigators now fully grasped the scope of the "Ted" crimes. But even as they sorted through the grim gleanings from the dumping grounds, the killings seemed to have stopped. Bob Keppel and the other investigators dared to hope that the horror had passed.

But it had not passed. It had moved. In September of 1974, Ted Bundy packed up his belongings and decamped for the University of Utah.

In Salt Lake City, he settled into an apartment and found a job as a dormitory manager. He kept in regular touch with Beth Archer back in Seattle, but he also began dating a number of other women. "Why should I want to attack women?" he would later say. "I had all the female companionship I wanted. I must have slept with at least a dozen women that first year in Utah, and all of them went to bed with me willingly." (Such logic was a sham, as Bundy himself well knew. He would eventually admit that sex was not his motive for killing. Sex was hardly more than an afterthought. Power and possession were the real motives.)

On October 2, 1974, he went hunting again. Sixteen-year-old Nancy Wilcox, a high-school cheerleader, disappeared from her neighborhood just south of Salt Lake City. She was last seen riding in a light-colored Volkswagen bug. Sixteen days later, 17-year-old Melissa Smith, the daughter of a local police chief, vanished on her way home from a pizza parlor. A third victim, 17-year-old Laura Aime, dropped out of sight 13 days later following a Halloween party.

Evidently Bundy took less care with his dumping grounds in Utah: The nude, battered bodies of both Melissa Smith and Laura Aime were soon recovered by police. Less than a month after she disappeared, Smith's body was found in a canyon in the Wasatch

Range, east of Salt Lake. A month later, Laura Aime's corpse was found alongside a trail in the same mountains. The skulls of the young women had been crushed by ferocious blows to the head, possibly from a crowbar. Both victims had also been strangled; nylon stockings were found tightly knotted around their necks. The coroner's report revealed that both had been raped and sodomized.

The attacks were more frequent now. On November 8, only eight days after the disappearance of Laura Aime, Carol DaRonch managed to escape the clutches of "Officer Roseland" at the Fashion Place Shopping Mall in Murray. And later that same night, even as DaRonch gave police a detailed description of her attacker, Bundy struck again.

At Viewmont High School in Bountiful, Utah, 17 miles from the Fashion Place Mall, parents and students crowded into the school auditorium to see the latest drama club production. Just before 8 p.m., as the curtain was about to go up, 24-year-old drama teacher Raelynne Shepard noticed a tall young man hanging around in a hallway backstage. The stranger, whom she would later describe as "very good looking," wanted to know if she would go with him to the school parking lot to identify a car. She declined. Undeterred, Bundy merely went after new game. Seventeen-year-old Debra Kent left the play early to pick up her brother at a skating rink. Soon after her departure, residents of an

Bundy and Seattle divorcée Beth Archer relax by the fire in this photo from the early 1970s. During the time that he courted Archer, Bundy killed about two dozen women who were strangers to him.

apartment complex across the street from the high school heard two short, piercing screams. Debra Kent's body would never be found.

In all, Ted Bundy would kill at least 11 times in Utah and neighboring Colorado. By the summer of 1975, his activities had put two dozen police agencies in four states—Washington, Oregon, Utah, and Colorado—on alert. But the separate investigations weren't coordinated; detectives didn't yet know they were all after the same man. That would soon change.

It was past 2 a.m. on August 16, 1975, when Sergeant Robert Hayward, a 23-year veteran of the Utah Highway Patrol, was ending his shift and returning to his home in the Salt Lake City suburb of Granger. He saw a gray Volkswagen bug cruise past him. Hayward's home was deep in a housing subdivision, along a maze of curving streets—an odd place to find an unfamiliar car circling aimlessly so late at night—so Hayward threw on his bright lights to try to catch a glimpse of the license plate. As he did this, the VW's driver killed his own lights and gunned his engine, pulling away fast. Hayward set off in pursuit and radioed for back-up. After a short chase, the VW pulled into an abandoned gas station. A tall man in jeans and a black turtleneck stepped out of the car.

"Can I see your license and registration?" Hayward asked. The man handed over his identification and Hayward glanced at the name: Theodore Robert Bundy. It meant nothing to him.

"What are you doing out here at this time of the morning?" the trooper asked. Bundy said that he was lost. He'd been to a movie at the nearby Valley Vu Drive-in Theater, then couldn't find his way home. He was oddly insistent on the story, so much so that Hayward suspected that he was lying. By this time, a second patrol car was on the scene.

"Mind if I look in your car?" Hayward asked.

"Go ahead," Bundy said. The beam from Hayward's flashlight played across the VW's interior, highlighting a small crowbar on the car's right side, where the passenger seat had been removed. A burglar's tool, Hayward thought. He called again for backup, this time for a detective. Shortly thereafter, Detective Daryle M. Ondrak of the Salt Lake County Sheriff's Office arrived. He took a closer look at the VW. Searching inside and in the trunk, Ondrak found an ice pick, a ski mask, a mask made out of pantyhose, some pieces of rope—and a pair of handcuffs. The detective ar-

rested Bundy. The suspect was soon freed on his own recognizance, but Ondrak told him to expect a warrant for possession of burglary tools.

Still, the detective had a hard time squaring the situation in his own mind. The items found in Bundy's car were suspicious in the extreme. On the other hand, the suspect himself was clean-cut, polite, obviously well-educated. Some of Ondrak's confusion was cleared up a couple of days later, when he attended the usual weekly gathering where area detectives discussed active cases and exchanged information. Toward the end of the meeting, Ondrak mentioned Bundy, the bright young law student who happened to get caught with some handcuffs and other strange gear in his Volkswagen.

Across the table, Homicide Detective Jerry Thompson of the Salt Lake County Sheriff's Office snapped to attention. For almost a year, Thompson had been investigating the murder of Melissa Smith. In connection with that case, he'd learned of Carol DaRonch's encounter with the mysterious Officer Roseland. He remembered the handcuffs, the Volkswagen, the polite and well-educated assailant. He remembered seeing Bundy's name on a police report from Seattle. The pieces fell together.

Over the next few weeks, Thompson worked feverishly trying to link Bundy to the DaRonch case. He flew to Seattle and interviewed Beth Archer, who told him the story that she'd tried to tell the Seattle police almost a year before: that her lover had a stash of plaster of paris, that he had a crowbar, that he occasionally sought her compliance for weird sex, that he had an unpredictable temper, and that sometimes she was afraid of him. Sensing he was on the right track, Thompson studied the trail of gasoline credit card receipts that placed Bundy near several crime scenes not in Utah, but in Colorado. A net of circumstantial evidence tightened. But while police in Utah, Colorado, and Washington may have found it convincing, they knew that they had nothing conclusive to take to court.

And Bundy, well aware that he was under suspicion, seemed to enjoy the contest of wits with authorities. It was a game he felt to be so weighted in his favor that he could toy with his pursuers, not troubling to hide his contempt for them. He nonchalantly allowed police to search his apartment. "Jerry, you do a pretty good job" he told Detective Thompson. "Keep going and one of these days you might make it." Meanwhile, he continued to polish his public

Bundy and Carol Bartholomew do the dishes after a birthday party. Bartholomew was one of several new friends Bundy made after he moved to Salt Lake City in 1974.

Bundy *(second from right)* got a quick haircut before appearing in this police line-up in Murray, Utah, on October 2, 1975. Despite his changed appearance, Carol DaRonch identified him as her assailant, and he was charged with kidnapping.

image. To the role of Bright Young Law Student, he added another: Devout Convert. Forsaking his Methodist upbringing, he joined the Mormon church—a politically savvy move in Utah.

But his roles did not win applause from all quarters. On October 2, Thompson, sure that Bundy was guilty, arranged for a police lineup, hoping that Carol DaRonch would be able to provide a positive identification. He also brought in Raelynne Shepard, the drama teacher from Viewmont High, as well as a student from the school who'd also spoken to the intrusive stranger that night. All three women picked Bundy out of the lineup. The suspect, his long hair newly shorn for the occasion, had come to the lineup expecting to be back in law school that afternoon. But in fact, he'd seen the last of law school: Thompson promptly charged him with the kidnapping and attempted murder of Carol DaRonch. Bail was set at $100,000, and up-and-coming young Ted found himself carted off to the Salt Lake County jail.

"My world is a cage," began one of Bundy's jail letters in typically florid style. "How many men before me have written these same words? How many have struggled vainly to describe the cruel metamorphosis that occurs in captivity?"

Melodrama aside, Bundy went through the "cruel metamorphosis" rather nicely. He adapted quickly to jail life, learning to hoard oranges and toilet paper, to roll his own cigarettes, to say "please" and "sir" to his jailers. Fellow inmates detested him, however. Lockups have a caste system all their own, and molesters of the young and innocent fall at the bottom. Vows of violence against the "baby raper" floated through the corridors. After seven weeks in this "caged human sea," as he called it, Bundy got his bail reduced to $15,000. Johnnie and Louise Bundy scraped together the money, and on November 26 their son started back to Seattle.

Having helped finger her ex-lover for police, Beth Archer was so frightened when she learned of his release that she made detectives promise to notify her the minute he crossed back into the state of Washington. But evidently even she had underestimated the persistence of her old romantic vision of Ted. Within two days of his return to Seattle, he'd convinced her of his innocence, rekindled the flame, and moved into her apartment.

Out on bail, Bundy reveled in his new notoriety; it added the role of Martyr to his repertoire. He taunted police officers who were assigned to follow him. He protested to all who would listen his outrage at the news coverage of his case. At a preliminary hearing in Salt Lake, he strolled into court carrying a copy of Alexander Solzhenitsyn's *The Gulag Archipelago,* likening his own ordeal to that of the persecuted Soviet novelist.

After three months of this behavior, Bundy went to trial on February 23, 1976, in the Salt Lake City courthouse. In the courtroom were Louise and Johnnie Bundy, along with several of Ted's newly acquired Mormon friends. Also there were the parents of Laura Aime and Debra Kent, and the father of Melissa Smith. Bundy was clearly implicated in the murders of all three girls, even though police felt that they lacked enough evidence at the time to charge him with those killings, or with any others. At issue was only the assault on Carol DaRonch.

Proceedings dragged on for several days, but DaRonch's testimony was the decisive factor. On February 27, Bundy was found guilty of aggravated kidnapping and ordered to undergo psychiatric examination before sentencing. (Dr. Van Austin, the Utah State Penitentiary psychiatrist, would conclude as follows: "I feel that Mr. Bundy is either a man who has no problems or is smart enough and clever enough to appear close to the edge of 'normal.' ") On June 30, 1976, Ted Bundy was sentenced to one to 15 years in Utah State Prison.

Once again, Bundy had to adapt to the "living hell" of prison life, but he made a great show of gamely making the best of it. To friends, he claimed he was a popular inmate, sought out by other convicts for legal advice. He seemed to be confident that the conviction—a "setback"—would soon be overturned.

This assessment reflected either pure bravado or a woeful inability to appraise reality. Already police were preparing to press further charges—murder charges—against him. Samples of hair found in his car were discovered to be, in the legal phrase, "microscopically indistinguishable" from

the hair of Melissa Smith, Carol DaRonch, and a third young woman, Caryn Campbell, who had been bludgeoned to death in Aspen, Colorado, in 1975. In January of 1977, Bundy waived extradition and was transferred to Colorado to stand trial for the murder of Caryn Campbell. He was held for two months in the quaint, somewhat antiquated Pitkin County jail in Aspen before being moved to a more modern facility, the Garfield County jail, 45 miles away in Glenwood Springs. Both homes suited him far better than the Utah lockup had. In Colorado, he enjoyed unlimited telephone privileges and developed an easy camaraderie with his jailers.

In fact, Bundy got along better with the prison staffs than he did with his own team of lawyers. The two-time law school dropout insisted on orchestrating his own defense and took an arrogant, bullying tone with the public defenders assigned to his case. "He is the most cocky person I have ever faced," said one prosecutor. "He tells his lawyers what to do. He arrives carrying armloads of books, as if he were an attorney himself."

Actually, Bundy's motive for taking control of his own defense transcended mere theatrics. Prisoners acting as their own lawyers are often permitted a certain freedom of movement. They are, for instance, allowed access to law books and such. Bundy expected to find this sort of freedom useful: He meant to escape.

On June 7, 1977, a police car transported Bundy from Glenwood Springs to the Pitkin County courthouse for a hearing. He was no stranger to the courthouse; he was taken there three times a week to use the law library. On this day, however, no one noticed that the prisoner was wearing several layers of clothes, covered with a loose sweater that hid a supply of vitamins, some matches, and a photograph of Beth Archer and her daughter.

Court convened at 9 a.m. As usual, Bundy's handcuffs and leg irons were removed inside the courthouse, leaving him free to move about the room. At 10:30, Judge George Lohr called a recess, and Bundy wandered casually to the law library at the back of the room. Deputy David Westerlund kept an eye on him from an open doorway, but there seemed no cause for alarm; the courtroom was on the second floor, 25 feet above the street. Bundy picked up a file and began pacing back and forth among the tall bookshelves. After a few minutes, Westerlund strolled into the hallway for a smoke.

Three minutes later, a woman walked into the courthouse with a confused look on her face. "Is it normal," she asked, "for people to jump out of windows around here?"

As news of Ted Bundy's escape hit the airwaves, police advised Aspen residents to lock their doors, garage their cars, and hide their children. Teams of local authorities fanned out to search the area. Louise Bundy, appearing on a news broadcast in Tacoma, Washington, pled emotionally for her son to turn himself in. Along with fear, black humor invaded Aspen. "Ted Bundy is a One Night Stand," read one T-shirt. "I am not Bundy," proclaimed a hitchhiker's sign. A local restaurant made news with its "Bundy Burger"—open the bun, and the meat is gone.

But Bundy himself had not gone far. Following his dramatic leap he'd simply peeled off his outer layer of clothes and walked boldly through town, attracting no notice. Then he headed for Aspen Mountain, where he broke into an unoccupied cabin and rested for a day, dining on crackers, brown sugar, and stewed tomatoes left by the owners. Refreshed, and toting a rifle that he stole from the cabin, Bundy headed south.

Unfortunately for the fugitive, he had a terrible sense of

Wearing several layers of clothes, Bundy is led into Colorado's Pitkin County courthouse *(right)* for a hearing on June 7, 1977, in preparation for his trial for the murder of Caryn Campbell. During a morning recess he would jump to freedom from a second-story window. Police immediately set up roadblocks and began checking cars *(opposite)*, but Bundy calmly stripped off a layer of street clothes and strolled through town before heading for the nearby mountains. He wandered for a week before being recaptured.

direction. For two days he roamed in circles, discarding the rifle when it became a burden. Suffering increasingly from fatigue, hunger, exposure, and a leg injury that he'd sustained early in his mountain climbing, he wandered around for nearly a week without making it out of the Aspen area. Exhausted and shivering, he was huddled in some bushes near a golf course when he spotted an old Cadillac parked nearby. He peered inside and saw that the keys were in the ignition. It was the break he'd been waiting for. Climbing inside, he started the car and headed east, away from town. Then, suddenly, he swung the car around and headed back toward the courthouse and the road to Glenwood Springs, a road he knew well from traveling it back and forth to jail for two months.

At 2 a.m. Monday, a pair of Pitkin County deputies noticed the Cadillac weaving back and forth across the road. One of the deputies, Gene Flatt, had served breakfast to Bundy in jail for several months. Flatt and his partner pulled the car over, expecting to find a drunk driver inside. Instead, there was Bundy, squinting against the glare of Flatt's flashlight. "Hello, Ted," the deputy said.

Bundy returned to jail under tightened security. He now wore handcuffs and leg irons whenever he left his cell. His spirits seemed muted, depressed by his capture and by the news that Beth Archer was considering marrying another man. He took the latter blow stoically. "I will always love her so I could never say that I do not dream of our life together," he wrote to a friend. "But this new development, like my capture, must be taken calmly."

Bundy enjoyed the role of Wounded Lover, but he played it without much depth. Even as he supposedly pined for Beth Archer, he was cultivating another woman. Carole Ann Boone, his former coworker from Olympia, had become devoted to him, perhaps won over by the prison poetry that he addressed to his "Tender Apparition of Loveliness." The woman who had once teased Bundy about his resemblance to the "Ted" police sketches now professed abiding faith in his innocence. Whenever she could, Boone visited him in jail, where he courted her through the wire-mesh window of his cell door.

Bundy's legal maneuvering, however, was far less effective than his romancing. On December 23, he learned that his murder trial would be moved south from Aspen to Colorado Springs, where the death penalty was handed out far more freely. In the courtroom, he couldn't control his anger at the decision. "You're sentencing me to death," he cried, pointing a finger at the judge.

The accusation was far from true. Prosecutors and police knew that the Caryn Campbell murder case was weak, perhaps fatally flawed. Had Bundy flowed with the legal stream, he might have served three years or so in the DaRonch case and then been free. But he didn't care to take the chance. A week after the change of venue was announced, he once again took matters into his own hands.

To this day, no one knows how Bundy got hold of the hacksaw he used, or exactly how long it took him to carve the small square out of the ceiling of his cell. When finished, the makeshift trapdoor would measure only one foot square, but Bundy had intentionally shed a great deal of weight—nearly 35 pounds. He could easily wriggle through the opening.

He worked only at night, so the sound of other prisoners showering would drown out the noise, and he sawed so carefully that he could replace the flap without so much as a seam showing. During the last two weeks of December he made several practice runs, climbing through the opening and crawling around in the dusty space above, half expecting the guards to be waiting, guns drawn, as he dropped back into his cell.

For more than a week he made a point of refusing breakfast, opting instead to sleep late after nights spent working on his legal briefs. The guards would not miss him, then, until lunchtime the following day. On the night of December 30, 1977, Bundy pulled on a pair of jeans, a turtleneck, a down vest, sneakers, and a cap. He had more than $500 in his pocket, probably given to him by friends. Pushing open his escape hatch, he pulled

Leg irons confine Bundy as he peers over a lawbook in the Pitkin County courthouse about a month after his recapture. He continued to act as his own attorney in preparation for his Colorado murder trial, but his legal maneuverings were mostly for effect: He was planning a second escape. Ironically, some experts say, the killer would have been better off sticking with the legal system. Many believe that had he gone to trial for Caryn Campbell's murder, he would have beaten the prosecution's weak case and won acquittal.

NO.5

1 BUNDY, TED *vocation*,

2 a W.O.L.

A waggish description of Bundy's "AWOL" status *(above)* appears on the blackboard at the Garfield County jail in Glenwood Springs after the prisoner's second Colorado jailbreak. Escaping on December 30, 1977, through a hole he'd cut in the ceiling of his cell *(right),* he managed to get a 17-hour head start on pursuers. On January 3, 1978, dogs were brought in to sniff Bundy's clothing and track his scent *(below).* But by then the trail had grown cold, and both dogs and police ran in circles while Bundy was already on his way to Atlanta, a stop-over on his way to Florida.

30

himself up through the opening and edged his way through a shallow crawlspace until he found himself over the apartment of one of the resident jailers. Then he dropped down through an opening in the ceiling of a linen closet. Luck was with him; the jailer and his wife were out for the evening. Calmly, the escapee strolled through the front door, found a sports car with the keys in the ignition, and was gone.

This time, Bundy had a 17-hour head start on his pursuers. Although the sports car broke down, he managed to catch a ride to a bus station and board a bus to Denver. From there he took a cab to the airport, generously treating three of his fellow bus passengers to a lift. By the time his absence was noted — with the discovery of his lawbooks and legal papers piled under the blanket on his jail cot — Bundy was in Chicago, having enjoyed a celebratory Scotch and soda on the plane.

From Chicago he headed by train to Ann Arbor, drawn by the thriving campus life at the University of Michigan. On January 2, he mingled with a rowdy tavern crowd to watch the Rose Bowl game on television. The beer hit hard after his long privations, and he spent the second half throwing up in the bathroom.

But Bundy had already grown tired of the frigid Michigan weather and decided to try a warmer climate. He stole a car and drove to Atlanta, where he hopped a bus for Florida. There, thousands of miles from the Northwest, where his escape was front-page news, he apparently planned to stop killing, cherish his freedom, remake his life. Or so he would say later. Jail, he felt, had damped the fires that drove him to kill. He had changed, he thought; he was in control now. He was wrong.

On January 7, 1978, Ted Bundy got off the bus in Tallahassee, home of Florida State University, hoping to once again lose himself in a campus environment by passing as a graduate student. His first priority would be a new identity, complete with a social security card and driver's license. He would also need several backup IDs so he could switch quickly if the need arose. Giving the name Chris Hagen, he rented a room at The Oaks, a ramshackle boardinghouse near the campus.

The next priority was to find work — something low-profile, possibly as a janitor or repairman. He applied for work at a construction site but was told that he needed identification. That was his only stab at job-hunting. His resolve to go straight lasted about two days. Then he started stealing — a bicycle, along with a television set, a radio, and a typewriter to furnish his room at The Oaks. Soon he was shoplifting in supermarkets and stealing credit cards from wallets that women left unattended in their shopping carts. At night he sat alone in his room drinking beer, trying to regain the weight he'd lost while he was in jail. He began growing a mustache, and whenever he went out he penciled a fake mole on his left cheek. Other than that, he made no effort at disguise.

Bundy found that he didn't really like Tallahassee — or perhaps he just missed the notoriety, the action, of his other life. In any case, abandoning the notion of finding work, he decided to move on as soon as he'd established a false identity. Had he done so, he might still be at large today. But in a sense, he sealed his own fate when he wriggled through the trapdoor in the ceiling of his Colorado jail cell. Ted Bundy could elude the authorities almost at will, it seemed, but he could not escape what he was. Already, the demons were stirring.

Saturday night, January 14, began typically enough at the Chi Omega sorority house, home of some of Florida State University's loveliest coeds. Many of the 36 young women who lived in the split-level structure had dates; others planned to attend campus parties alone. A few were staying home.

Early that evening, Karen Chandler went to her parents' home to cook dinner for her mother, who was ill with the flu. Then she returned to the sorority house to work on a sewing project. Her roommate, Kathy Kleiner, went out to dinner with her fiancé that evening. Margaret Bowman, a 21-year-old student from St. Petersburg, had a blind date arranged by another sorority sister, Melanie Nelson. Nelson had no plans of her own, so she grabbed another Chi O, Lisa Levy, and went next door to a popular campus bar called Sherrod's. Also in the crowded bar that night was a thin, brown-haired man in his early thirties, eying various women with cold appraisal.

Shortly after 2 a.m., Melanie Nelson left Sherrod's. Lisa Levy had come home earlier. When Nelson arrived at the back entrance of the sorority house, she found that the sliding glass door, which was usually secured with a combination lock, was ajar. This was troubling, but it was not unheard of; the girls had had trouble with the lock earlier in the week.

Margaret Bowman and Lisa Levy died and two other young women were gravely hurt during Ted Bundy's 1978 rampage through the Chi Omega sorority house at Florida State University.

MARGARET BOWMAN

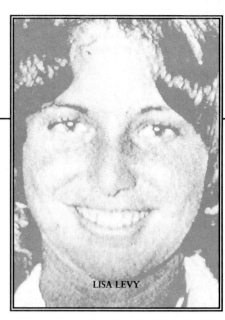

LISA LEVY

Inside the house, Nelson ran into Margaret Bowman, who was anxious to talk about her blind date. The two coeds went upstairs to Bowman's room, where they chatted until after 2:35. Melanie Nelson went back to her own room, and at 2:45 she turned out the light.

At 3 a.m. Nita Neary returned to the house, saying good night to her boyfriend at the back door. She, too, was surprised to find the door open. As she stepped inside, securing the door behind her, she heard running footsteps in the corridor above, heading for the stairway in front of her. A tall, slender man appeared on the stairs. He was wearing a dark jacket and a blue knit cap pulled down low over his face. In his right hand he clutched a large, rough club. It looked like a log. Neary caught only a glimpse of the intruder's profile as he rushed past her, but she would remember his long, straight nose and thin lips. In an instant, the man slipped through the front door and vanished.

At first, Neary thought the house might have been burglarized. She darted upstairs and woke her roommate, Nancy Dowdy. One of them grabbed an umbrella to use as a weapon, and the two went downstairs to see if everything was secure. It was. They went back upstairs and woke the Chi Omega house president, Jacqueline McGill. As the three women stood talking in a hallway, Karen Chandler stumbled out of her room, crashing heavily against a wall as if she were drunk. Her three sorority sisters called out to her. Chandler turned. Her face was covered with blood. Her skull, jawbone, both cheeks, and the orbit of her right eye were shattered. She tried to speak and couldn't; her mouth was full of blood.

Screams filled the house as McGill dashed into Chandler's room. Chandler's roommate, Kathy Kleiner, sat propped up in her bed, holding her head in her hands and moaning. Blood gushed from several head wounds, oozing through her fingers onto the bed. Pieces of oak bark were strewn over the pillows and bedding. The spray of gore had reached even to the walls and ceiling. Several teeth lay scattered on Kleiner's bloody sheets.

At 3:23 a.m., Tallahassee Police Officer Oscar Brannon was the first to reach the scene. Three minutes later, he was joined by FSU police officers Ray Crew and Bill Taylor. A team of paramedics arrived within minutes and started working on the injured women, trying to clear their airways. Both victims were in danger of choking to death on their own blood.

The scene was chaos: Terrified young women scurried in all directions; more police and paramedics kept arriving. Trying to establish some order, police attempted to corral the coeds in one upstairs room. Officer Crew went door-to-door upstairs, checking the bedrooms, waking anyone who had somehow managed thus far to sleep through the horror. The door to Lisa Levy's room was closed. Crew pushed it open.

"Lisa?" he called. There was no answer. Crew stepped inside. The room was dark. He turned on a light. The young woman was lying in bed with her back toward him. The covers were pulled up around her shoulders. Mary Crenshaw, the housemother, hovered in the doorway as Crew stepped over to the bed. He reached down and shook Levy by the shoulder. There was no response. He rolled her onto her back and saw a small bloodstain at breast level on the sheet. Crew thought that there was a gunshot wound. "Get the medics," he said.

The emergency team rushed to Levy's bedside and tried frantically to revive her, but at first they couldn't even locate the source of her injuries. As they cut off her nightgown, however, even the case-hardened medical technicians could not hide their horror. Lisa Levy's right nipple had been bitten almost completely off; it dangled by a thin strand of tissue. And there was more blood, much more.

Officer Crew knew then that it was too late to save her; the body was already growing cold. Later, investigators would discover a savage double bite mark on Levy's left buttock, where the attacker had torn at her flesh with his

A coed gazes warily from the Chi Omega house the morning after the killings.

KIMBERLY LEACH

Twelve-year-old Kimberly Leach,
Bundy's last victim, was abducted from
Lake City Junior High School
in Florida on February 9, 1978.

teeth, and extensive ripping and slashing of the victim's vagina and rectum. The cause of these last injuries would not be known for several days, until police discovered an aerosol hair spray bottle coated with blood, fecal matter, and matted hair.

While the paramedics hooked up a cardiac monitor and futilely threaded a breathing tube down Lisa Levy's throat, Crew moved on, the housemother still trailing behind him. They came to Margaret Bowman's room. The door was ajar. Crew pushed it open. The glow of a street lamp outside the window dimly outlined the coed's figure lying in bed, her long, dark hair spread out against her white pillow.

Crew stepped into the room and looked down at the bed. Margaret Bowman lay face down with the covers pulled up around her neck. A bubble of red ooze had welled up and hardened over the right side of her head. Her skull was shattered; Crew could see her brain. He turned and pushed Mary Crenshaw back out into the hallway, shutting the door behind her.

Stepping back to the bed, Crew pulled down the blanket that covered Margaret Bowman's body. There was a nylon stocking knotted around her neck, biting into the flesh. A gold necklace was tangled in the folds of nylon. Crew knew there was no point in trying to revive her.

Karen Chandler and Kathy Kleiner were rushed to the Tallahassee hospital for emergency surgery. Both women would survive. Lisa Levy was pronounced dead on arrival in the hospital's emergency room. Margaret Bowman was taken directly to the hospital morgue.

It would take several days to sort out the carnage at the Chi Omega house, but a few facts seemed fairly clear. The assaults had all taken place within a span of only 15 minutes, within earshot of about three dozen people. The killer had snatched up a heavy oak log from a woodpile at the back of the house to use as a club. Apparently he had also brought along his own supply of pantyhose to use as garrotes. And after killing two girls in the most savage way imaginable, he covered their bodies almost tenderly with their own blankets.

Incredibly, Ted Bundy's night was not yet over.

Debbie Ciccarelli and Nancy Young shared an apartment in half of an old frame duplex a few blocks away from the Chi O house. Earlier that night, the young women had been out dancing with a friend, Cheryl Thomas, who lived in the other half of the duplex. About 4 a.m. the roommates were jolted awake by loud thumping noises coming through the wall that separated their apartment from Thomas's. They picked up the phone and dialed her number. They could hear the phone ringing in the other apartment, but it went unanswered. Through the thin wall, they heard moans and a crashing sound. "Okay, that's it," Young said. "Call the police—*now!*"

Spurred by the horror at the Chi Omega house, the Tallahassee police were out in force that night. Within three minutes, a dozen patrol cars screeched to a halt in front of the duplex. Several officers banged on the door of Thomas's apartment, while others circled around back to surround the house. When Thomas failed to answer, her housemates opened her door with a spare key. Guns drawn, the police entered the apartment.

Cheryl Thomas lay diagonally across her bed, her face and hair wet with blood. She wore only a pair of thin cotton underpants; a sweater lay beside her. Tangled in her bedclothes was a crude mask, complete with eye holes, fashioned from a pair of pantyhose. "My God," breathed one of the officers. "She's still alive!"

Within minutes, the young woman was on her way to the Tallahassee hospital. Her skull had been fractured in five places by furious blows from a club. In time she would recover—at least partially. Nerve damage left her deaf in one ear, and she suffered a permanent loss of balance. Cheryl Thomas had come to Florida State to study dance.

Ted Bundy, the charming young law student, was no more. In his place was a predator, completely in thrall to his own rage. Gone was the finesse that had once marked some of his earlier abductions. His object now was slaughter, as fast and furious as possible.

It was all Bundy could do to keep from bragging about his atrocities. The day after the Chi O killings, some board-

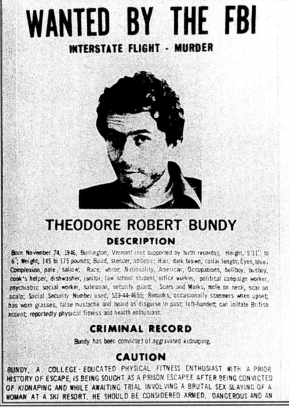

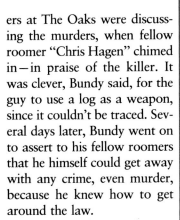

WANTED BY THE FBI

INTERSTATE FLIGHT - MURDER

THEODORE ROBERT BUNDY

DESCRIPTION

Born November 24, 1946, Burlington, Vermont (not supported by birth records); Height, 5'11" to 6'; Weight, 145 to 175 pounds; Build, slender, athletic; Hair, dark brown, collar length; Eyes, blue; Complexion, pale / sallow; Race, white; Nationality, American; Occupations, bellboy, busboy, cook's helper, dishwasher, janitor, law school student; office worker, political campaign worker, psychiatric social worker, salesman, security guard; Scars and Marks, mole on neck, scar on scalp; Social Security Number used, 533-44-4655; Remarks, occasionally stammers when upset; has worn glasses, false mustache and beard as disguise in past; left-handed; can imitate British accent; reportedly physical fitness and health enthusiast.

CRIMINAL RECORD

Bundy has been convicted of aggravated kidnaping.

CAUTION

BUNDY, A COLLEGE-EDUCATED PHYSICAL FITNESS ENTHUSIAST WITH A PRIOR HISTORY OF ESCAPE, IS BEING SOUGHT AS A PRISON ESCAPEE AFTER BEING CONVICTED OF KIDNAPING AND WHILE AWAITING TRIAL INVOLVING A BRUTAL SEX SLAYING OF A WOMAN AT A SKI RESORT. HE SHOULD BE CONSIDERED ARMED, DANGEROUS AND AN

Bundy made the FBI's most wanted list just five days before his arrest in Pensacola, Florida, on February 15, 1978.

ers at The Oaks were discussing the murders, when fellow roomer "Chris Hagen" chimed in—in praise of the killer. It was clever, Bundy said, for the guy to use a log as a weapon, since it couldn't be traced. Several days later, Bundy went on to assert to his fellow roomers that he himself could get away with any crime, even murder, because he knew how to get around the law.

Witnesses who saw him in those days were struck by his slurred speech and shambling gait. Bundy, who had once hidden behind such an attractive mask, could no longer offer even the pretense of normalcy.

He was inexplicably reckless. Although he had not yet gotten a job or paid his rent, he used stolen credit cards to buy trifles: a belt, luggage, underwear, a pipe and tobacco, and—most frequently—socks. Bundy found it necessary to charge at least 30 pairs of socks on his stolen cards. "One of my fondest dreams," he once said, "is to have all the underwear and socks I ever could conceivably use. It's one of my fantasies." (Fetishism involving footwear is common in severe cases of sexual deviance.)

Presumably, Bundy was wearing fresh socks on Monday, February 6, as he headed east toward Jacksonville in a stolen Dodge van. He seemed in no particular hurry, stopping along the way to charge more merchandise and meals on his credit cards—including, at one stop, $8.58 worth of pastries and cookies. At night he put in at motels, skipping out on the bill when morning came. He did not yet know where he was going.

On February 9, Kimberly Diane Leach was in a hurry to get to class at Lake City Junior High School. A fresh-faced 12-year-old girl with dark hair, Kimberly had been elected first runner-up to the queen at the school's annual Valentine's Day Dance. In her excitement over the honor, she left her purse behind when she went from her homeroom to gym class. It was raining outside, but nevertheless

Kimberly ran across the school courtyard to retrieve the purse. A friend later remembered seeing a stranger beckoning Kimberly toward a white van.

In his spiraling disintegration, Ted Bundy had become less particular in his choice of victims. Pretty coeds were preferable, certainly, but in a pinch, a little girl would serve. After all—as authorities would eventually find out—he'd already killed at least one other little girl.

It would be nearly two months before Florida State Trooper Kenneth Robinson, searching for Kimberly Leach's body in a remote and swampy state park, noticed something unusual beneath an abandoned hog shed. The site had for years served as a dumping ground for a local meat packer, and animal bones and debris were scattered everywhere, attracting buzzards and other kinds of scavengers. The bone that caught Robinson's attention, however, was protruding from a small sneaker.

Bundy had taken his 12-year-old victim into a deserted pigsty and killed her there, leaving her clothes folded in a neat stack beside her. Little was left of the body after eight weeks of exposure, but the coroner's inquest revealed a severe neck wound and massive damage to the pelvic region. These facts, and the position of the remains when they were found, implied that the child had been on her hands and knees when Bundy slit her throat from behind, as if he were butchering a hog.

The killer returned to Tallahassee on the same day that Kimberly Leach disappeared. He ditched the van and stole a Toyota. If he feared discovery, changing vehicles was the only sign of it. Previously, he'd resolved to leave the city as soon as he'd established a new identity. When he returned to The Oaks there was a false birth certificate waiting for him in his mailbox—his ticket out, as it were. Still, Bundy didn't leave. He took a date to an expensive French restaurant for dinner.

During the 1979 Chi Omega murder trial in Miami, forensic odontologist Richard Souviron points to a picture of Ted Bundy's teeth. The teeth matched bite marks in Lisa Levy's flesh.

After his date, Bundy pulled the Toyota up to The Oaks in preparation for loading it: He was going to leave. At precisely that moment, a police officer approached him. With the Chi Omega murders fresh on their minds, the police were quick to pick up on anything out of the ordinary, including a man who was out late at night for no apparent reason. The officer asked to see a driver's license; Bundy had none. When the officer walked back to his squad car to call in the license plate number, Bundy bolted on foot and escaped.

He'd been within an arm's reach of capture and, incredibly, he didn't flee. The next morning, as though he hadn't a care in the world, he was out playing racquetball and riding his bicycle. While he was out, a police officer called at his boardinghouse, canvassing the neighborhood for leads in the Chi Omega killings. Bundy knew the officer had been there, and still he chose to stay put. He seemed either to relish the danger he courted, or to be oblivious to it. It's possible that he was by now so caught up in his imagined superiority that he simply found the idea of his own capture inconceivable.

Finally, on February 12, barely one month after arriving in Florida, Bundy decided he'd overstayed his welcome. He gathered up his stolen possessions, gave away a box of cookies to a woman who lived down the hall, wiped his room clean of fingerprints, and slipped out of town. True to form, he stole a VW bug and drove west out of the city. He didn't get far.

At 1:30 a.m. on February 15, David Lee, a Pensacola patrolman, was cruising his route when he noticed an orange VW pulling out from an alley alongside a restaurant parking lot. Since the restaurant was closed, Lee decided to investigate. At first he was simply curious to see who was in the car. But as he turned on his flashing blue lights, the VW started to pull away. Lee radioed in the license number. A computer check came up positive; the car was stolen. Lee gave chase, signaling the Volkswagen to pull over. Instead, it picked up speed. Lee ran the car down and pulled it over about a mile down the road. Stepping out of his squad car, the patrolman drew his revolver and approached from behind. He ordered the driver to get out and lie face down on the pavement.

Two and a half years earlier, in Utah, Ted Bundy had smiled engagingly at an arresting officer and tried to bluff his way out. Now he chose to fight. As Officer Lee bent down and snapped his handcuffs onto the suspect's left wrist, Bundy rolled over and kicked the policeman's legs out from under him. The two struggled on the ground briefly before Lee fired a warning shot into the air. Bundy jumped up and ran. Lee shouted after him to halt, but Bundy kept running. The policeman saw a glint from the handcuffs on

Bundy's wrist and mistook it for a gun. He leveled his revolver and fired again.

Bundy hit the ground and lay still. Lee approached warily. "When I rolled him over to see how badly he was hurt," the officer later reported, "that's when he came back 'alive,' trying to take my pistol from me." The fight resumed, but finally Lee managed to subdue his suspect, handcuffing Bundy's hands behind his back. Lee had no idea that he had collared a notorious killer. He was just relieved that the somewhat sloppy arrest was over. As for Bundy, all the fight had gone out of him. Sitting in the back of Lee's patrol car, he kept mumbling one phrase over and over. "I wish you had killed me," he said. "I wish you had killed me." The statement was typically theatrical—and almost certainly false. In the months and years to come, Bundy would strive mightily to stay alive.

Jailed on a variety of charges, including automobile theft, he refused for two days to give his real name. But police connected the alias he gave—Kenneth Misner—with its real owner, a man living in Tallahassee. Bundy had stolen Misner's student identification and used it to send off for the duplicate birth certificate that he wanted. Once a Tallahassee connection was established, detectives from that city and from Leon County, where Kimberly Leach had disappeared, hurried to Pensacola. The Chi Omega murders and the little girl's fate were very much on their minds.

Bundy, still silent about his real identity, was fingerprinted, and the prints were sent to the local FBI office. Results were not yet in on the night of February 16, when the suspect finally announced his name in return for access to a phone and some other minor privileges. Doubtless he expected these local cops to greet his revelation with something akin to awe: Here they were with a big-time celebrity killer in their grasp. To his astonishment and utter deflation, he got only blank stares. None of them knew who he was.

They soon learned. The FBI confirmed that the suspected car thief was indeed Ted Bundy, who'd just attained a spot on the bureau's most wanted list. By now, authorities in the Northwest, veterans of the Bundy case, had been alerted. They began phoning frantically to fill in their Florida counterparts on exactly what sort of creature they had netted. And Detectives Norman Chapman of the Pensacola police, Don Patchen from Tallahassee, and Stephen Bodiford of the Leon County Sheriff's Office began questioning their man in earnest.

Just after midnight on February 17, Bundy began to talk—and to haggle. Without confessing to anything, he implied that he could help the investigators out with the Florida cases, not to mention a number of murders in several states out West. He was vague about exactly what he wanted in return, although a clear goal was to avoid eventual execution. His avowed hope was to be institutionalized, preferably back home in Washington where he could be near his mother.

The interrogation went on for hours at a time over the next several days, with Ted usually controlling its diverse directions. Given his rapt and captive audience, he explored with relish his own character and habits, his likes and dislikes. If not especially pertinent, some of the exposition was telling. Speaking of his night-owl existence, Bundy said with a smile, "Sometimes I feel like a vampire." He discussed his "problem," as he termed it, indicating that it involved a taste for pornography.

At one point, a detective suggested to Bundy that he might prove his good intentions by telling them what happened to Kimberly Leach. It would, the officer said, be a comfort to the child's family. Bundy seemed to think the idea over for a minute. He crumpled an empty cigarette pack and tossed it onto the floor. Then he looked up at his interrogators. "But I'm the most cold-blooded sonofabitch you'll ever meet," he said.

In July of 1978, Bundy was indicted for the murders of Margaret Bowman, Lisa Levy, and Kimberly Diane Leach. There would be two separate trials, and they would have similar conclusions.

The Miami trial of Ted Bundy for the Chi Omega killings proved to be one of the most complicated and bizarre proceedings in legal history. As in Utah, Bundy's courtroom histrionics in Florida only added to the confusion. At one point, the jurors were bewildered to find him filling three roles at once—defendant, defense attorney, and witness for the defense.

As his own defense lawyer, Bundy could, and did, summon prospective witnesses to be interviewed by him at his new home, the Leon County jail. These included the Chi Omega coeds who had survived his deadly Saturday night visit to their sorority house. Even Karen Chandler had to submit to this frightening indignity. Her answers to Bundy's questions were sometimes hard to understand, per-

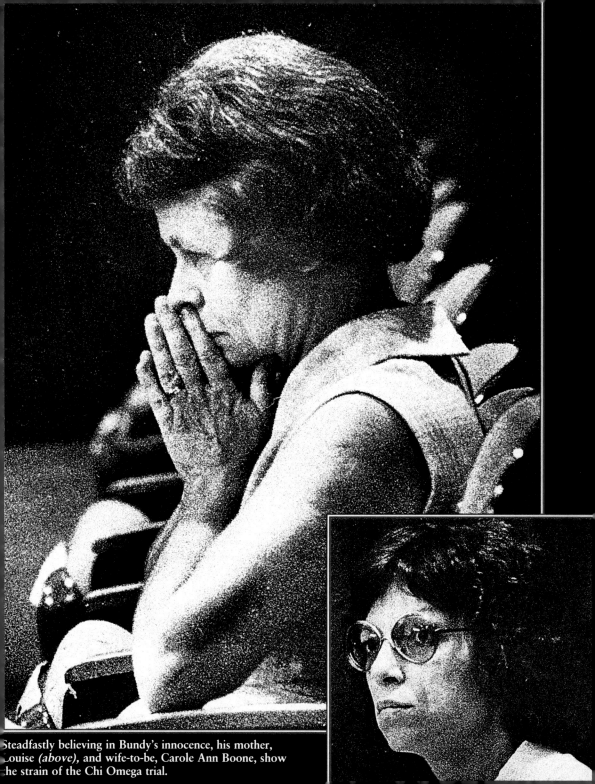

Steadfastly believing in Bundy's innocence, his mother, Louise *(above),* and wife-to-be, Carole Ann Boone, show the strain of the Chi Omega trial.

haps because her jaw had been smashed, courtesy of her inquisitor.

In the end, it would take more than a failed law student's cruel games and courtroom antics to overcome the accumulation of damning evidence. Karen Chandler, Kathy Kleiner, and Cheryl Thomas each delivered eyewitness testimony. These, the jury was reminded, were the lucky ones, the ones Bundy had not managed to kill. From the witness stand, Nita Neary identified Bundy as the man she had seen run out the front door of the Chi Omega house the night of the killings. A parade of experts followed, presenting a blitz of forensic evidence. Their strongest proof came in the form of photographs—pictures of the teeth marks Bundy left in the flesh of Lisa Levy. The marks, when matched to a plaster impression of Bundy's teeth, had a powerful effect on the jury.

Yet even as the details of his depravity accumulated, Bundy somehow managed to attract women. "Ted's Groupies," as they were known, jammed the visitor's gallery throughout the trial, their eyes riveted on their hero. From time to time he would turn and flash them a smile.

The court, however, was not charmed by the defendant. His posturing and bickering served to alienate not only the judge and jury but also his own lawyers. As a result, he would pass up a chance to save his own skin. After protracted plea bargaining between prosecution and defense, Bundy walked into court one day holding an envelope that contained his confessions to the Chi Omega and Kimberly Leach killings. These were part of an agreement that would have meant life in prison but would have spared him the death penalty.

Rather than merely submitting the confessions and letting the legal system take its course, however, Bundy could not resist an attack on his own lawyer, public defender Mike Minerva. Minerva was, in fact, a highly ethical and able lawyer; his real sin was that he believed his client was guilty and had told him so. Bundy moved to dismiss him, telling the judge that Minerva was inept and defeatist. At this point, prosecutors silently signaled the defense table that the plea bargain deal was off: The prosecution wasn't about to take a chance that Bundy's confessions would be invalidated on appeal over the issue of his appointed attorney's competence.

More than three years after Carol DaRonch *(top)* helped send Ted Bundy to prison for kidnapping in Utah, she appears in court in Miami to read a statement during the sentencing phase of the Chi Omega murder trial. Earlier in the proceedings, Kathy Kleiner DeShields, a survivor of the sorority house bloodletting, testifies about the injuries she sustained when Bundy bludgeoned her.

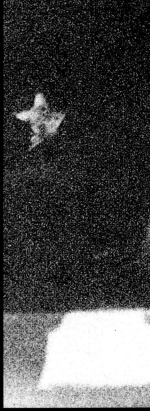

Starring in his own courtroom drama of legal maneuverings prior to the Chi Omega murder trial, Ted Bundy displays a range of moods—amiably arguing a legal point on his own behalf *(top left)*, purposefully preparing for his courtroom defense *(top center)*, joking with newsmen as he leaves the Leon County courthouse *(top right)*, and grimly contemplating jury selection.

During the Chi Omega trial, Bundy takes a close look *(above)* at pictures comparing his teeth to the bite marks left on one of the murder victims. The dental forensic evidence was particularly damning. Later, a much subdued Bundy *(above, right)* absorbs the jury's recommendation that he be sentenced to death for the sorority house killings. The convicted slayer had lost some of his theatrical flair by the time of his 1980 trial for the murder of Kimberly Leach, but he still managed to applaud a courtroom joke.

His lawyers and Carole Ann Boone counseled Bundy against such injudicious behavior, but the advice fell on deaf ears. Bundy's arrogance was such that he simply could not grasp the seriousness of his situation. "I'll be there when I feel like it," he would tell jailers when they arrived to take him to court. On one occasion, with the jury absent from the courtroom, he mugged for news cameras in a way that beggared the very notion of bad taste: holding a model of his own teeth against an enlarged photograph of the bite marks on Lisa Levy's body.

For all the courtroom dramatics, the trial ultimately wound to a conclusion so tedious that two of the jurors actually dozed in their chairs during closing arguments. On July 23, 1979, after barely six hours of deliberation, the jury convicted Bundy on two counts of first-degree murder in the Chi Omega slayings.

"I will tell the court that I am not really able to accept the verdict," he informed Judge Edward Cowart, "because all the verdict found in part was that these crimes had been committed. They erred in finding who committed them." The verdict was acceptable to the judge, however, and he sentenced Bundy to death by electrocution for the murders of Margaret Bowman and Lisa Levy.

The following year, Bundy received an additional death sentence for the murder of Kimberly Leach. His groupies were still in attendance at the second murder trial, but by this time their idol's deterioration was plain for all to see. The man who had once shed 35 pounds to prepare himself for a jailbreak had bloated up to 190, and his temper flared easily. After one outburst, as an enraged Bundy tried to stalk out of the courtroom, five court officers surrounded him to stop him. He spun out of control. With television cameras whirring, Bundy reared up like a trapped animal, his mouth gaping, his face contorted with rage *(page 6)*. "You know how far you can push me!" he snarled. After a few moments he regained his composure and resumed his seat, but the damage was done. Ted Bundy had shown his true face.

It took the jury approximately seven hours to conclude that the defendant had, in fact, killed the little girl. His guilt had never really been in doubt. Thus the most memorable part of the Leach trial was not the deliberation of guilt, but the penalty phase. When Carole Ann Boone took the witness stand to plead for the life of her beloved Ted, there began one of the strangest episodes in the history of Florida jurisprudence.

In his guise as his own defense attorney, Bundy rose to question Boone about her relationship with him.

"Is it serious?" he asked.

"Serious enough," she said, "that I want to marry him."

"*Will* you marry me?" asked Bundy.

"Yes!" Boone answered with a giggle.

"Then I *do* hereby marry you," Bundy declared.

Before anyone in the stunned courtroom could react, Carole Ann Boone had become the wife of the nation's most famous serial killer. After careful research, she'd learned that Florida law allowed a public declaration in open court, if properly phrased, to constitute a legal wedding ceremony. A notary public was standing by with a marriage certificate. The bride was wearing a white blouse and a black skirt and sweater. The groom sported a bow tie, a blue jacket, khaki slacks, and argyle socks. The judge could only shake his head in astonishment.

The jury was apparently unswayed by this demonstration of love in bloom, or by Bundy's rambling 40-minute-long summation pleading for his own life. The sentence was death. Once again, the defendant had trouble accepting the decision. Jumping to his feet, he shouted, "Tell the jury they were wrong!"

The bridegroom soon departed, not on his honeymoon, but on a helicopter trip to death row. Even so, he was not entirely dismayed. The road to execution in America was long, and not particularly sure, as Bundy well knew. The game was not over.

In the Florida State Penitentiary at Starke, Bundy enjoyed his assumed status as the world's foremost authority on serial murder. It flattered his outsized ego that so many psychiatrists, reporters, and writers were interested in interviewing him, and he did his best to oblige. "It became almost like acting a role," he told one interviewer, describing the repetition and frequency of his crimes. "It wasn't difficult. The more an actor acts in a role, the better he becomes at it, the more he is apt to feel comfortable in it, to be able to do things spontaneously. And get better, as it were, in his role."

In a remarkable series of interviews with authors Stephen G. Michaud and Hugh Aynesworth, Bundy adopted the coy device of speculating on how some hypothetical third-person serial murderer might have killed. The charade sheltered Bundy from any possible legal repercussions that might have resulted from the interviews, but there was no doubt that he was talking about himself. He spoke of a sinister "entity" that bore the true responsibility for his crimes.

"The initial sexual encounter would be more or less a voluntary one," he said of one of the murders, "but one which did not wholly gratify the full spectrum of desires that he had intended. And so, after the first sexual encounter, gradually his sexual desire builds back up and joins, as it were, these other unfulfilled desires—this other need to totally possess her, after she's passed out, as she lay there in a state somewhere between coma and sleep, he strangled her to death."

These "other unfulfilled desires" became a recurring theme, but one that Bundy never could fully explain. "The sexual act—in the larger scheme of things—was sort of obligatory conduct," he insisted. "Not in itself, you know, the sexual act was not the, the . . . the principal source of gratification."

Every so often, as he struggled to elucidate the real "source of gratification" and the course of its development, Bundy seemed to reveal more than he intended. "And when he's 15," he said of the moment of killing, "it'd be a much more mystical, exciting, intense, overwhelming experience . . . than when he's 50." The statement had a frightening resonance for authorities who remembered an eight-year-old girl named Ann Marie Burr, who had vanished from her home in Tacoma, Washington, on August 31, 1961. A few blocks away lived Ted Bundy, just shy of his 15th birthday. Bundy would deny committing that particular murder.

In his veiled disclosures, the killer's manner was as chilling as his words. He was by turns intense, gloating, excited, nonchalant, indifferent, even amused. He described quite merrily how he had his "own garbage disposal" method at the dumping grounds where he left his kills—a "whole bunch of little beasties who would, in effect, destroy every last shred of the victim."

Sometimes Bundy had trouble keeping his many victims straight; he couldn't remember their names. "Terrible with

I'm the most cold-blooded sonofabitch you'll ever meet.

names," he smirked. "And faces." He even seemed surprised that the killings caused such a furor, that the young women he murdered were mourned so deeply by the people who'd loved them. "What's one less person on the face of the earth anyway?" he shrugged.

The question of just how many people he killed would surface again and again. Bundy would eventually confess officially to 30. Others close to the case placed the number at 36. Once, when a policeman expressed shock that one person had killed 36 women, Bundy shook his head. "Add one digit to that," he said, "and you'll have it."

It may never be clear what he meant by the remark. He may have been saying that the tally was off by one victim, but he may also have meant that the figure was far too low—that the actual number was more than 100. Some investigators, Seattle's Bob Keppel among them, believe the latter interpretation.

Writers and psychiatrists were not Bundy's only visitors on death row. Carole Ann, his wife, stood by him through his early years of imprisonment. The stark, brightly lighted visitor's room didn't make for a terribly romantic setting. Nevertheless, the prisoner managed to impregnate his wife there. Ted Bundy's daughter was born in October 1982. For a time, Carole Bundy would bring the baby along when she visited her husband in prison. Then, in 1986, she left the state to comfort a sick relative and never returned.

Meanwhile, Bundy had abandoned his Mormonism to become a Hindu, although once again his motivation was practical rather than spiritual. As a Hindu he was entitled to a diet consisting of fish and vegetables, vastly preferable to the usual prison fare.

By the end of 1988, however, Bundy was harking back to his Protestant roots, wondering aloud whether his soul had a chance of entering heaven. The timing was not coincidental. After almost nine years on death row, he was running out of appeals, running out of time. His execution date was set: January 24, 1989.

One confidant in Bundy's spiritual discussions was William Hagmaier *(pages 44-45),* an agent attached to the

Federal Bureau of Investigation's Behavioral Sciences Unit in Quantico, Virginia. The unit has since become famous for its pioneer work in probing the psychopathic mind. Hagmaier clearly struck Bundy as a worthy audience for the deepest insights of a killer.

True to his notions of grandeur, the murderer adorned his savagery in metaphysical trappings: He told Hagmaier of the spiritual oneness he achieved with his victims. "You *feel* the last bit of breath leaving their body," Bundy said. "You're looking into their eyes. A person in that situation is God! You then possess them and they shall forever be a part of you. And the grounds where you kill them or leave them become sacred to you, and you will always be drawn back to them." These were the same grounds he'd described earlier as places where the "little beasties" helped him dispose of his garbage.

Sacred unions aside, toward the end Bundy had no compunction whatever about using his victims' bodies one last time: He cynically bartered them, trading the awful details of their deaths in an effort to prolong the only life that had ever mattered to him—his. Agents for the convicted killer hastily contacted various investigators in the Bundy case, promising to provide details of unresolved murders if the detectives would urge Florida governor Robert Martinez to delay the execution. The victims' family members were given the same offer: the truth about how their daughters died, in exchange for a good word on the killer's behalf. Bob Keppel and several other detectives showed up to hear the confessions, although they were vague about commitments to intercede with the governor. Among the families, not a single person agreed to say or do anything that might prolong Bundy's life.

The confessions, when they finally came, left even the hardened detectives cold with contempt and disgust. Bundy told of luring his victims by affecting some injury, playing on their kindness to get them to come within striking range. He told of clubbing them with a crowbar, of handcuffing them, of chatting with them once they regained consciousness. Sometimes it amused him, he said, to pretend that someone else had attacked them and that he was a good Samaritan taking them to a hospital. (Bundy had already described for Bill Hagmaier how, before killing, he sometimes used his victims to animate his sick fantasies. Given sufficient leisure, he would make them dress in certain clothes and pose in ways that re-created pornographic im-

ages that appealed to him. Many of the images came from the covers of the cheap detective magazines that Bundy liked to read. Sometimes he took Polaroid snapshots of the young women during these sessions and kept them as souvenirs. "When you work hard to do something right," he confided, "you don't want to forget it." Also, Bundy confirmed for Hagmaier a horror that other investigators had long sus-

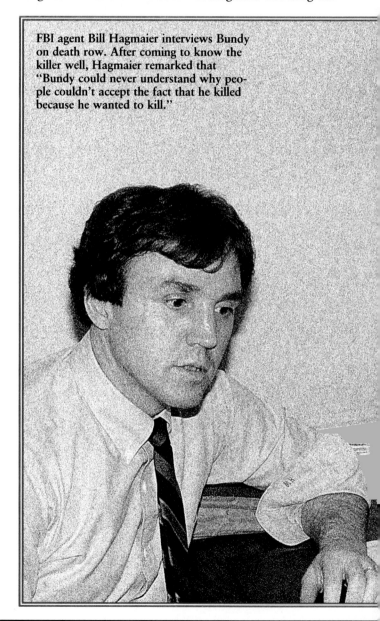

FBI agent Bill Hagmaier interviews Bundy on death row. After coming to know the killer well, Hagmaier remarked that "Bundy could never understand why people couldn't accept the fact that he killed because he wanted to kill."

pected: On the day that he kidnapped Janice Ott and Denise Naslund from Lake Sammamish, he kept both alive for a while. One had to watch the other die.)

In his official confessions, Bundy told how he strangled his victims with lengths of rope, sometimes even as he raped them. After killing, he said, he beheaded at least a dozen of the corpses with hacksaws. Sometimes he cut off the

Rehearsal for Death

After murdering so many, Ted Bundy finally had a change of heart about killing. Hours away from death in Florida's electric chair, he decided not to kill himself.

Suicide was a possibility he discussed with Special Agent William Hagmaier of the FBI's Behavioral Sciences Unit—a law officer who ironically, Bundy came to call his "best friend." The men met in 1985; Bundy was on death row, and Hagmaier was working on the FBI's ongoing mission of interviewing serial killers. On different sides of the law, they nevertheless had certain things in common. They were about the same age, both intelligent—and each, in his own way, an expert on serial murder. A unique rapport developed, and Bundy shared with the agent thoughts and fears he apparently entrusted to no one else.

Bundy "thought about suicide," Hagmaier said. "Alternatives to sitting down in the chair were discussed. He opted to sit down in the chair." Part of suicide's appeal, the agent said, was that Bundy "didn't want to give others the satisfaction of watching him crumble." But Hagmaier added, there was another dimension to the killer's thinking. Concerned about the fate of his soul, Bundy "didn't think it would be appropriate to take another life." To Hagmaier, Bundy's dread of death or seemed real: "In the end, it was he who ended up crying and asking me what to say to God," the agent recalled.

Still, the condemned man greatly feared the pain of electrocution. He turned to Hagmaier for comfort, and the agent, who had researched some 20 executions, offered what help he could. "We rehearsed his death," Hagmaier said, recalling how he tried "to describe the room, to describe the chair, to describe the procedure" so Bundy would be better prepared and less afraid.

The agent and the murderer last saw each other on Monday, January 23, 1989. The next day at 7 a.m. Bundy entered the Florida State Prison death chamber. He looked haggard but he was also calm. Hagmaier didn't witness the execution, but he said he heard from some who did that Bundy's last words "were very simple, very clear."

The words were: "I'd like you to give my love to my family and friends." About 16 minutes later, Bundy was declared dead.

hands as well. Part of his motive for this was to impede identification of the dead. Evidently, however, that was not the only reason: He carried the heads around with him for days. There were some things he would not discuss for the record—whether he had sex with any of the women after they were dead, for instance. Several investigators believed that he did.

In all, Bundy confessed officially to 11 murders in Washington, 8 in Utah, 3 in Colorado, 3 in Florida, 2 in Oregon, 2 in Idaho, and 1 in California. (Off the record, he had hinted earlier at two more killings: During his brief 1969 stint as a student at Temple University, he implied to a psychologist, he traveled from Philadelphia to kill two young women in nearby Atlantic City, New Jersey.) Of the official tally of 30, Bundy had long been a suspect in some of the cases; others came as a surprise to police. His first killing—first, at least, among those he admitted for the record—was in May of 1973, earlier than most investigators had thought. The victim was an unidentified hitchhiker whom Bundy picked up near Olympia, Washington. It also turned out that little Kimberly Leach was his second 12-year-old victim. The first was Lynette Culver, kidnapped from her junior high school in Pocatello, Idaho, on May 6, 1975. Some of the dead Bundy could not identify. Some have never been identified.

In the last days of his life, Bundy did not even bother to feign remorse for the lives he took. He was lavish, however, in his self-pity. While talking to Bob Keppel, he burst into tears, then went on to beg for "sixty, ninety days. A few months." Sometime earlier, there had been a similarly weepy scene with Bill Hagmaier. Bundy's eyes had filled with tears and he said, "You know, they want to kill me." He seemed amazed.

Bundy reserved some time on his last night to videotape a segment with Dr. James Dobson, an evangelist. On the tape, the killer warns against pornography, which, he says, led him into his violent ways. It is his own version of the "devil made me do it" defense.

Bundy also talked to his mother that night.

"I'm sorry I've given you such grief," he told her. "A part of me was hidden all the time."

"You'll always be my precious son," Louise Bundy answered. "We just want you to know how much we love you and always will."

Bundy spent what was left of his last night in a 14-by-9-foot "death watch" cell, less than 30 feet from the Florida electric chair (opposite). In the morning, guards brought him a last meal of steak, eggs, hash-brown potatoes, and coffee. Bundy left the tray untouched. As the appointed hour drew closer, the prison barber arrived to shave Bundy's head and his right calf so that the electrodes could be attached.

Outside the prison, while turkey vultures circled overhead, more than a thousand people gathered to await the execution. Some demonstrators carried signs reading "Bundy BBQ" and "Fry, Ted, Fry." A large truck circled the jubilant crowd, carrying an effigy of Bundy strapped to an electric chair. A local radio station gleefully anticipated the day's event, complete with the sound of bacon sizzling in a hot pan.

Inside, Bundy was given loose-fitting blue pants and a light blue shirt. A few minutes before 7 a.m., a pair of guards arrived to lead the condemned man down a short hallway to the gray death chamber. By now, no trace of the killer's former arrogant manner remained. "He was weak-kneed, if not wobbly," a witness observed. "He looked old, tired, and gaunt."

A steel cap clamped down on Bundy's shaved head as the guards strapped him into the chair. Behind him, a hooded executioner stood waiting. Beneath the hood, witnesses claimed, were long, curling eyelashes; Bundy's executioner, it seemed, was a woman.

At 7:06 a.m., Prison Superintendent Thomas Barton gave a nod to the executioner. She reached out and pressed a button. Bundy's fists clenched as 2,000 volts of electricity coursed through his body. After 10 minutes, Dr. Frank Kilgo stepped forward and shone a small flashlight into Bundy's pupils. "He's dead," the doctor announced.

Outside, the crowd reacted with frenzied delight. And in homes stretching from the northwestern United States to Florida, families of victims who had died so young, with so much promise unfulfilled, factored into the equations of their private grief whatever comfort could be had from Ted Bundy's death.

For one person, certainly, his death marked the end of a long nightmare. "He lived too long, if you ask me," said Carol DaRonch, who was 33 years old when Bundy died. "If they'd have asked me, I probably would have pulled that switch myself." ◆

I'm sorry I've given you such grief. A part of me was hidden all the time.

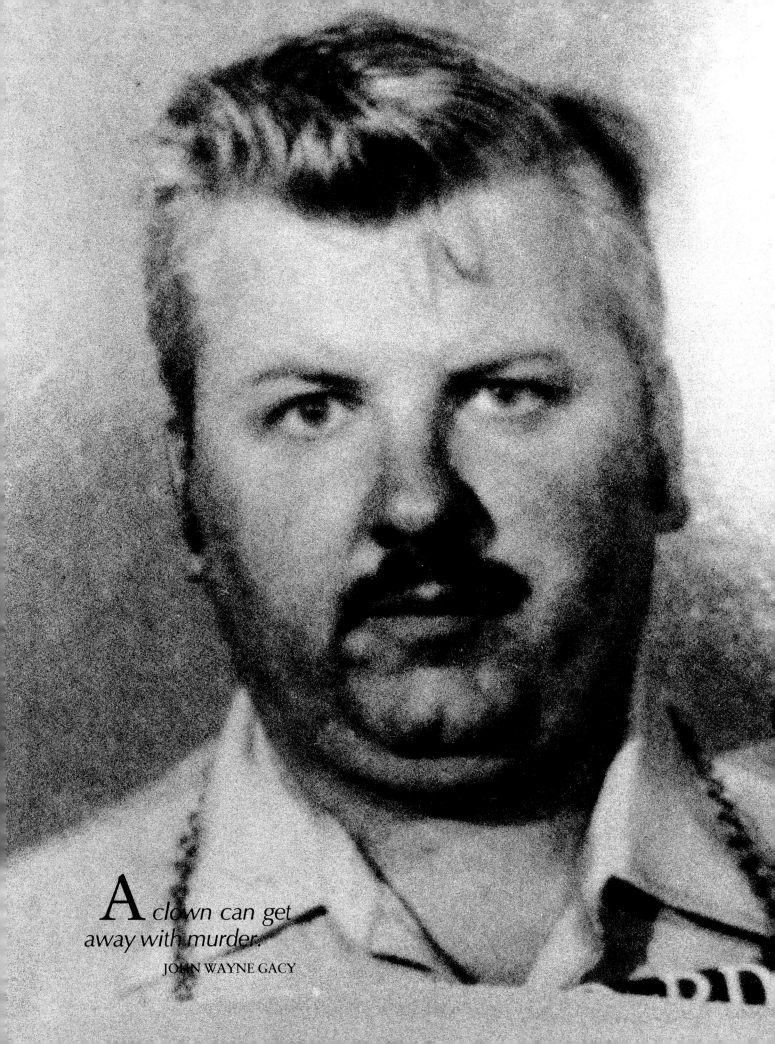

A clown can get
away with murder.
JOHN WAYNE GACY

2

Crawlspace

---

ortunetelling afforded Florece Branson a pretty good living. A veteran of the craft, she practiced it four nights a week at a restaurant, saw clients at her home, and performed at private parties. Branson's business usually boomed during the Christmas season, and this was the case in 1978 when holiday festivities got into high gear in well-tended Norwood Park Township, a suburb just northwest of Chicago. On December 2 Branson set up shop in the home of her friends Ron and Gloria Rhode, who were throwing a party for about a dozen guests.

As usual, Branson worked hard at her trade. Her main implement was a 24-card euchre deck that each of her subjects would shuffle, imparting a sort of individual imprint to the cards. Then she would lay the cards out in a certain pattern and divine their meaning. Along with knowing the message of each card, she brought to bear her presumed psychic powers to get the reading right. And, like many colleagues in her line of work, she was adept at picking up clues to character and circumstance from the physical traits of her subject—a tone of voice, a nervous twitch, a quirk of posture or grooming, a mode of dress. People could reveal a lot about themselves to a psychic while scarcely saying a word.

Settled at a card table in a small room that the Rhodes used as an office, Branson went about her duties. It was a pleasant enough evening, she recalls. She liked her host and hostess, and she knew most of their guests. She'd read the cards for about half of them when a stranger lowered his bulk into the chair across from her and introduced himself: John Gacy was the name.

The psychic gave him a quick professional once-over. He was a big man—not especially tall, but heavy: about five feet seven and a good 225 pounds. He bulged beneath his wrinkled, gray-and-brown checkered sports coat and brown polyester pants. When Branson looked at his bloated face she saw exhaustion. Blue eyes stared unblinkingly from under hooded lids; jowls and a double chin sagged heavily on his shirt collar. There was something un-

healthy about this one, Branson concluded, something dissipated—or worse.

She handed over the cards and watched while he gave them a quick shuffle. His fingers were thick and stubby. A gaudy gold and diamond ring gleamed on his left hand.

As Branson remembers it, the rest of the reading went this way: She retrieved the deck and turned up the top 12 cards, revealing in quick succession the ace of hearts—the card of love—surrounded by jacks that were separated by spades. The jacks, she interpreted, meant that the man had boyfriends, many of them; the spades suggested darkness. Branson had experienced a vague unease about this man from the minute she saw him; now she felt distinct dread.

"You have boyfriends," she ventured.

"You mean friends, people I drink with?" he asked.

"No, I mean young men you have a . . . a different interest in. You're attracted to them romantically."

"That's just something I fantasize about," he said quietly. She didn't pursue the subject.

She turned up the ace of spades; it was inverted, denoting danger. Then came another ace, the ace of clubs, indicating jail time or trouble with the law. The cards lay there, mutely telling of danger to the jacks—the boyfriends—maybe even of crimes committed against them. Florece Branson's stomach churned.

Gacy was asking about whether there was a business deal or a woman in the cards. Ah, yes, Branson said. There were riches in his future. She followed this cliché with a quick wrap-up of the reading, and as soon as he left her table she put the cards in her purse. She wouldn't use that deck again, she decided, not that night or ever.

As Branson tells the story, the party ended and she made her way into the night, vastly relieved to be done with the job. On her way home she stopped her car and climbed out into the freezing air. With the fleshy face of John Gacy looming in her mind, she staggered to the side of the highway and vomited.

Florece Branson knew with intuitive certainty that she'd

been in the presence of evil that night, but she didn't know the details. Psychic or not, she could not have known about the crawlspace. She could not even have imagined.

About three weeks later, police armed with a search warrant visited John Wayne Gacy's ranch-style brick house at 8213 West Summerdale Avenue in Norwood Park. They went inside and made their way directly to a closet off the foyer. Inside it was a small plywood trapdoor that led down beneath the house. An evidence technician named Daniel Genty peered through the door and saw that the crawlspace was covered with standing water, so he waited a quarter of an hour or so for a sump pump to drain the surface.

With the water gone, Genty dropped down into the crawlspace and found himself on a surface of cold mud crusted over with a moist, pale coating of lime. He shone his flashlight through the gloom, dimly illuminating an area 28 by 38 feet and only about two and a half feet high. Wearing coveralls and firefighter's boots, Genty began crawling on his hands and knees through the muck, making his way to

the southeast corner of the crawlspace, against the foundation of the house. His light played over two shallow troughs parallel to the wall. Each was about six feet long and less than two feet wide — grave size. The technician crossed the crawlspace diagonally to the northwest corner, then to the southwest. The beam from his flashlight picked out three puddles of water, each only a few inches across. Two of the pools were alive with worms, hundreds of them, squirming into the mud to escape the light.

Genty decided to start digging in the southwest corner. As he thrust his trenching tool into the soggy ground, a sickening stench exploded from the earth and flooded the crawlspace. Genty turned over another spadeful of sodden soil and saw there amid the clumps of dirt a white, lardlike lump. It was rotted flesh.

It would take weeks for the authorities to finish their work in the chill, dank hell of the crawlspace. When they were done, they had recovered all that was left of 27 young men, murdered by Gacy and left to rot underneath the innocent-looking suburban house. Another body was found crammed into a pit in Gacy's garage and covered with con-

The exterior of John Wayne Gacy's house in a quiet Chicago suburb gave no hint of the atrocities its owner had been hiding. While making renovations and keeping up the appearance of the place, Gacy was also busy burying bodies in the crawlspace *(inset)*.

crete, and another corpse lay under the driveway. Four other victims were recovered from a nearby river. Thirty-three youths in all—sodomized, raped, and tortured, used in unspeakable ways, and then consigned to watery graves or to crude earthen trenches like so much garbage to a landfill. When all was said and done, the grisly toll would constitute a grim record: the most victims officially laid at the door of any one serial killer in American history. John Wayne Gacy liked to do things in a big way.

The news about the crawlspace burst on the public like an erupting infection, but most people who knew John Gacy had a hard time believing it. He was, after all, a local pillar of the community—a successful contractor, a ward heeler of some influence in Democratic party circles, a considerate and thoughtful neighbor, a tireless volunteer for good causes. One of his favorite activities was to deck himself out in circus regalia and, as Pogo the Clown, entertain hospitalized children or senior citizens. Gacy was an organizer, a joiner, and a doer, a hale and hearty good fellow. He was by no means a known homosexual, much less a sexual sadist; twice married and twice divorced, he had the aura of

a man's man, the sort of guy who liked to banter with the other boys about sexual exploits with women.

But John Wayne Gacy was also a man of secrets. He had dark appetites and hidden desires, things that no one else could know, things that he could hardly face himself. He kept some of his secrets under the house. His beloved father, although he was not a killer like the son, had done much the same thing.

John Wayne Gacy was born March 17, 1942, the second of Marion and John Stanley Gacy's three children and their only son. His was the shakiest of starts in this world, as he barely lived through a difficult breech birth. The family of this infant survivor lived on Opal Street in a western section of Chicago that gave a nod to suburbia—there were six houses on the street—but maintained its rural charm. Prairie grass grew in all directions, and the neighbors kept chickens and goats and tended vegetable gardens.

Marion Gacy was a gregarious woman from Racine, Wisconsin. She loved to sing and dance and was not averse to sharing a few drinks with her friends. Marion was also, by nature, a hard worker; she supported herself as a pharmacist prior to her marriage at the age of 30. Her husband was a Chicago native, the son of Polish immigrants. The elder John Gacy was serious and self-contained, a silent, somber individual who seemed largely incapable of displaying the gentler emotions such as happiness or sorrow. He could do anything with his hands—making repairs around the house, painting, even creating his own tools—with order and precision. He worked hard as a machinist, a perfectionist in a perfectionist's trade, and made good money. But he was also impatient and quick-tempered, and he could explode with little warning. At the dinner table he would lunge with a punishing hand at anyone who said a word that displeased him. He drank, he beat his wife, and he believed that to spare the rod was to spoil the child.

John Stanley Gacy expected a lot from his only son. Theirs was the story of generations: The first one to leave the old country just wants to survive; the second generation wants to make good. John Stanley Gacy had made good, and for the third generation he wanted even more. But Johnny's father had little patience with childhood. One of John Wayne Gacy's earliest memories was of angering him

An aerial view of 8213 West Summerdale Avenue shows police and onlookers converging on Gacy's home after news spread of the burial ground in the crawlspace. On December 28, 1978—seven days after the first body was found—police and the media were still camped out around the house *(inset, far left)*, and the body count had reached 22. Remains of the dead were removed in bags *(inset, near left)* and taken to the Cook County morgue for the difficult task of identification.

one day as John Stanley puttered with the car. The son was only four years old and wanted to help, but he bumbled into a collection of parts that his father had neatly laid down in a specific order. John Stanley Gacy liked things orderly. He was expected to deal with tolerances of a thousandth of an inch at the factory where he worked, and that, in his view, was the way things should be at home as well. He yelled at his son and gave him a whipping to remember; he kept a belt for just that purpose. He had to teach the boy a lesson.

Coupled with the physical punishment the father meted out over the years was a pitiless campaign of emotional abuse. John Stanley Gacy never missed an opportunity to let his son know he was a disappointment. The elder Gacy berated the boy for the slightest childish miscue, calling him "dumb and stupid," and the redundant expression fixed itself in Johnny Gacy's psyche like an unwelcome mantra. The child was overweight, clumsy, and inclined to be dreamy and imaginative. He wasn't good at sports, he wasn't good with his hands, and he was sickly.

Johnny's mother told him he had a heart problem from birth, an "enlarged bottleneck heart" she called it, that kept him from the rough-and-tumble play of childhood. The family doctors could find nothing of the sort, but they did have cause to wonder. At about five, the time when a boy begins to care what his classmates think of him, Johnny started to have seizures. He'd pass out for no reason at all. The physicians who examined him did not immediately settle on a precise diagnosis; nevertheless, they prescribed strong barbiturates, such as Dilantin and phenobarbital, that are used to treat seizures. It was not until the boy was 10 that a doctor identified his malady as a form of psychomotor epilepsy. By then, Johnny had already been taking the powerful antiseizure drugs for about five years.

John Stanley Gacy, meanwhile, had his own ideas about what caused the seizures. The father—who would never admit to an illness, even during a pneumonia attack that nearly killed him—believed that the son was playing sick to get out of school or to get attention. Marion Gacy thought differently. Her boy was sick and she did her best to protect him—though her efforts were flawed in at least one way: As an experienced pharmacist, she probably should have realized that her preadolescent son was growing steadily more dependent on the painless highs of mood-altering drugs. But apparently her chief concern in those days was not Johnny's growing addiction, but the ceaseless friction between the boy and his father. Marion tried to be a buffer between them, and she succeeded to such an extent that John Stanley Gacy taunted Johnny about being a "mama's boy" and told him he was "going to be a queer." Calling the child a "he-she" was another favored note of derision.

When he was little more than a toddler, John Wayne Gacy later recalled, a neighbor's 15-year-old mildly retarded daughter took him out into the long prairie grass and pulled his pants down. Johnny told his mother what happened, and afterward there was a lot of yelling between his parents. The child didn't know exactly what the fight was about, but he sensed that he himself was the cause and that he'd done something wrong. Johnny fell prey to an experience every bit as confusing when he was no more than nine years old. One of his father's friends, a contractor, began taking him for rides in his pickup truck, and the rides always included episodes of tickling and wrestling. Invariably, these sessions would end with the boy's face caught between the grown man's legs. Johnny knew in some obscure way that he was being victimized, but he felt powerless to do anything about it. Telling his father was out of the question: More than any physical abuse he could suffer at the hands of a family friend, Johnny feared the sting of his father's taunts about being a "queer."

When Johnny Gacy was about 10 the family moved to a larger house, closer to Chicago. A notable feature of the new place was its spacious basement, an area that became the father's special retreat. It was off-limits to the youngsters and even to Marion Gacy. Every afternoon when John Stanley Gacy came home he descended to the basement to soak up a little classical music—he was partial to the floridly heroic works of German romantic composer Richard Wagner—and pursue projects such as painting by the numbers. All the while, he'd soak up liquor as well. Sometimes, after the drink began to take hold, the family could hear John Stanley talking to himself in two different voices. The household was well aware that he did his hard drinking down there. But no one really knew exactly what else went on in the basement, and everyone was afraid to ask.

If the father had a private lair, the son had already found similar comfort in a playhouse of his own. It was a crawl-space of sorts, a space under the porch at the old house. From there Johnny Gacy could see others but not be seen himself. What he did under the porch was his secret—until the day the boy took his mother's underwear to his playhouse and hid it there in a paper bag. In later years Gacy would tell interviewers that he hadn't taken the lingerie for sexual reasons; as he told his parents, he just liked the feel of it. This excuse won no sympathy from John Stanley, who whipped the boy; but that wasn't the end of the underwear incidents. The adult John Gacy couldn't remember exactly when it happened, but there was a time his younger sister, Karen, found panties in his bed. And once—to humiliate him and to try to end this troubling habit—his mother made him wear women's panties to school under his clothes.

Marion Gacy told her husband about only one of the underwear episodes—the first one. After that she kept silent. But Johnny Gacy believed that his father knew anyway. His father could see straight through him, Johnny thought, could tell when he was lying, could read his secret thoughts. The boy keenly felt his father's disappointment, as well as his own helplessness to hide his flaws and meet the older man's expectations. Johnny was good at some things: He did passably well in school, and he kept himself neat and his room orderly. But these weren't the things John Stanley Gacy was looking for. The father wanted a son who shared his interests, a son who did things just the way he did. When Johnny Gacy was about 11, his father took him on a two-week fishing trip to Wisconsin, just the two of them. It was what the boy had been waiting for: a chance to prove himself to his father and get close to him. But it rained the entire time. "So," Gacy later recalled, "he drank. And the more he drank, the more he figured the rain was my fault." The trip seemed to finalize the rift between father and son, at least from the father's point of view; John Stanley Gacy never took his son fishing again.

Still, a child seldom stops trying to win a parent's affection, and John Wayne Gacy was no exception. If he feared his father, he also loved him, and he desperately needed his approval. John Stanley Gacy was a hard worker and admired that attribute in others, so Johnny set out to prove he could work hard too. At school he ran errands for teachers and helped the school truant officer by phoning parents to check up on absent children. He took on odd jobs after school: He had a paper route, mowed lawns, and at 14 got his first salaried job, delivering groceries for a supermarket. He helped his mother paint rooms and do housework. All this wasn't enough, so he eventually took on more. He learned early that people admired volunteer workers and trusted and respected public servants such as policemen and firemen. So Gacy organized a civil defense squad at his high school and made himself captain. It was most satisfying. He got to put a flashing blue light on his dashboard, and, according to his sisters, he delighted in playing cop, racing off to a fire or traffic accident with the blue light pulsing.

John Wayne Gacy liked the sense of belonging and acceptance that came with his high-profile activities. But in one area he still considered himself a failure—girls. Mostly they just didn't notice him, and if they did, they never thought of him in any romantic way. He was friendly and earnest, but at the age of 18, a time when physical appearance seems to hold the key to almost everything, Gacy had a doughy, shapeless look that held little appeal for teenage females. When he did arrive at sexual initiation at about that age, he fluffed it, and the shame of the experience burned into his mind. After groping at each other in his car for a while, he and the girl had gotten as far as taking her clothes off when Gacy fainted. He passed out, just as he'd done many times before at moments of stress. The girl was shocked; Gacy was mortified—even more so later when he blurted out the incident to his father during an argument. John Stanley Gacy just stared at him, his eyes filled with contempt—and suspicion.

The father ridiculed sissies and weaklings, and according to Marion Gacy, he hated homosexuals. John Wayne Gacy, soft and unathletic, had felt some disturbing sexual stirrings from childhood. Sometimes he wondered how it would feel to hold another boy in his arms. But to please his father—he remembered the taunt about growing up "queer"—he learned to act tough. He bragged with pitiful bravado about his sexual conquests, conquests that never happened.

Still looking for a way to please his father, John Wayne Gacy got into politics. When he was 18 he threw himself into volunteer campaign work for an alderman candidate in the 45th Ward. It was important work, widely recognized, but his father still knocked it. Politicos were phonies, John Stanley Gacy said, and his son was a patsy to work for them for free. Even so, Gacy enjoyed the campaign. His life was not really in high school, he decided, and he dropped out in 1961, in his senior year, at 19.

Gacy's political abilities carried over to other aspects of his life, including his labors on behalf of the Roman Catholic church. As a member of the St. John Berchmann's parish bowling team—bowling was the one sport at which he showed some promise—he recognized that the church was

Young John Gacy: Mask and Reality

Like many other serial killers, John Wayne Gacy led a life that was a study in deception: normal on the outside, twisted at the core. These snapshots from the Gacy family's photograph album, showing the future killer as a child and as a young man, are almost emblematic of his nature: perfectly ordinary on the surface, but hinting at troubled depths.

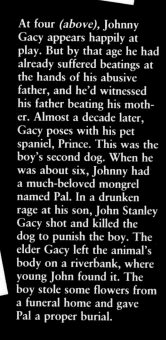

At four *(above),* Johnny Gacy appears happily at play. But by that age he had already suffered beatings at the hands of his abusive father, and he'd witnessed his father beating his mother. Almost a decade later, Gacy poses with his pet spaniel, Prince. This was the boy's second dog. When he was about six, Johnny had a much-beloved mongrel named Pal. In a drunken rage at his son, John Stanley Gacy shot and killed the dog to punish the boy. The elder Gacy left the animal's body on a riverbank, where young John found it. The boy stole some flowers from a funeral home and gave Pal a proper burial.

In 1950 an eight-year-old John Gacy, wearing a robe for a graduation ceremony, smiles for the camera in the yard of his family's Opal Street home. He looks robust, but he was already a sickly child.

Gacy was a high-school dropout, but in 1958 his father humiliated him by forcing him to dress up for this picture holding his sister's diploma. Appearances—even when they were false—were very important to the elder Gacy. The photo was taken outside the Gacy residence on Chicago's Marmora Avenue.

By the time he was 18, Gacy's favorite attire was the uniform of his local civil defense squad, and his greatest thrill involved driving around town acting like a government official. Ironically, the homicidal Gacy was always fascinated by law enforcement and by the trappings of established authority.

not meeting the needs of some parishioners, particularly young ones. So he formed a young adults group called the Chi Ro Club. He organized events, including a formal winter dance, that were moderate successes. Moreover, he endeared himself to the priests by doing odd jobs around the church. He spent so much time there, in fact, that he considered the priesthood. Becoming a priest would not only relieve his nagging concerns regarding his sexual orientation, he reasoned, it would place him above criticism from his father. Sometimes during confession he'd try to nudge the subject around to his calling, but the priests tended to turn the conversation toward practical problems of carpentry and plumbing. Gacy remembered with some chagrin spending an eyebrow-raising amount of time in the confessional—not to detail his sins (for these were few) but to discuss building repairs with the father confessor.

But for all his efforts to please, things were no better at home. He was 19 years old and owed his father payments on a new 1960 Chevy Impala, an arrangement that had seemed good at the time, but that ultimately gave the father more control over the son's life. Once, after a disagreement, the old man grounded his son by taking the car's distributor cap and keeping it for three days. This was the last, most humiliating straw for Gacy. He was debilitated by it, becoming physically and emotionally ill. From a practical standpoint, he was unable to get to work; it never occurred to him to buy another distributor cap at an auto-parts store. The day that the father replaced the hostage part, Gacy picked his mother up from her job, dropped her at home, and told her he needed to go out to get some air in his tires. He didn't come back for three months.

His parents' first contact with him after his departure came in the form of a medical bill from his insurance company. Marion Gacy called the hospital and found out that her son was paying off the bill by working in Las Vegas at a place called the Palm Mortuary. Gacy had been originally signed on as part of the funeral home's ambulance crew; he'd always liked the flashing lights, the urgency, the commanding presence of paramedics at the scenes of accidents or death. But the funeral-home director soon found out that Gacy was too young to work on the ambulances—you had to be 21—and assigned him to the mortuary. There, during a three-month stint, Gacy observed the detached professionalism of the morticians as they went about their work. He learned how bodies are cleaned, treated, embalmed, and

prepared for their final moments aboveground. He even slept on the premises, behind the embalming room. He was often alone with the dead bodies, and he was curious.

When Gacy abruptly quit his job at the mortuary, it was after a run-in with his employer. The boss, it seemed, had been finding bodies entrusted to the mortuary undressed for no apparent reason. On each occasion, the corpse's clothes were found neatly folded next to its casket, and the funeral-home director had come to the conclusion that his new employee was prone to unnatural acts. The director told the police of his suspicions, but Gacy quit his job and the matter was never pursued. Whatever the truth, the accused necrophile had had enough of mortuaries. He called his mother and asked if it would be all right for him to come home.

Oddly enough, the time in Las Vegas seemed to have made more of a man of Gacy in some ways. He'd proved he could make his own way, and he'd apparently found some practical ambitions as well: Back in Chicago, he managed to get himself enrolled in a year-long course at a local business college, even though he had no high-school diploma. When he finished his schooling he found an opening as a management trainee for Nunn-Bush, a large shoe company. It was 1963, and Gacy was 21 years old.

He was a natural, an instant hit as a shoe salesman, and soon he had a job handling the Nunn-Bush line at Robinson's department store in Springfield, Illinois. Gacy's life suddenly seemed to emerge from darkness and doubt onto a shining plain. Living with his maternal uncle and aunt and away from his father's scorn, he found himself. Becoming ever more sociable, he dabbled in local politics. More important, he discovered the Junior Chamber of Commerce—the Jaycees—a group of active, under-30 businessmen. The organization proved a perfect base for the gregarious Gacy. Here up-and-comers involved themselves in charitable works and held meetings to honor one member or another for achievement. *Honor* and *achievement* were Jaycee watchwords. Gacy quickly learned that in such company, drive and energy could make a reputation, and he had plenty of both. He soon won respect as a go-getter, a doer, an organization man who would take on any job to help the group. So well did he mold himself to the Jaycees ideal that he won the Key Man award for April 1964. He'd only been in Springfield for a couple of months.

Gacy reveled in the recognition. It seemed everything was

At the 1967 Christmas party thrown by the Waterloo, Iowa, Jaycees, a cheery John Gacy socializes in the buffet line *(below)*. His first wife, Marlynn, is on his right. In the photograph at left, Marlynn *(circled)* chats with other club wives at a June 1968 Jaycees luau.

finally going his way. He'd even met a woman he liked, a colleague at the department store where he worked. Only one incident—a homosexual encounter—clouded his otherwise hopeful view of the future.

Gacy had been out drinking with an acquaintance of his, someone a few years older than he. When they decided to call it a night, the man invited Gacy to his house for coffee. "But instead we had more drinks," Gacy remembers, "at least I did." The conversation turned to sex, and the man suggested it didn't matter who handed it out—male or female. "If I strike out with women," Gacy recalled him saying, "I pick up a guy. Which means on any given night, I got twice the chance to score that you do." Whether it was that seeming logic, the alcohol, or Gacy's own slumbering feelings, one thing soon led to another. The two men ended up naked, with the other man performing oral sex on Gacy.

"It felt good," Gacy admitted, "which, I suppose, is one of the reasons I didn't stop him." But later the younger man felt shamed and violated. He was also humiliated that he'd been manipulated, outsmarted by his partner—victimized. He didn't tell anyone. He locked the episode away; it was just another of life's little secrets.

Later that same year, in September 1964, John Gacy married Marlynn Myers, his coworker at the department store and the daughter of a successful franchiser of Kentucky Fried Chicken. The next year was good to the Gacys: John was named first vice president of the Jaycees, the outstanding first-year Jaycee in his area, and the organization's third outstanding member statewide. Marlynn became pregnant with their first child. And John even forged a reconciliation of sorts with his father. Even if he didn't say it in so many words, John Stanley Gacy had to be suitably impressed by his son's accomplishments.

Life was good, and it seemed to keep getting better. Gacy's new father-in-law wasn't crazy about his daughter's choice of a husband, but Fred Myers adored his only daughter and wanted her near him. He offered the young couple a house and his son-in-law a job managing three chicken franchises in Waterloo, Iowa. Gacy could see that this was a prime opportunity—it paid $15,000 per year, plus a percentage of profits—and he jumped at it. He took the course at Kentucky Fried Chicken University, joined the Waterloo

Three generations of Gacys—John Stanley, Michael, and John Wayne—seem the model of family unity in this 1966 photo. Michael's birth, along with business success operating Kentucky Fried Chicken outlets in Waterloo, seemed to bring Gacy a measure of much-needed approval from his stern father.

Jaycees, and settled down to the best years of his life.

Early in 1966 his son Michael was born, and a year and a half later Marlynn gave birth to a baby girl, Christine. But Gacy had scant time for family life. He worked at the chicken business 10 to 14 hours a day and kept up his hectic labors for the Jaycees—organizing events, recruiting new members, coordinating fund-raising efforts, and donating his skills to community projects. At meetings or events he usually arrived with buckets of chicken, combining a little public relations with good works. He also joined the Waterloo Merchant Patrol, a kind of auxiliary made up of citizens who helped augment police protection of businesses. Gacy carried a gun, too. It was easy to get one in Iowa, and it came in handy when he was on patrol at night or taking cash from the chicken stores to the bank. Gacy was fascinated with the police; he even had a red flashing light put on the dashboard of his car.

He seemed on a permanent high. He was voted the Jaycees' outstanding member for 1967, and he was chaplain of the local organization. He was clearly in line for a shot at president of the Waterloo club in 1968. Gacy had his house in order. He had political connections, friends in the fire station and on the police force. What next? The state senate? That would impress his father.

Then it all caved in. The problem arose from the strange sexual stirrings that Gacy couldn't control. This time the demon took the form of a blond 15-year-old named Donald Voorhees. It was late summer, at the end of a busy day. Gacy was driving down the highway when he heard a kid yell, "Hey, Mr. Gacy." John Gacy stopped, recognizing the boy as the son of a fellow Jaycee. It was innocent enough, he reasoned, giving the kid a ride. The boy had been at his girlfriend's house, he explained, and was walking home. That brought the conversation around to girls and then to sex, and Gacy mentioned some stag films that some of the Jaycees—including Gacy, the club chaplain—had been showing in their homes. The kid said he'd never seen such a film. Gacy's mind raced. What could it hurt? Marlynn was out of town, and besides, she was open-minded. There'd been a bit of wife swapping going on between some of the younger Jaycees, and the Gacys were in the thick of it.

Gacy and the boy went to his house and watched a film. After it was over, Gacy manipulated the boy into exchanging acts of oral sex. He had sex with young Voorhees a few more times and, at the boy's request, paid him for it. The hidden adventure may not have meant much in Gacy's mind—no more than a fair exchange of cash for sex—and besides, it was soon over. The whole matter blew up in his face in March 1968, however, when Donald Voorhees told his father what had happened. It might never have come up except that Gacy was planning to run for Jaycees president and wanted the boy's father to be his campaign manager.

The father went to the police, and the next thing Gacy knew, officers arrived at his house with a search warrant. They found the stag films—films that showed oral sex—and Gacy was charged with sodomy. When the case got to the grand jury, it wasn't just the Voorhees boy who sealed Gacy's fate. The jurors heard that in late August 1967, Edward Lynch, a 16-year-old employee of one of the chicken franchises that Gacy managed, had received a similar ride from the boss. He, too, had gone to the Gacy home while Marlynn was away. The boy said Gacy had suggested gambling on a pool game in the basement rec room, with the prize being oral sex. When the boy—who won the game—balked, Gacy showed the pornographic films. Then he suggested they go upstairs, where he pulled out a kitchen knife. He ordered the boy to a bedroom, and when Lynch resisted, the two struggled. Lynch was slightly cut before he managed to wrest the knife from Gacy. Then all aggression seemed to go out of the older man. He apologized and brought the boy a bandage. Gacy pressed Lynch with apologies and offered to show another film.

Lynch wanted only to go home, but Gacy insisted on showing the film, making it a reward, a part of the apology, and Lynch reluctantly agreed. The next thing he knew, Gacy had produced a padlock and a length of chain; he wanted to bind the boy's hands. "Let me try something," Lynch recalled him saying. The boy did what his boss asked, but when Gacy tried to sit on his lap, face-to-face, Lynch butted him with his head. Gacy then tried to force him face-down onto a cot and began to choke him. He released his hold only when the boy fell unconscious for a few seconds.

Suddenly, Gacy was full of apologies again. He released the boy and took him home. A few days later, however, he fired Lynch from his job at Kentucky Fried Chicken.

When Lynch made his allegations, Gacy claimed it was all a frame-up and offered to take a polygraph test. He failed it—twice—but his willingness to take the test at all rallied some Jaycees to his support. In spite of the charges, he still

had a chance of winning the presidency of the club. No one could believe that Gacy, who professed to be a hearty midwestern homophobe, could be a molester of young men. For his part, Gacy claimed that his political enemies in the Jaycees had framed him. He stayed in the running for club president until the election meeting, but, once nominated, emotionally announced his withdrawal from the race "in the interests of the organization and my family."

Gacy's friends continued to support him, but events soon undermined their confidence. In September Gacy hired an 18-year-old named Russell Schroeder to persuade Voorhees not to testify. Schroeder was to beat up Voorhees and warn him more was coming if he didn't withdraw as a witness. Without Voorhees, Gacy reasoned, the jury would have only the wild story of Edward Lynch—dirty movies, chains, and assault (but no sex) to consider. Case dismissed.

Gacy promised Schroeder to pay off a $300 loan on his car if he did the job. Schroeder succeeded in terrifying Voorhees and burning him in the face with Mace, but Voorhees went straight to the police. Schroeder eventually confessed that Gacy had put him up to the deed, and Gacy now faced additional charges.

Investigators preparing the sodomy case against Gacy now found witnesses coming out of the woodwork. One was Richard Westphal, 17, another Kentucky Fried Chicken employee. He claimed Gacy occasionally offered to play pool with him for oral sex, which the boy declined. Gacy also joked about the youth sleeping with his wife, Marlynn, saying that if he ever caught the two together, Westphal would be obliged to have sex with him, too. According to Westphal, in January 1967 he'd been helping Gacy late into the night with a project at the man's house. Gacy told Westphal he could sleep in the guest room. Soon after Westphal went to bed, Marlynn Gacy joined him. It was the hapless boy's first time, and he was easily seduced. Just as they were concluding, John Gacy walked into the room, as if on cue, and announced to Westphal that he owed him one. A few days later, Westphal said, he was "more or less coerced" into making good on the debt.

An 18-year-old boy who worked at the same restaurant as Westphal reported that Gacy threatened him with a pistol and played a bluff game of Russian roulette with him because the boy knew too much about Gacy's sex life. Yet another boy, aged 15, said that Gacy paid him and others $5 each for helping out with sexual "experiments" that

Convicted of sodomy in 1968, John Gacy served 18 months at the grimly ornate Iowa State Reformatory for Men at Anamosa. A tireless organizer and worker even in jail, Gacy spearheaded the construction of a minia-ture golf course *(inset)* for the use of the inmates.

Gacy claimed to be conducting for the governor of Iowa.

Gacy was finished in Waterloo. He was jailed because he couldn't make his $10,000 bond, and he was sent to the Psychopathic Hospital at the State University of Iowa to await trial. Doctors at the hospital examined him for 17 days with considerable interest. A physical exam showed that aside from being overweight, he had no chronic ailments and no "bottleneck heart." All his internal organs, in fact, were judged to be fine.

The mental picture, on the other hand, was far murkier. On the positive side, Gacy had an IQ of 118 — "bright normal." But the doctors also concluded that he enjoyed a total denial of responsibility for anything that went wrong in his life. He had an excuse for every accusation, every wayward move; he would always twist the truth to deflect blame from himself and make himself look good, however damning the circumstances. As to molesting boys, Gacy had "no remorse over the admitted deeds," Dr. L. D. Amick wrote in his report to the trial court. "We regard Mr. Gacy as an antisocial personality, a diagnostic term for individuals who are basically unsocialized and whose behavior pattern brings them repeatedly into conflict with society." No known medical treatment could help such people, the report said, because they "do not learn from experience."

Just before his trial, Gacy decided to plead guilty to the sodomy charge. He expected a sentence of probation, since the psychiatrists had reported that supervision would serve as well as prison in his case. Gacy also promised to relocate to Illinois. Even the investigating probation officer, Jack Harker, recommended probation, noting that the defendant was 26 and had never been in serious trouble before.

Nevertheless, Judge Peter Van Metre would have none of it. Influenced, perhaps, by the prosecution's argument that Gacy showed a pattern of molestation, the judge sentenced him to 10 years in the Iowa State Reformatory for Men at Anamosa. Marlynn filed for divorce the day the sentence was read. Gacy would never again see his son or daughter. Marlynn later remarried, and her new husband adopted the children. The book closed on John Gacy's life in Waterloo as he became prisoner No. 26526.

Even in prison, Gacy was an organizer and doer, setting out with enthusiasm to impress officials and fellow inmates alike. While incarcerated, he passed the exam for a high school equivalency diploma and even took college credits in psychology. He immersed himself in work in the prison kitchen, and he was delighted to find that the facility had a Jaycee chapter. He toiled feverishly on any number of projects, ranging from installing a donated miniature golf course on the prison grounds to preparing Jaycee banquets. His tireless efforts earned him a number of Jaycee honors, including the club's Sound Citizens Award and the roles of chaplain and legal counsel. A model prisoner, Gacy won parole, and on June 18, 1970, after serving only 18 months of his sentence, he walked out of prison a free man — although subject to provisions of parole.

He was glad to be out, but his joy was somewhat dimmed by the many things that had changed while he was locked away. He'd lost his home, his family, his position in the community. Most important, perhaps, he'd lost his father. On Christmas Day, 1969, John Stanley Gacy had died of cirrhosis of the liver. The elder Gacy had been devastated by his son's disgrace in Waterloo. He'd broken down and cried, for one of the few times in his life, and the son would always regret this ultimate proof that he'd let his father down. For reasons that are unclear, John Wayne Gacy was not informed of his father's death until a week after the funeral. His desolation was total. Thereafter, Christmas would always remind him of his failure as a son.

When Gacy left prison, he returned to the Chicago area to live with his mother in the condominium she and her husband had bought as a retirement home. The parolee found a job as a cook at a popular restaurant called Bruno's.

Gacy did well. He liked the restaurant and its patrons — some members of the Chicago Black Hawks hockey team came there regularly, as did many Cook County police officers. One cop in particular became a fixation with Gacy. James Hanley was a detective with the hit-and-run unit of the force. He and Gacy were not friends, but they did speak on occasion. In any case, it was not the real flesh-and-blood Hanley who became an obsession for Gacy, but a fictionalized *Jack* Hanley, a tough homicide cop who existed only in Gacy's mind. Jack was all the things Gacy was not — muscular, commanding, and a devoted hater of homosexuals. Jack Hanley was the punishing type of lawman that Gacy both admired and feared. He became kind of a mental partner for Gacy, an alter ego — and, later, a scapegoat.

When Gacy got to drinking or taking drugs, it seemed, Jack would take over and do things that Gacy would never do sober. Gacy would eventually explain in confessions to

Police took this photo of Gacy on June 22, 1972, as they booked him in Northbrook, Illinois, on charges of aggravated battery. The incident stemmed from an accusation that Gacy had fought with one of his sex partners, then attempted to run the boy down with his car. The charges were eventually dropped for lack of evidence.

police that when he couldn't really remember the details of his crimes—exactly what he'd done with some of the bodies before he buried them under his house—it was because Jack had been in charge.

According to Gacy, however, Jack did not emerge as a separate personality until 1975. The alter ego was not on the scene, therefore, in February of 1971 when Gacy picked up a teenage boy near the Greyhound bus station and tried to force him into sex. Only eight months out of prison and still on parole, Gacy claimed that it was the kid who wanted sex and that he, Gacy, threw him out of his car. Gacy was arrested and charged with assault, but the case was dis-

missed when the youth failed to show up in court to testify. Somehow, news of the arrest and charge never made its way to Iowa, where it could have endangered Gacy's parole. Eight months later, in October of 1971, he was released from parole. Restoration of full rights of citizenship, under the Iowa law for first offenders, came through a little over a month later.

By that time Gacy was involved personally and professionally with a young street hustler named Mickel Ried. The older man had picked up Ried on a street corner in November 1970, and after sex, the two talked of working together. Ried needed a job, and Gacy was thinking of quit-

Nine days after his arrest in Northbrook, Gacy appears untroubled at his wedding to his second wife, Carole Hoff. The two knew each other in high school and got reacquainted after Gacy's release from Anamosa.

ting the restaurant and working full-time at his own business. He'd started taking on painting jobs in his spare hours and wanted to get into the business of light construction. Painting, decorating, maintenance —those were his principal interests, and PDM was the name that Marion Gacy suggested for his company. The work was going well, and Gacy and Ried talked of forming a partnership.

It was because of the growing business that Gacy and his mother decided to move from the condo—where paint cans and lumber were beginning to stack up—into a house with a garage. They found a tract home in the suburbs at 8213 West Summerdale Avenue. It was a strange group that settled there: Marion Gacy; her son John, now counting the weeks until he could abandon his career as a cook; Mickel Ried, who needed a place to stay and a job; and Roger, one of the chefs at Bruno's.

Ried and Gacy parted ways just a few months later. As Ried remembers it, one evening the two men were handling supplies in the garage, and Gacy came at him from behind with a hammer. Ried, who suffered a cut on the head, couldn't recall what had provoked Gacy. He only knew that his partner had hit him, and when he resisted a possible second blow, Gacy stopped and started apologizing, a wild look fading from his eyes. The incident terrified Ried, however, and he lost no time in moving out.

While he was having homosexual encounters in Illinois, Gacy was also courting a young woman named Carole Hoff. Growing up, she'd been friendly with Gacy's two sisters and had even had one date with Gacy when they were in high school. In 1971 Hoff was newly divorced, and she was renewing old ties. She found Gacy "a very warm, understanding person, very easy to talk to." He was comforting to her and gentle with her two children from her first marriage. As she and Gacy became closer, he confessed to her that he was bisexual. Hoff didn't

take him very seriously on that point, however, and in the summer of 1972 she married him. Gacy's mother moved to an apartment, and Carole Hoff Gacy, her mother, and her two little girls moved into the house on West Summerdale.

It wasn't long before the new bride noticed a strange odor emanating from the crawlspace under the house.

The killing had started about seven months before the wedding, at the beginning of 1972. On New Year's Day Gacy joined his mother at a family party, where they drank, gossiped, and played cards. The party broke up sometime after midnight, but Marion Gacy refused to drive home with her son; he'd had too much to drink, she said. She stayed with her relatives. Gacy walked out to his car and disappeared into the night.

Even after all the Scotch he'd drunk, the cold air suddenly made him feel wide awake; he decided to go "looking around," as he put it. He drove down to central Chicago, and near the Greyhound bus station he picked up a light-haired young man whose name he couldn't remember. He would eventually come to refer to him simply as "the Greyhound Bus Boy." (The youth was eventually identified as Tim McCoy of Omaha, Nebraska.) Gacy drove the young man to his house, where they had a few drinks and sandwiches, followed by sex. According to Gacy's later statement to police, both men then went to sleep—Gacy in his bedroom, the boy in the guest room.

The next morning, Gacy claimed, he woke to find his young guest walking toward him with a butcher knife in his hand. Gacy leaped from the bed and grabbed for the knife. He gave authorities varying accounts of what happened next: At one point he claimed that in the ensuing struggle the boy fell on the knife and stabbed himself to death. Later he amended the story. According to the second version, the boy didn't fight back; rather, he seemed surprised and frightened. As Gacy grappled for the knife, he was accidentally cut on the arm and felt "a surge of power from my toes to my brain." Then, he said, he plunged the knife into the boy's chest. When it was all over, he looked down at the pants he'd worn to bed. They were covered with blood—but with something else, too. During the struggle he'd experienced a powerful sexual release.

Gacy was in a quandary, he said. He felt he couldn't call the police; they'd never believe a story of self-defense. He'd have to take care of this himself. He cleaned up the blood, dragged the body to the foyer closet, and pushed it through the crawlspace trapdoor. He would bury it later, before his mother came home. Only when he went to the kitchen did the full import of the incident strike him: On the counter were a carton of eggs and a slab of unsliced bacon. The young man with the knife had been planning not a vicious attack, but breakfast for his host.

However dark the hidden recesses of his life, Gacy managed to keep his outward image intact. For the most part, his marriage remained fairly untroubled for the first year. Moreover, his business was picking up. In June 1973 he was able to quit his job at Bruno's and devote himself full-time to his construction firm, PDM. On his business cards he added a Jr. to his name, reasoning that John Gacy, Jr., had a more professional ring to it. Or so he explained. Perhaps, consciously or not, he was also trying once again to link himself to his loved and hated father.

Always industrious, John Wayne Gacy, Jr., turned into a complete workaholic; and while business thrived, his marriage began to suffer. He no longer spent much time with his wife or his stepdaughters. He began scheduling business meetings at all hours of the night. Often after grabbing a quick dinner he'd do paperwork until midnight, then go out to appointments, returning only to fall asleep on a couch for an hour or two before starting the cycle again.

His marital sex life was in limbo. Gacy was always "too tired," and Carole Gacy began finding worrisome reminders of her husband's homosexual proclivities. There were magazines under the kitchen sink showing nude men, and she found stained silk bikini male underwear behind the bedroom dresser and under the bed. For the first time, the couple argued violently. She taunted him about masturbating; he shoved her across the room.

More and more often Gacy slept on the couch in the rec room, which he'd outfitted with a bar and a pool table. One night Carole Gacy couldn't sleep and was in the rec room watching TV when her husband appeared. Gacy came into the house and then nervously retreated, saying he'd just come to get something. His strange behavior roused her curiosity, and she looked out the window and saw Gacy getting into his car with a blond boy. After they drove away, she found a blanket on the garage floor. Later she learned that Gacy was having sex with young men, some of them PDM employees. Not all were compliant. One husky youth beat Gacy up in the driveway. Gacy told his wife it was a dispute over money, but years later, after everything had come out, she learned that Gacy had raped the youth.

On Mother's Day, 1975, Gacy announced to his wife that their sex life was over. He said that he hoped they could go on living together in some sort of platonic relationship, but in fact, both parties knew that it was only a matter of time before the union dissolved completely. They were fighting more often, Gacy was gone almost every night, and his wife suspected he was out looking for sex. It was about this time that John Wayne Gacy split irrevocably in two, and the pieces began to spin out of control.

On the one hand, there was Gacy the successful contractor, the long-winded but thoughtful neighbor and friend, the community organizer. On the other hand, he was a secret sadist whose murderous compulsions were growing.

Gacy was well-liked in his neighborhood. Some acquaintances found him a loudmouth and a braggart, but no one could deny that he was the first person on hand to help when a snowy driveway needed shoveling or a neighbor needed a ride. And he was a popular host. He threw theme parties each summer beginning in 1974, and sometimes as many as 300 people crowded to these affairs.

His reputation was growing in the wider community as well; at one function—the groundbreaking of a retirement center he'd helped raise money for—the contractor had his photograph taken with then-mayor Michael Bilandic. Police would puzzle over the picture when they searched his house only seven months later.

Of course Gacy could never be an elected politician himself, not with his criminal record. But he was able to nourish his longstanding taste for politics in small ways. With the help of Robert Martwick, a Norwood Park neighbor and Democratic party organizer, in 1975 Gacy achieved an appointed post, his first political position: secretary-treasurer

Dressed in colonial garb in honor of America's bicentennial, Gacy welcomed scores of neighbors and friends to his home for a barbecue on July 4, 1976. As he prospered in business and expanded his social contacts, Gacy made an annual event of his backyard theme parties.

of the Norwood Park Township Street Lighting District.

Martwick also suggested that Gacy involve himself with community projects, and the eager pupil responded with verve. He headed up Chicago's Polish Constitution Day Parade, and it went like clockwork. He joined the River Grove Moose Lodge—at 33 he was too old to be a Jaycee—and as part of the organization's Jolly Jokers Club he developed the character Pogo the Clown. As Pogo, he joined the other Jokers in trips to hospitals to cheer up sick children. Pogo also took part in parades, store openings, Democratic picnics—wherever there was an audience to applaud the rotund clown's antics. Gacy liked this image so much that he started collecting pictures of clowns. He savored the irony of the smiling face painted over the sad one underneath.

The irony was, perhaps, deeper than he admitted to himself. He, like the clowns, had two faces: Beneath the facade of the successful public man, the dark side of John Gacy was blossoming too. There was the fantasy detective Jack Hanley, Gacy's alter ego, who made nightly forays into the seamy parts of Chicago, picking up a steady stream of boys. Most of the youths no doubt soothed Gacy's sexual demons and then moved on. But there were others, the ones who caused trouble for him, the ones he thought tried to trick him and take advantage of him, the boys who had to be taken care of—the boys who needed to be taught a lesson.

Tony Antonucci was one of those boys, although he was not an anonymous pickup from the bus station. Tony was a family friend. Gacy had hired the 14-year-old in May 1975, and one night about a month later the two were working alone, cleaning offices at the local Democratic party headquarters. According to Antonucci, Gacy first asked if he could perform oral sex on him, then offered money when the boy refused. Gacy tried to laugh off the incident as a test of the young man's morals. But a month later he visited the youth at home when the boy's parents were out. Antonucci was laid up with an injured foot, and Gacy brought wine, his film projector, and some heterosexual pornographic films. Before long the older man was wrestling with the boy and had locked handcuffs on his wrists. The youth was able to somehow slip out of the cuffs and he fought back; he wrested the key from Gacy and soon had his boss locked in the manacles. Gacy simply lay there until Antonucci let him up, after Gacy promised to leave. Antonucci went on working for PDM for nine months after this incident.

For entertaining hospitalized children and doing other good works, Gacy created two clown characters. One was the tattered Patches, shown in this colorful publicity shot. The killer lovingly devised his own makeup and costume for Patches, as well as for his better-known clown alter ego, Pogo. Gacy described Pogo, his first creation, as a happy clown; Patches, he said, was more serious. Gacy's interest in clowns took the form of collecting paintings of them and, eventually, painting them himself. A psychologically interesting example of his artwork *(inset)* shows a child-sized Gacy sitting on the lap of a monstrously large Pogo. It seems as though the real man is about to be overwhelmed by his fantasy creation.

Three of Gacy's victims were Samuel Stapleton, Gregory Godzik, and John Szyc. Stapleton disappeared on May 14, 1976; Godzik and Szyc vanished within a two-month period in the winter of 1976-1977.

SAMUEL STAPLETON

GREGORY GODZIK

Another PDM employee, 18-year-old John Butkovich, was not as lucky as Antonucci. Butkovich worked almost a year for Gacy and was a favorite of both John and Carole. He was easygoing and a hard worker, but he quarreled with Gacy over money. On July 31, 1975, Butkovich disappeared. Gacy told his wife that the boy had quit, but he later confessed to police that he'd brought Butkovich to the house, ostensibly to give him some past-due money. Carole was away from home. There had been some heavy drinking, some threats from the boy about collecting his pay, and then Gacy put the handcuffs on Butkovich—to subdue him, he said, nothing more. In the morning, however, when Gacy got out of bed, he saw the boy's body just where he'd left it: lying on the floor, hands cuffed behind the back—and with a rope around his neck. Bad Jack must have done it, Gacy reasoned.

Gacy rolled the body in a tarp and dragged it out to the garage, where he left it for a day or two, planning to bury it in the crawlspace when he had time. Then Carole came home, and he couldn't get the body under the house unnoticed. So Gacy dug a hole in the only part of the garage floor that wasn't covered by concrete—a section only three feet long by one and a half feet wide, where he'd planned to install a drain. When Gacy tried to fit the body into the small opening he had to jump on the stiffened corpse to bend it double so it would go into the hole. He then covered the grave with concrete. It was Gacy's second murder, and the first victim whose name he could remember.

As Gacy himself continued to deteriorate, so did his marriage. Carole Gacy asked for her freedom, and her husband didn't fight it. In fact, he sent her to his own lawyer and helped her move. He kept in touch with her and even dated her after the 1976 divorce. Although divorce actually seemed to improve the relationship between John and Carole—restoring them to friendship, at least—Gacy was depressed by the split and took to drinking ever more heavily. He also stepped up his intake of drugs, some of which he stole from the pharmacies that hired him to do remodeling. And when Gacy drank or got too strung out on pharmaceuticals, Bad Jack tended to visit.

By the summer of 1977, at least 12 young men had passed through Gacy's hands to graves in the damp subsoil of the crawlspace. How it had happened, Gacy could not explain clearly. But he came to admit to himself that he had needs that could be met only by these violent encounters. They began, he said, partly because of Bad Jack, the fantasy detective who wanted to crack down on the little hustlers and cheats who thrived on certain city streets, and partly because Gacy needed to prove he was smarter than those boys were. They couldn't hustle him. He'd teach them a lesson.

Gacy couldn't remember the particulars of the young men who died in 1976. Darrell Sampson disappeared April 6. Randall Reffett and Samuel Stapleton disappeared May 14; they were found buried together in the crawlspace. On June 3 Michael Bonnin, 17, went to help paint a friend's garage; he never arrived. William Carroll, 16, vanished on June 13. Rick Johnston, 17, went to a concert on August 6 and never came home.

But Gacy did remember Gregory Godzik. The 17-year-old boy, who'd worked for him for two weeks, came to Gacy's home on the night of December 12, 1976. Godzik had agreed to buy some marijuana for the boss, but he'd had some difficulty in making good on this promise. The next morning the boy was dead—sitting in a chair in his underwear with a rope around his neck. Godzik ended up in the crawlspace with the others, still in a sitting position. Police interviewed Gacy about the boy's disappearance, but they never ran a background check on the contractor.

Then there was John Szyc. Gacy would remember him because of the weird, vowelless surname—and the car. It was January 1977, and Gacy was cruising North Chicago. John Szyc, 19, was a street hustler who explained to Gacy

JOHN SZYC

that he had a Plymouth Satellite for sale. Gacy told him he was interested and inquired about the title to the car. Then the two of them agreed to go to Gacy's house to settle the deal. Szyc died that night; he was buried in the crawlspace. The next morning Gacy and a longtime employee and friend named Mike Rossi went to fetch the car outside a gay movie house where Szyc had parked it. (Rossi apparently had slept at Gacy's house the night of the murder, but later testified that he'd never met John Szyc and knew nothing of the young man's death.) Rossi and Gacy soon struck a deal of their own: Rossi would buy the dead boy's car from Gacy for $300. According to Gacy, Rossi forged the title, signing the vehicle over to the two of them. (Rossi would later deny the forgery, and he was never charged with it.) A television and a clock radio, found in the trunk, went home with Gacy, but Szyc's offbeat wardrobe of women's dresses and wigs was left behind in a dumpster.

In 1977 nine young men were murdered in Gacy's home and buried under the house, and it seemed that part of their killer was dying as well. Gacy's dark side — the cruising, the drinking, and the pills that helped him sustain his energy — was pushing much of his normal existence aside. His life was taking on a frenzied, reckless quality. But if anyone noticed, no one cared enough to do anything to help him. Nor did authorities heed the stories of those few victims who escaped, who endured rape and torture at the hands of the affable businessman and lived to tell their stories.

One of those survivors was a 19-year-old department-store employee named Robert Donnelly. It was 1977, after midnight at the end of December — the last dregs of the Christmas season that always so depressed John Gacy. Donnelly was walking along a northwest Chicago sidewalk on his way to a bus stop when a black Oldsmobile pulled over to the curb. The boy suddenly found himself fixed in a spotlight shining from the driver's side of the car. Gacy played tough cop and asked for identification, then pointed a gun at Donnelly. "Get in or I'll blow you away," he said.

Maintaining the cop act, Gacy handcuffed the youth and drove him back to West Summerdale, forced whiskey down his throat when he refused a drink, and anally raped him. Gacy then hauled the young man into the bathroom and repeatedly dunked his head into a bathtub full of water until the boy lost consciousness. After Donnelly came to, Gacy urinated on him, dragged him back into the rec room to watch homosexual movies, and continued the torture. Donnelly would later testify in court that Gacy made him play Russian roulette with a revolver, spinning the cylinder and pulling the trigger 10 to 15 times until the gun finally went off. It was loaded with a blank shell. Gacy then bound and gagged his terrified victim and raped him once more. His rage nearly spent, Gacy ordered the weakened youth to take a shower and get dressed, then put him in the car for what he promised would be Donnelly's last ride. "How's it feel, knowing you're going to die?" he taunted as he drove Donnelly back downtown. But then, inexplicably, Gacy released his captive with one last threat: "If you go to the cops," he said, "I'll hunt you down."

Nevertheless, Donnelly did report the attack, describing to police the black car and the distinctive vanity license plate that read "PDM." As had happened three times before, police took the report and interviewed Gacy. In this instance, Gacy corroborated the details of Donnelly's horrific story, but with one difference. He said the sex was consensual — a slave routine. After reviewing the case, an assistant state's attorney declined to prosecute, perhaps doubting the persuasiveness of the lone witness: Donnelly was afflicted with a stutter and had been receiving treatment from a psychiatrist following the death of his father.

Gacy was not noticeably cowed by his close call with the police. Just three months later, in March 1978, he again left a bruised witness to his torture games. Jeff Rignall, a 26-year-old homosexual, was walking to a Chicago gay bar when a bulky man in a black Oldsmobile picked him up. Though Rignall willingly got into the car, Gacy chloroformed him for the drive to West Summerdale. There he removed Rignall's clothes and strapped him to what the victim would describe as a pillory device that held his neck and arms immobile. His attacker then forced him to perform oral sex and repeatedly raped him with a number of objects. At one point, according to Rignall, there was an-

other person in the room who participated in the sodomy, but he never saw the man's face.

Rignall was later dumped at the base of a statue in a downtown Chicago park. He was bleeding from the rectum and his face felt like it was on fire; he had suffered facial burns and liver damage from the chloroform.

The attack transformed Jeff Rignall into an avenger bent on tracking Gacy down. Once the police realized Rignall was homosexual, he says, they lost interest in the case. When he hired a lawyer and sued in civil court, Gacy countercharged that Rignall had abused him verbally and shoved him. In September Gacy settled the suit for $3,000.

While Rignall was doggedly pursuing every legal avenue available to bring his attacker to justice, Gacy was keeping up his public image. He was in charge of the May 1978 Polish Constitution Day parade, which was attended by Rosalynn Carter, wife of then-president Jimmy Carter. Gacy was in his element. At a reception he was even photographed shaking hands with the smiling First Lady. The picture shows the contractor wearing a gold *S* on his lapel — a sign that he'd been cleared by the Secret Service.

Throughout 1978, even as Gacy planned for his photo opportunity with Rosalynn Carter, the killings continued. In January 19-year-old William Kindred disappeared from

Jeff Rignall, seated at the left with his attorney, survived a brutal beating by Gacy and sued his attacker in civil court. Rignall secured a $3,000 settlement from Gacy. The photographs in the foreground show some of Rignall's injuries, notably facial burns caused by chloroform that Gacy used on him.

North Chicago after telling his girlfriend he was going to a bar. In the spring of 1978 Tim O'Rourke went out for cigarettes. He was found in June, floating facedown in the Des Plaines River. On November 4 Frank Landingin, a 19-year-old hustler and drug user just out of jail on a battery charge, went for a walk with plans to visit his girlfriend. He was found dead in the Des Plaines eight days later. Near the end of the month 20-year-old James Mazzara left his parents' home after Thanksgiving dinner and disappeared. His bloated body was found a month later in the river.

And on December 11, 1978, fifteen-year-old Rob Piest vanished into the night. He went to see a man about a contracting job and never came back.

When card reader Florece Branson met John Gacy at the Rhodes' holiday party, he was only days away from killing Rob Piest, his last victim. In hindsight Gacy realized that killing Piest was a crucial mistake in every way. Not only would the killer leave a trail of clues that begged for discovery, but he picked the wrong victim. With the Piest boy, Gacy broke his usual pattern of seizing on strays and hustlers, runaways and troublemakers—the boys he would later describe as "worthless little queers and punks."

Robert Piest was a good kid. He worked hard, got good grades, loved—and was loved by—his family and his friends. He was a few merit badges short of being an eagle scout, and he held down a $2.85-an-hour job after school at the Nisson Pharmacy in Des Plaines. He was trying to make enough money to buy a Jeep. When Piest got off work at 9 o'clock each weeknight, one of his parents would pick him up at the store. December 11, 1978, was unusual only in that it was his mother's birthday, and there would be a family party that evening after Rob got home.

When Elizabeth Piest walked into Nisson's that night her son wasn't quite ready to go. "Some contractor wants to talk to me about a job," he explained, grabbing his parka and running out the door. She hung around the store waiting for him to return.

Gacy was the contractor. He'd visited the drugstore twice that evening, taking measurements for an alteration to the display shelves. As was his habit he was loud and chatty and long-winded; he mentioned his practice of hiring teenagers and paying them well—"$5.00 an hour," he boasted, within earshot of Piest. Then he'd left and Piest vanished, leaving his mother waiting inside the store.

By 9:20 p.m. the boy still hadn't returned. A worried Elizabeth Piest went home, leaving instructions with the clerk at the register for Rob to call when he got back to the store. When she got home, she called the pharmacy. Rob still wasn't there, but the store owner, Phil Torf, gave Mrs. Piest John Gacy's name. By 10 p.m. the Piests were beside themselves with worry. At the insistence of Rob's father, Harold Piest, Torf called the house on West Summerdale; he got the answering machine. The Piests went to the police, but the officer on duty told the distraught parents he had no one available to investigate until the following morning.

To Rob Piest's parents it was obvious that Gacy was linked to their son's disappearance, but the police didn't see it quite so clearly at first. For one thing, most missing kids return in a day or two. And John Wayne Gacy was a man with a business and connections; he even had ties to the local Democratic party power structure. Attitudes began to shift the day after the boy's disappearance, however, when the Des Plaines police discovered Gacy's

As director of the Polish Constitution Day parade in 1978, Gacy was photographed with First Lady Rosalynn Carter. But even as he enjoyed this honor, one of his victims, Jeff Rignall, was sorting through other pictures—police mug shots—hoping to identify his attacker.

ROBERT PIEST

After running out of burial room on his own property, Gacy began disposing of his victims' bodies by throwing them off this bridge over the Des Plaines River. Robert Piest *(inset)*, whose death eventually led police to Gacy's door, was the fourth victim to be tossed into the river.

felony conviction from 1968, a battery charge from 1972, and another battery charge in July 1978. But even with this information in hand, they proceeded cautiously.

Lieutenant Joseph Kozenczak, commander of the Criminal Investigation Division, and three other detectives visited Gacy the night of December 12, asking for help in the matter of the missing Piest boy. Gacy invited Kozenczak in, volunteered that he had indeed been at the Nisson Pharmacy the night the boy vanished, but said he knew nothing about the case. He said he'd do all he could to help, even come to the station to make a statement. But it would have to be later, he told the officers. Family troubles—an uncle had just died—were his first priority. When police insisted on a statement sooner rather than later, Gacy grew testy: "Don't you have any respect for the dead?" he snapped as he shut the door. Even as he spoke, the dead body of Rob Piest lay above their heads in an attic storage area.

Something about Gacy's manner worried the Des Plaines chief of detectives, who thought the suspect might even be holding the Piest boy captive in his home. Kozenczak decided this was no ordinary missing kid case and took the unusual step of ordering a search warrant. On December 13, detectives took the warrant to Gacy's house while the increasingly annoyed Gacy sat at the station writing a report and answering the same questions about the Piest case over and over. Ostensibly miffed about delays and lost business, he demanded to talk to his lawyers. Officers tried to stall him, well aware that unless the search of his house produced something, they had no legal way of holding him.

The search team found no clear-cut evidence of guilt at the house, although in the bedroom they discovered handcuffs, jewelry, a high-school ring with the intials J.A.S., and a curious contraption made of a three-foot-long two-by-four with holes drilled in each end. This last item looked to the detectives like some kind of bondage device. The cursory search also uncovered sex books, a starter's pistol, a spot of dried blood on the carpet near the bathroom—and a customer's receipt from the Nisson Pharmacy for photo development. And there was something else disquieting—a low, pervasive odor of decay and stagnation that filled the house.

Edward Grexa, a helpful neighbor drawn by the strange cars at 8213 West Summerdale, told police: "If you're searching for something, you know there's an attic and a crawlspace in there." But the police had already looked at the crawlspace. Two officers with flashlights had entered

the area and noted no disturbed earth, only a thick coating of white material, apparently lime that had been spread to dispel the musty sewage odors plaguing the house. In the attic they'd found police badges and an 18-inch rubber dildo—strange, but not necessarily incriminating.

Unknown to police, the day before their search Gacy had bundled Rob Piest's body out of the attic and into the trunk of the Oldsmobile. He stopped at the bridge over the Des Plaines River and heaved the corpse into the frigid water.

The odd gleanings from Gacy's house had given police only one item, seemingly insignificant amid the sex paraphernalia and other suspicious gear, to link the contractor to Rob Piest: the photo receipt from the Nisson Pharmacy. The receipt corresponded to an order listed in the name of Kim Byers, Piest's friend and coworker at the store. On the night the boy disappeared, Kim Byers had borrowed his coat, a blue down parka. While she had it on she placed in the pocket, then forgot, the photo receipt. None of this would be known, however, for about another week. Nevertheless, the team of detectives was convinced of two facts—that the boy they sought had been inside Gacy's house or car, and that Gacy was lying about it. They also knew another fact: They didn't have enough evidence to arrest Gacy or charge him.

The third day since Rob Piest's disappearance was passing. Kozenczak had no body, not even any proof that a murder had been committed. The detective had exhausted Gacy's cooperation without concrete results. So, despite the meager resources of the tiny Des Plaines police force, he ordered round-the-clock surveillance of the suspect. He hoped that under the pressure of being constantly watched, Gacy would somehow panic, give something away, or lead detectives to a witness.

The surveillance quickly took its toll. For years Gacy had been sinking into the habits of a confirmed pill abuser, gulping handfuls of Valiums to calm down, then amphetamines to pep himself up. He swilled beer and whiskey every evening in increasing amounts. During his last week of freedom he was on a roller-coaster ride of liquor and drugs. Nevertheless, he was able for a time to hide his disintegration from police, remaining for them a wily and infuriating quarry.

Gacy seemed to sense the odd freedom of the hunted. He somehow knew that the officers tailing him would be extremely reluctant to arrest him on any relatively trivial

A file drawer confiscated during a police search of Gacy's house contained, among other things, a young merchant seaman's identity card. In the house police also found wallets, jewelry, and other items owned by boys Gacy killed, as well as goods apparently left behind by youths who survived visits with the serial slayer.

charge, so he openly defied traffic laws, puffed marijuana, and drank heavily as he led the surveillance teams on a merry chase. He introduced his police escorts to his pals from the Moose Lodge, calling them his bodyguards. He also delighted in eluding his pursuers and succeeded on a number of occasions. Once, after openly joking with his attorney about taking a long vacation, Gacy vanished, and a squad car rushed to O'Hare Airport to block his departure. It was only a trick; Gacy had spent the time driving around, making a brief stop to see a friend who sold Christmas trees.

But even as he remained free, police were slowly adding to their store of evidence against Gacy through a string of interviews. They talked to a young employee, David Cram, who'd lived with Gacy briefly in 1976. Cram said that Gacy had shown off a box filled with men's watches, rings, and other jewelry. He'd even given Cram one of the watches—along with a lecture on punctuality—explaining that he'd gotten the watch "from a dead person."

On another front, Mike Rossi, who had worked for Gacy off and on for four years, told police that his boss had sold him John Szyc's car. This was the second crucial clue pertaining to Szyc's disappearance in the spring of 1977: Police had already surmised that a high-school ring engraved J.A.S. and found in Gacy's bureau drawer could well have been Szyc's. When officers found that the vehicle identification number of Rossi's car matched that of Szyc's car, they knew Gacy was involved in more than one disappearance—and perhaps more than one murder.

Police interviewed Gacy's former wife, Carole, who had remarried right around the time of Rob Piest's disappearance. She stressed how her ex-husband would fall into deep depression around the Christmas holidays every year. Gacy, she said, gradually became open about his sexual preferences and how he couldn't help "slipping the other way." He'd described to her the type of men who appealed to him—young blonds of a wiry, compact body type.

Meanwhile, officers tailing Gacy were being dragged about to bars and business sites where he'd either boast to them about his social and business success or mock and curse them. Gacy would invite them to a restaurant for dinner, pump them for information about the case, and drop the names of his important friends. On one of these bizarre forays, Gacy treated two detectives to dinner, during which he regaled them with stories of his success as Pogo the Clown. The plight of sick children particularly affected him, he said, because he'd been sickly himself as a youth, still suffered from heart disease, and was dying of leukemia. (His imagined diseases were apparently merely a melodramatic bid for pity.) And while he waxed sentimental about Pogo's role in cheering up sick children, he also boasted about how the clown was able to take advantage of women. As Pogo, he said, he could drift along the sidelines of parades and fondle the female spectators, who would only giggle. Then he made a statement that was indelibly etched into the minds of his listeners. "You know," he said portentously, "clowns can get away with murder."

When he was not being affable, Gacy was often threatening. He filed a $750,000 federal court suit against the City of Des Plaines, claiming that Kozenczak and several other officers had violated his civil rights. The suit claimed the investigation and surveillance of him infringed on his right to privacy and that his home had been searched illegally. His attorney in this matter was Sam Amirante, who'd shared duty with Gacy as a member of the Norwood Park Township Lighting District.

On December 19, the day the suit was filed, Gacy once again became generous with his pursuers and invited the two officers on duty in front of his house to come inside to warm up. The air feed from the furnace was blasting heat, and a putrid stench permeated the rooms. Detective Robert Schultz was hoping for a chance to get a look at the serial number on a television set in Gacy's bedroom—he suspected that the set had once belonged to the missing John Szyc—so he excused himself to go to a bathroom near the bedroom. In that part of the house the objectionable odor was particularly noticeable, and Schultz recognized it. He'd smelled it dozens of times before when investigating homicides and accidental deaths. It was the smell of rotting flesh. Gacy—whether unconsciously begging to be caught or simply accustomed to the reek—seemed not to notice.

The surveillance teams on duty that day noted that Gacy's mood swings were growing worse. Where he'd once joked sarcastically with them, he now snarled. He seemed particularly agitated by police contact with Mike Rossi and David Cram. The thought that his two trusted employees and former roommates might incriminate him caused deep cracks in Gacy's veneer of rational behavior.

The suspect was right to be concerned; investigators were working the stratagem of pitting Rossi and Cram against each other. They hoped for a breakthrough with the tough and cynical Rossi, since they believed he was in a position to know more than he was telling. They thought he was either Gacy's lover (which proved to be true), had assisted Gacy in some way with the Piest boy, or at the very least was hiding facts. To whipsaw him, they implied that David Cram was already giving evidence and that Gacy had been telling them a few things about him.

Detective Kozenczak told Rossi that police believed Syzc, whose car Rossi was driving, was dead. Apparently fearing that he was implicated in the murder, Rossi tearfully agreed to take a polygraph test. He swore that he knew nothing about the disappearances of John Szyc or Rob Piest. The results of the lie detector test were inconclusive.

David Cram, however, was yielding some very interesting new information. He told police that Gacy had directed him and Rossi on a couple of occasions to dig trenches for drainage pipes under Gacy's crawlspace. The trenches were about two feet wide, two feet deep, and six feet long.

Although he didn't know precisely what Rossi and Cram were saying, the fact that they were being questioned seemed to drive Gacy into a frenzy. On the evening of December 20, 1978, he drove like a man possessed to the Park Ridge office of his criminal lawyer, Sam Amirante. Gacy's business lawyer, LeRoy Stevens, joined them. Gacy spent the night in Amirante's office, drinking Scotch, babbling, and finally falling into a stuporous sleep at 3:30 a.m. All the while, the surveillance team was watching the shadows within the office from the other side of a frosted glass wall. When Gacy went to sleep, the tired lawyers stepped out of the office and approached the detectives. The attorneys hinted openly that Gacy should be taken into custody.

On his way home the next morning Gacy stopped at his usual service station, filled his car with gasoline, and then stuffed a plastic bag of marijuana into the pocket of a teenage attendant, knowing full well that he was being watched by police. Detectives snatched the drugs as evidence just moments later. At home, Gacy deposited his pet dog, Patches, with neighbors, then drove to the house of Ron and Gloria Rhode, where earlier in the month he'd had his fortune read. Ron Rhode later told police that Gacy was shaky and unshaven. He asked for a Scotch and water, then sat at the kitchen table and moaned about being a "bad boy."

"What the hell are you talking about?" Rhode demanded.

"The end is near," Gacy told him, "I killed 30 people, give or take two or three." The contractor went on to explain to his stunned neighbor that the victims were "bad people," who'd been blackmailing him. "They deserved to die," he said. Gacy slumped against Rhode and began to cry.

When Rhode asked him if he knew anything about the Piest boy, Gacy replied, "If Piest walked through the door right now, I wouldn't know him." With that, he stumbled out of the house, clutching a rosary.

Police watched as the tear-stained Gacy got into his car and careened down the expressway to David Cram's house. Rossi was there, too. Gacy informed his two employees that he had confessed to 30 mob-related killings and had come to say goodbye. (The reference to the mob was not particularly surprising. Gacy sometimes hinted darkly to his intimates of connections to organized crime.)

The contractor told his two young associates that he wanted to meet with his business lawyer, then visit his father's grave at Maryhill Cemetery. According to Cram, he was also babbling about "the end" and gobbling Valiums. Cram offered to drive Gacy, and while his boss talked with Stevens at a North Side restaurant, Cram slipped outside to

JOHN BUTKOVICH

A police officer checks out John Gacy's garage and driveway *(right)* during a search on December 22, 1978—the day after the first bodies were found in the slayer's crawlspace. During the above-ground inspection, Gacy spray-painted an *X* on the floor of the garage to mark the grave site of John Butkovich *(inset),* who had worked for him for about a year and then disappeared. Police uncovered his body shortly after the killer gave them its location. They also dug up a body buried beneath the driveway.

tell surveillance detectives about the confessions of murder: "Don't lose us," he warned. "I'm really afraid the guy might try to kill himself and kill me with him."

The police team was suddenly faced with an urgent decision: Arrest Gacy on the marijuana charge or continue to follow him and risk the possibility that he might commit suicide. At 12:15 p.m. on Thursday, December 21, they arrested him on the felony charge of "delivery of marijuana." They were hoping to buy enough time to get a warrant for a second search of Gacy's home. This time they wanted to have a closer look at the crawlspace.

The search team entered the crawlspace expecting horrors, but the reality, if anything, exceeded their worst forebodings. What they found was a hellish graveyard that assaulted both their senses and their sanity. In the first hours of discovery under the Gacy house, police had a hard time believing what they saw. As they dug for evidence, ice-cold ground water kept seeping into the crawlspace, turning the search area into a sea of soupy mud. They brought in submersible pumps, but the devices continually clogged on the bits of floating, greasy, soaplike flesh—called adipocere—that filled the crawlspace. The searchers discarded the pumps and bailed the water out with buckets.

Floodlights illuminated the work and made it more ghastly. The men laboring in the lurid glow wore heavy protective clothing, including surgical gloves: Contact with the noxious matter that they were unearthing made blood poisoning and gas gangrene dangerous possibilities. But the flimsy gloves were soon torn by the bones and grav-

el, exposing the workers' hands to the sting of the many bags of lime that Gacy had poured into the area. Wearing thicker rubber gloves, the men shoveled the foul earth into plastic buckets that were hoisted up to the living room. There, on the floor, a second crew sifted for bone fragments and other evidence.

Right from the start authorities tried to impose some order on the chaos. Police sawed through the flooring and subflooring to gain easier access to the burial space. They divided the search area into a grid, and when a bucket was lifted from a particular grid it was taken behind the house and placed in a corresponding grid to dry. This plan had one flaw: In the icy winter air the mud froze instead of drying.

It was not possible to methodically remove bodies one at a time; in most cases, decay had left little intact. Technicians merely searched through the mush for bones. The bones were then crudely rinsed—using a bucket of water and Gacy's own deep-fry basket—before they were passed along for inspection by Dr. Robert Stein, the Cook County medical examiner, who was directing the excavation project. It soon became clear that small bones from wrists, fingers, and toes would be lost. Only when shoes or socks survived could technicians recover the tiny remains.

Identifying the bodies was a nightmare: Only after developing a technique of defining each grave site by depth and length could searchers be reasonably sure they were lifting parts of one corpse and not another as they explored. In some graves Gacy had buried one body atop another. In one depression the skeletons were so jumbled together that two skulls were almost touching. The technician digging there simply placed body bags on each side of the plot and deposited alternate handfuls of soil in each.

The first body positively identified did not come from the crawlspace but from under the garage. It was that of John Butkovich, the Gacy employee who'd argued with his boss about money and then disappeared in July 1975. Gacy himself led searchers to the grave.

In custody on the drug charge, the contractor was also booked for murder shortly after technician Daniel Genty spaded up the first bit of rotting flesh from the crawlspace. On December 22, a day after his arrest, the suspect agreed to return to his house in exchange for an opportunity to visit his father's grave. Police coaxed Gacy to spray-paint an *X* on the spot where he'd poured concrete over Butkovich's grave. The body, preceded by a cloud of stinking gas, was chipped out of the garage floor.

Incredibly, after marking Butkovich's grave, Gacy started railing at police for making a mess of his house: the mud on the carpet, the houseplants displaced, his neatly ordered tools disarranged. He began cleaning up, petulantly announcing that he wouldn't cooperate with the police anymore if they were going to be so careless. That was enough for State's Attorney Terry Sullivan, in charge of building the prosecution's case: "Cuff him," Sullivan screamed in rage, and Gacy was removed from the premises.

The next day the prisoner was still cranky, but he continued to cooperate. He'd already outlined for police his method of stalking young men, handcuffing them, and strangling them with rope. Gacy had also provided a map showing the layout of graves in the crawlspace. He'd labored over this guide, which was sketched on the back of a phone-message sheet. The map was amazingly accurate.

During the first week of the excavation hardly a day passed without a loathsome revelation. The necks of some of the victims were still encircled by the ropes used to murder them; other bodies had wadded fabric — sometimes their own underwear — jammed into what was left of their throats. Still other corpses had foreign objects — in one case a prescription bottle — lodged in their dissolving pelvic regions, indicating to the medical examiner that Gacy had thrust them into his victims' anuses. Investigators later discovered from interviews with surviving victims that Gacy frequently tortured his captives in that way.

The horrors multiplied as fear of infection spread. Men started shaving only at night to give nicks a chance to heal

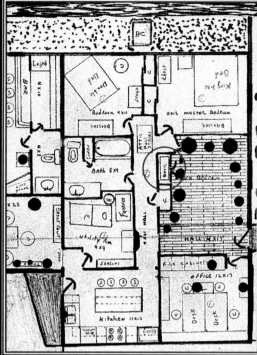

Working with a builder's precision, John Wayne Gacy drew a floor plan of his house *(above)* as it appeared prior to his arrest. Originally, the entrance to the crawlspace was in a closet near the front door *(circled, above),* but investigators excavating beneath the house made many changes. Among other things, they ripped out most of the flooring in order to have better access to the burial ground *(right).*

Numbered stakes *(right)* mark the locations where skulls were unearthed from the crawlspace. The stakes were part of an elaborate system police established to help identify the bodies of Gacy's victims. The grave site marked with a 6 *(far right)* yielded up remains identified as those of Samuel Stapleton, who had disappeared in May of 1976.

An investigator comes up for air *(right)*, repelled by the reek of the crawlspace. Excavators of the burial ground had to contend not only with noxious working conditions but with the public clamor for names of the victims. Many parents with missing sons feared that their loved ones might have ended up in the crawlspace.

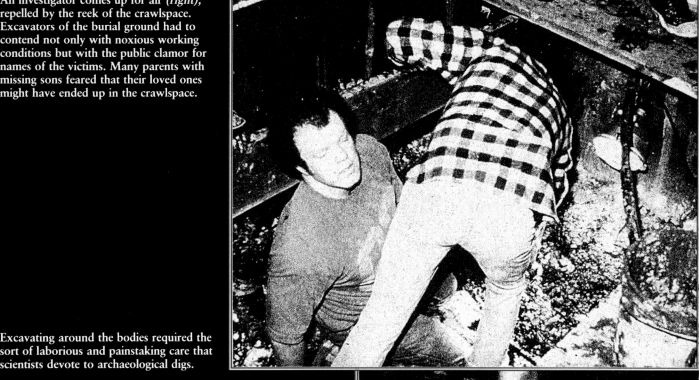

Excavating around the bodies required the sort of laborious and painstaking care that scientists devote to archaeological digs.

Police did their own schematic of Gacy's house on West Summerdale Avenue, marking black rectangles on the sites where bodies
were recovered. The grave positions matched closely with a sketch
Gacy had provided during his confession. Sanitary schematics
did little to convey the actual horror of decomposed bodies *(bottom)* awaiting removal from the crawlspace.

A rumpled and weary-looking John Gacy is
escorted into court by police officer Walter
Lang on December 22, 1978, to be formally
charged with murder.

over before exposure to the pathogens in the crawlspace.
Any digger who suffered a cut was sent out immediately for
a tetanus shot. As it turned out, no one contracted tetanus
or other infections associated with the corpses; but between
the bitter cold of Chicago's winter and the furnace heat that
made work possible, many of the diggers came down with
colds and other respiratory infections. In a way, head colds
were a blessing. They helped muffle the smell.

Dr. Stein, the medical examiner, worked methodically.
He matched the bones from body bags with what he presumed to be the appropriate skulls, which were wrapped
separately. As the law prescribed, he pronounced each
corpse dead and wrote a death certificate. Then he and
assistants piled the bags near the front door to be picked up
for daily delivery to the morgue. Each body was reduced to
a number, each number was placed on a wooden stake, and
the stake was driven into the mud of the crawlspace as near
as possible to where the skull had been found. As the graves
emptied and the stakes went up, the chill ground water
seeped relentlessly in, pooling around the posts.

The searchers fought the horror of their work with black
humor. Officers warned against throwing chicken bones
into the pit, saying that Dr. Stein might flip out. Then there
were the inevitable John Gacy jokes: Gacy wouldn't be going out this New Year's because he couldn't dig up a date.
Officers held a "ghoul pool" on the total number of bodies.
The guesses ranged from 5 to 24—all too low.

Police looted the house of souvenirs such as bricks, ball-
point pens with the PDM logo, and Gacy's business cards.
Photos of the diggers and technicians were taken for pos-
terity. They posed in front of a huge blow-up of Gacy
adorned with Polish flags and a collection of dildos. Officers
postured before this grotesque background, their riot hel-
mets under their arms, while a colleague displayed the day's
body count on a film-style chalk clapper board.

Officers tore the house apart and found more evidence of
Gacy's past crimes and proclivities—more IDs, more sex
books and magazines, marijuana pipes, and phony police
badges. And jammed under the floor of the utility room
they found Rob Piest's blue down-filled parka. Gacy had
suggested that it might be there.

The searchers took brief breaks over Christmas and New
Year's. By December 29 the 27th body had been recovered
from the West Summerdale house. After the holidays, heavy
snows blanketed the upper Midwest, effectively stopping

outside work. Later, highway equipment excavated the entire crawlspace down to undisturbed clay. Gradually the
swarms of reporters and onlookers drifted away, and gradually the number of police on the site diminished. In April
of 1979 the house, now unsafe from all the digging around
the foundation, was razed. The digging continued.

The total number of bodies unearthed from the house, the
driveway, and the garage eventually came to 29. Six of the
corpses have never been identified.

The excavations over, investigators turned their attention
anew to the other bodies—the imprecise number that had
been thrown, like Rob Piest's, into the Des Plaines River
after the crawlspace was full. Unfortunately, Gacy, who'd
been in police custody throughout the long winter excavation of his home, was muddled when it came to names,
faces, or dates. He wasn't sure exactly how many bodies
were under the house, or how many were in the river. The
total number of corpses thrown into the river was eventually set by investigators at four.

The contractor had started confessing to police at about
11 o'clock the night of his arrest. He described in broad
terms killing 25 or 30 young men. "I want to clear the air,"
Gacy said. "I know that the game is over. The lime was used
to cover the smell. The bodies have been down there a long
time. And there are more bodies off the property." But even
as he confessed to everything, he held himself totally blameless. All his victims, he said, deserved what they got. They
were hustlers, he claimed, homosexuals who sold their bodies for cash, then tried to trick the client who'd paid them.
Gacy denied his own homosexuality, insisting proudly that
he was bisexual. Incredibly, he also asserted that he never
made anyone do anything that he didn't want to do. "I
never used force," he said. "It was always by consent." He
also claimed that Rossi and Cram were involved in his
crimes, an accusation authorities did not substantiate.

Police made no audiotapes or videotapes of Gacy's confessions, perhaps fearing that the suspect would put on a
performance or alter the content of his revelations to bolster
an insanity plea. Instead of tapes, authorities relied on the
notes taken by the small circle of Des Plaines police and
representatives from the sheriff's office.

But according to those notes, the words came pouring
out. Gacy said that he used the same method for all but one
of his victims; he called it the rope trick. He would loop a
rope around the victim's neck, then slip a hammer handle

A Workaholic on Death Row

With sole proprietorship of a growing business, a calendar filled with charitable works, an active hand in local politics, and a criminal life that routinely spilled over into the small hours of the morning, John Wayne Gacy functioned at a pace that far outstripped the energies of the people around him. A boundless but woefully misguided vigor had seized him as a young adult. And it never let go, even in the aftermath of his murder convictions.

At the Menard Correctional Center in southern Illinois, where Gacy occupies a cell on death row, he devotes a portion of his time to painting with oils. He is not a particularly gifted artist, but he is extremely prolific. A mail-order graphic-art dealer peddles Gacy's moderately priced portraits of clowns, along with renderings of the Seven Dwarfs and studies on religious themes. Proceeds from the sales support a second outlet for Gacy's pent-up energy—a massive and wide-ranging correspondence. Since he has regular pen pals in 38 states and numerous foreign countries, the postal charges alone would make the letter writing impractical if Gacy did not have the income from his painting.

The convicted killer receives letters from people in many walks of life. In addition to a steady stream of interview requests from journalists, psychology students, and filmmakers, he gets letters from children, notes from female admirers, and inquiries from a wide variety of people who are simply curious. Some of the correspondents send their best wishes and offer religious counseling, others convey only their deep-seated loathing. Whatever the nature of the mail he receives, Gacy usually responds to the letters. When he feels that he has grounds for in-depth communication, he sometimes sends along a questionnaire to be filled out by the correspondent. In one instance, he reciprocated by completing the form himself *(right)*.

Letter writing and painting are merely diversions, however. In his 12th year of life as a condemned man—and in the final stages of his appeals—Gacy's central preoccupation is his legal defense. And this is where the true creativity comes into play: Although 29 bodies were unearthed on his property, although wallets and other personal effects of the deceased were discovered among his belongings, although he confessed to his crimes before a roomful of Des Plaines police and Cook County authorities, Gacy would now have the world believe he had nothing to do with the murders. "Anyone that I've had sex with," he asserts, "so far as I know, is still alive."

Recasting his personal history is a familiar game for John Wayne Gacy. He has been doing it all his life. In his memories, he is always the victim. When it comes to the killings, he claims to be the sacrificial lamb in an elaborate police conspiracy—one that was aided and abetted by his defense lawyer, who was hoping to write a book about the trial. According to Gacy, the confessions never happened; they were invented by the police. If boys were killed at his home, it was not by his hand. After all, he argues, several other people had keys to his house, and he was frequently away on business.

Given the evidence that was presented at his trial, it is difficult to imagine a court of appeals accepting Gacy's new scenario. But the convicted killer has a history of imposing his will through sheer hardheadedness and unstinting labor. With absolutely nothing to lose, he will probably follow that strategy right to the bitter end.

Divulging likes, dislikes, and pet peeves on a "Bio Review" form of his own devising, Gacy depicts himself as openminded but—down deep—a softy and a straight arrow. He has taken to using the questionnaire to draw out his pen pals.

Bio Review

Full Name: John Wayne Michael Gacy   Date of Birth: March 17th, 1942

Age, HT., Wt.: 50, 5'9", 220

Maritial Status: Twice divorced   Home: Menard,Deathrow,Chester,Ill.

Wheels: last car 79 oldsmobile 4 dr.   Family: 2 sisters, 5 children

Most Treasured Honor: 3 times man of the year Jaycees 3 different cities   Brothers: none   Sisters: two

Perfect woman or man: woman, independant, thinker, self starter, mind of her own. Man:Bright,bold, honest dependable says what he is thinking.

Childhood Hero: J.F. Kennedy,R.J.Daley.Current Hero: M Cuomo, Donald Trump.

Favoirte TV shows: Unsolved Mysteries, National Gepgraphic specials

Favorite movies: Once Upon a time in American, Good fellas,Ten Commandments

Favorite song: Send in the clowns, amazing grace

Favorite singers: Judy Collins, Bob Dylan, Neil Diamond.Roy Orbison,Sha na na

Favorite Musicians: REO Speedwagon Elton John, Zamfir

Hobbies:Correspondance, oil painting, study of human interests.

Favorite Meals:Fried Chicken, deboned lake perch drawn in butter, salad. Tea.

Why you wrote JW Gacy: I don't I just answer for him.

Recommended Reading: Texas Connection, Question of Doubt

Last Book read: Naked Lunch and Wild boys William S Burroughs

Ideal Evening: Dinner and concert or live show, drinks and a quiet walk by lake

Every Jan1st I resolve: Correct things that I let go year before.

Nobody Knows I'm: a character who love to tease and joke around

My Biggest regret: being so trusting and gullible, taken advantage of.

It I were President I'd: Make sure the people of this country had jobs and a place to live before worrying about other countrie

My advice to children:Be yourself, think positive respect parents

What I don't like about People: Phonies, people who don't keep their word.

My Biggest Fear: Dying before I have a chance to clear my name with truth.

Pet Peeves: People who say things they have no intentions in doing.

Superstitions: none its for negative people

Friends like me because: I am outspoken and honest, fun loving,dependable

Coffins holding the remains of John Wayne Gacy's unidentified victims stand in front of a mausoleum at the Oakridge Cemetery in the Chicago suburb of Hillside. A memorial service for these nameless dead was held at Oakridge on June 12, 1981. After the service, the bodies were dispersed to several different cemeteries. Authorities feared that burying them in one place might create a macabre tourist attraction.

through the loop and turn it to tighten the noose. (Later he would demonstrate the deadly manuever on a policeman's wrist. Lacking a hammer for this exhibition, he used a pen. And in the absence of a rope, he used another substitute: a rosary.) Piest, he told the investigators, had been handcuffed and roped in that way and left gasping while Gacy calmly took two business calls. When Gacy returned to where Piest lay in the bedroom, he was surprised—and a bit angry—that the boy seemed to be dead. Gacy observed with a sneer that if Piest had only wriggled a little and ducked his head away from the hammer handle, the twisted rope would have released. Rob Piest didn't need to die, according to Gacy; he more or less killed himself.

The killer claimed he never had sex with Rob Piest that night, although he left open the possibility that Jack Hanley may have done so. Gacy did admit to sleeping in the bed next to the boy's corpse and to moving Piest's body to the attic the next morning—where it lay hidden when the Des Plaines detectives paid their first call to the contractor's home. Gacy later loaded the body into the trunk of his car, took it to the I-55 bridge over the Des Plaines River, and dumped it into the water below.

Gacy spoke to the group of detectives and officials calmly and quietly. It had all started, he said, in 1972. He claimed that he'd lost count of the number of victims. Two or three times, he'd killed more than once in a single evening. Some bodies he'd soaked with acid, others he'd covered with lime before burying them under the house in shallow graves. He'd sometimes simply thrown away their clothes, but he had also on occasion given items of apparel to favored employees or made a donation to the Salvation Army.

Gacy said he killed his next-to-last victim, James Mazzara, because the youth wanted an extra $20 for sex acts. Another victim, he said, had tried to take money from his wallet and had pulled a knife on him, but Gacy countered by showing him some feats of magic—ending with the rope trick. With one victim, he told the officers, he'd read the 23rd Psalm—"Yea, though I walk through the valley of the shadow of death"—as he twisted the rope.

Throughout his confession Gacy made occasional references to "Jack" as the actual perpetrator. He also explained that the name was handy for his "cruising" identity as a cop who would first feign arrest of a youth and then offer to let him off in exchange for sex.

Gacy's revelations at first left police dumbfounded. He

must be lying, they thought. How could one person kill so many? But as the crawlspace yielded up body after body, the truth of his story became horribly plain. On December 28 a body was found floating in the Des Plaines River. Thinking that it might be the remains of Rob Piest, police raced to the scene. It was a young male and bore all the signs of being a Gacy victim, but it wasn't the young pharmacy clerk. It was James Mazzara, who had disappeared on Thanksgiving. In the months before Gacy's arrest, two other bodies had been discovered in the icy water; now they, too, were linked to the contractor. It was not until April 9, 1979—some four months after Rob Piest's disappearance—that his body was discovered by a man strolling the river's towpath, five and a half miles downstream from the I-55 bridge.

The fame of Gacy's case spread like a wave across the country. Then, as such things will, the notoriety gradually receded, leaving Gacy curiously stranded. He spent his days at Cermak Hospital, the medical wing of the Cook County jail, shuttling between interviews with the police and meetings with doctors and mental-health professionals assigned to examine him.

Meanwhile, for Gacy, a transformation typical of psychopathic killers was taking place. As the days passed, his belief in his own innocence grew. From the outset he'd held himself blameless because, he reasoned, his victims were worthless little hustlers who got what was coming to them. Now, he went a step further: He was not guilty because, he believed, the state had little real proof that he was. This logic, coupled with Gacy's view of his own importance, left him feeling fairly confident in the face of his upcoming trial—an event he dubbed "the largest case in Illinois history."

In the view of his defense lawyers, the insanity defense seemed the only logical strategy. Under the Illinois statute, Gacy could concede that he'd killed the youths but still escape prison and a possible death penalty. He would be confined to a mental hospital if he could prove that he was mentally ill at the time of each killing. But Gacy recoiled from such an image of himself. Before long he was repudiating his confessions—after all, he reasoned, there were no witnesses to his crimes—and suggesting that other people, the real killers, could have gotten into his house without his knowledge and buried the bodies there. As Gacy later fumed in his thus-far-unpublished manuscript *Question of*

Doubt, "I honestly felt that the state's case against me wouldn't wash. The evidence was circumstantial, insubstantial. The charges could not stand up under the questioning, explanation, the clearing testimony that I felt would certainly emerge during the course of a trial."

Gacy was right on one count: The evidence was circumstantial—as is much of the evidence presented in countless trials every year. But it was hardly insubstantial. Twenty-nine corpses on one's property constituted, after all, a most extraordinary circumstance. Moreover, such revelations as Gacy's possession of Piest's parka and the photo receipt; Gacy's confessions and his descriptions of victims John Szyc, Gregory Godzik, and John Butkovich; and the emotional testimony of friends and relatives of the victims were more than enough to convince a jury.

The trial began February 6, 1980, and the opposing attorneys spent six weeks painting conflicting portraits of the same man. According to prosecutors, Gacy was an evil man who lured innocent, vulnerable young men to his home and played death games with them. The defense countered that Gacy was "a deeply sick individual" who was "crazy all the time." He tried unsuccessfully to control his murderous impulses, the defense attorneys argued, by working obsessively at his business and at his political and charitable activities.

It took the jury only one hour and 50 minutes to find Gacy guilty of 33 counts of murder. On March 13, one day after the verdict, the same 12 jurors deliberated just over two hours to decide the convicted man's sentence: death.

By the following day, John Wayne Gacy was behind locked doors on death row at Menard Correctional Center in southern Illinois. He has been there ever since. By the summer of 1992, appeals had delayed his execution for more than 12 years, and during that time he proved that even death row could not dampen his entrepreneurial spirit: Gacy kept up a lively correspondence with the many people who wrote him letters, and he wrote his autobiography. In addition, he took up a hobby that might call to mind the long-ago days when his father, John Stanley Gacy, locked himself away in his basement and muttered darkly while daubing paint onto the numbered patches that, when complete, made a coherent picture. In prison, John Wayne Gacy taught himself to paint with oils—but not by the numbers. His designs were original, even if their subject matter was repetitious. The favored subject of his artwork was himself, dressed as a clown. ◆

Gallery of Evil

Murder is neither new nor rare. It has occurred in societies everywhere, throughout history. Serial killing is not new either, but it is dramatically more common than it used to be. In fact, the term *serial killer* only entered the language in the 1970s. In the decade before that, there were perhaps five such slayers in the United States. In the 1980s there were, by some counts, around 90. The American numbers are telling, since the United States breeds far more serial murderers than any other country, trailed distantly by other nations of the industrialized West. It seems that something about modern life — mobility, alienation, permissiveness, a decline in emphasis on individual responsibility, a glorification of violence — triggers the latent evil in human misfits who kill for pleasure.

Whatever their time and place, serial killers come in many guises: a sadistic French aristocrat, a bloodthirsty German factory worker, a demented American farmer. Meet these and other examples of the deadly species on pages 92 to 115.

The Bestial Baron

Among history's most notorious serial killers was 15th-century French aristocrat Gilles de Rais, a man whose life was a study in extremes. He was by turns immensely rich and bankrupt, a military hero and a moral leper, a pious Christian and a secret killer.

In his best days, Gilles was personal bodyguard to Joan of Arc. Fighting by her side in the Hundred Years' War, he rose to the supreme rank of Marshal of France, an honor that swelled his massive family fortune. But blood, more than booty, held war's chief allure for him, and when hostilities paused in 1433, he looked toward new outlets for his lust for torture.

In a grisly routine that varied only in details, two of the baron de Rais's trusted servants would bring a peasant youngster to their master, who used the child sexually, then murdered it or watched its murder, laughing all the while at the victim's agony. He then caressed and dismembered the still-warm corpse before having it burned in a fireplace or tossed into his castle's latrine or a lime pit. Most of the slaughtered children were small, fair-haired boys, although little girls were not immune. While killing with abandon, Gilles was also squandering his fortune in ostentatious displays of hospitality and religiosity, and he eventually turned to devil worship in hopes of rebuilding his lost wealth.

The baron's crimes were rumored in the countryside for years, but they went uninvestigated until he ran afoul of a powerful political enemy, the bishop of Nantes. The result was trial by both ecclesiastical and secular courts. Threatened with excommunication and torture, the murderer became lavishly penitent, tearfully blaming his crimes on a permissive upbringing. Gilles confessed in vivid detail and was convicted of heresy, sodomy, and murdering 140 children. The actual total may have been much higher.

Contrite or not, Gilles was executed in Nantes in 1440 at the age of 36. He was hanged, then his body was tossed onto a blazing pyre. Before the corpse could be consumed, it was plucked out, to be interred in a church in accord with his Christian wishes. ◆

Victorious on medieval battlefields, French nobleman Gilles de Rais later turned his bloodlust toward the ritual torture and murder of children.

The Fiend of Whitechapel

London's Whitechapel district in the 1880s was a seething slum of poverty and crime where the cry of "Murder" was commonplace. But the murders that were committed there by an unknown psychopath dubbed Jack the Ripper brought into stark relief the social rot lying near the heart of the great British Empire.

The victims were prostitutes. Usually their throats and faces were slashed, their bodies slit open, and their viscera torn out. The number of murder-mutilations attributed to the so-called Whitechapel Fiend has ranged between 4 and 14, but the generally accepted toll is 5. The first, Mary Ann Nichols, was found on August 31, 1888, in a gateway leading to some stables. The last, Mary Jane Kelly, was the most thoroughly savaged, killed in her room and disemboweled at leisure on November 9.

Shortly after the Ripper's 10-week killing spree, journalists received several grisly, cheerful notes signed "Jack the Ripper." It was never known whether the real killer sent them, but the nickname stuck.

An intensive police investigation turned up numerous suspects—a rich cross section of London society—but no one was ever brought to court in the sensational case. By 1894 there were three chief suspects: Montague Druitt, a barrister and schoolteacher who was found drowned in the Thames River several weeks after the fifth murder; Aaron Kosminski, a Polish Jew who lived in the neighborhood and reputedly hated women; and Michael Ostrog, a confidence man and sneak thief who sometimes posed as a Russian doctor.

Still, after more than a century, the case remains open, and it continues to excite the public imagination. Over the years, histo-

In this photograph, taken around the turn of the century, slumdwellers congregate in front of a rooming house just blocks from where Jack the Ripper murdered two of his victims. The tenement was one of many on prostitute-infested Flower and Dean Street, known as the wicked quarter mile.

rians and criminologists, both amateur and professional, have put forward more than 100 suspects and have proposed conspiracies and cover-ups involving Freemasons, Catholics, Jews, the government, and royalty. Most likely, the case will never be solved, nor, it seems, will interest in it ever die. Jack the Ripper was not a prolific serial killer, but his deeds, trumpeted by the media, focused indelible attention on the depravity and poverty that lay beneath the sleek veneer of Victorian England. ◆

At his Chicago hotel for young ladies *(right)*, con artist, swindler, and polygamist Herman Mudgett *(below)* trapped some 100 victims, one by one, then gassed or tortured them to death.

The Murder Castle

A charming swindler and ingenious crook, Herman Webster Mudgett would stop at nothing to make a dollar. His greed and cunning made his life a labyrinth of confidence games, forgery, and fraud. Of his countless victims, scores lost not only their money but their lives, in a macabre killing machine he called his Castle.

As pieced together later by detectives and reporters, Mudgett's life began in New Hampshire in 1860. He married the first of his three wives there when he was 18 and attended medical school at her expense. He practiced legitimate medicine only briefly after graduation, however, opting instead for a variety of quasi-medical and entrepreneurial scams. These included a bogus cure for alcoholism, some energetic real-estate ripoffs, and at least one clever pseudoscientific hustle: He rigged up a tankful of smelly liquid with wires, pulleys, and hoses, one of which secretly tapped a city gas main. He claimed that this "invention" turned water to natural gas and sold the contraption for $2,000. Mudgett conducted most of these nefarious enterprises under his favorite alias, H. H. Holmes.

Mudgett's first steps toward mass murder were apparently taken in Chicago in 1887. Hired to help run a pharmacy, "Dr. Holmes" first made himself indispensable to the widowed owner, then somehow got rid of the woman and laid claim to her property. With the drugstore as a respectable base, he piled scheme upon swindle and soon was able to begin, on a huge lot across the street, the crowning jewel of his wicked empire.

Presiding over an ever-shifting stream of itinerant workmen—none of whom knew the overall plan of the building—he created a conjoined row of turreted, three-story buildings. Their ground floor was devoted to shops, the top to Mudgett's office and private apartments. In between, Mudgett had built a nightmare maze of 100 windowless rooms, stairways to nowhere, secret doors, and chutes that led to a torture room and mortuary in the basement. The Castle opened its doors as a hotel in time for the World's Columbian Exposition in 1893.

Handsome and suave, the proprietor of the grand edifice placed newspaper advertisements offering women lucrative work or advantageous marriage in a large city. One after another, pretty applicants responded to the ads, and Mudgett persuaded each of them to bring him all she possessed, as he bargained or wooed her into captivity.

Over the next three years, a steady procession of gullible young women took up residence in the Castle, which proved to harbor a warren of soundproof, escape-proof death chambers. Peepholes were everywhere, doors were wired to activate a buzzer if the prisoners opened them, and gas lines permitted the murderer to asphyxiate an inmate at will. Transformed abruptly from mistress to corpse, the victim could be shoved through a secret door in Mudgett's apartment, to fall without ceremony to the basement.

Mudgett took some of the sufferers belowstairs while they were still alive, there to torture them if he felt they still had riches to reveal. Once they were dead, he had many means of disposal. A metal door in the dirt floor hid a large lime pit, and behind one wall was a furnace big enough and hot enough to serve as a crematorium. There he processed corpses in numbers impossible to reconstruct with absolute accuracy. Wringing every last cent from his victims, Mudgett even arranged to sell several bodies, as cadavers or as cleaned skeletons, to a nearby medical school for anatomical classes.

Ironically, it was not murder but fraud that eventually led to the slayer's undoing. Investigating an East Coast insurance scam, authorities discovered that Mudgett had dispatched a Philadelphia man who was his partner in the scheme. While the killer was in custody in Philadelphia, part of his castle burned. Despite the fire, police amassed evidence of slaughter through the summer, and the list of suspected victims grew to 20. Authorities later placed the likely toll at closer to 100, including men and children as well as women.

But Mudgett was never charged with the Chicago atrocities; Philadelphia authorities would not extradite him. They tried him for murder, and he confessed not only to the slaying of his partner but also to 27 other killings and an additional six attempted homicides. In at least one case, he reported with evident shock, he killed even though there was no money in it. "I committed this and other crimes for the pleasure of killing my fellow beings," he confessed, "to hear their cries for mercy." He had become, he said, "a moral idiot." Fittingly, his confession itself was yet another swindle, omitting known victims and naming several women still living.

Mudgett was hanged on May 7, 1896, in Philadelphia, even while investigators still pieced together his regime of evil, not only in Chicago, but in Indianapolis and Toronto as well. Even in death, he remained unique. At his request, his body, encased in a pine casket, was embedded in cement and buried 10 feet deep under another two feet of cement. He wished, he had said, to be safe from graverobbers and medical science. ◆

The Vampire of Düsseldorf

Factory worker Peter Kürten *(left)* was a quiet man whose harmless hobby was bird-watching. He was unassuming, neatly groomed, impeccably polite—and a monster. Behind his gentle mask was a seething rage thirsting for victims; in both numbers and savagery, his killings easily eclipsed those of his idol, England's Jack the Ripper *(page 93)*.

Through the summer of 1929, Kürten held the city of Düsseldorf, Germany, in a vise of fear, although the citizens did not yet know the name of their tormenter. But they knew all too well that a killer was on the loose; almost every week a fresh corpse was found, horribly slashed or bludgeoned to death, sometimes sexually assaulted. Most of the victims were young women, but older women, men, and children also fell prey, often in clusters of attacks. One August day brought news of the sadistic murders of two foster sisters, aged 5 and 14, and the attempted murder and rape of a 26-year-old domestic worker.

Months of terror stretched to a year as police searched for the killer. Parents forbade their children to play outdoors, friends distrusted one another, everyone feared to go out at night. Police received tips from all over Germany and questioned 9,000 citizens in Düsseldorf alone.

As for the killer, he sent friendly letters notifying the police of corpses so far undiscovered; once he even sent a map. And his crimes continued, until the 15-month total of murders and murderous attacks climbed above 30.

An assault charge brought police to Kürten's door in May of 1930. What they found was a man who, however meek he seemed, had a criminal record spanning 30 years. Once in custody, the prisoner confessed freely, not merely to assault, but to multiple murder, after warning his listeners, "you will hear many gruesome things from me."

Kürten said he liked to kill, "the more people the better. Yes, if I had had the means of doing so," he told authorities, "I would have killed whole masses of people—brought about catastrophes." He prowled for victims nightly, he said, and he found sexual gratification in slaying.

The prisoner was scrutinized for keys to his twisted character. He was the oldest of 10 children, and between beatings by his alcoholic father, the youngster developed a taste for tormenting animals and for watching houses burn. At nine he pushed a playmate off a raft into the Rhine River and, when a third child went to the rescue, kept them both submerged until they drowned. In his midteens, Kürten later recalled, "I found out what pleasure it gave me to try and strangle a girl I took out with me into the woods."

At 16, caught stealing, he was jailed for the first of 17 sentences that would add up to nearly 20 years in prison for arson and theft. It was during this time that he took to poring over the exploits of Jack the Ripper. "I thought what pleasure it would give me to do things of that kind once I got out again," he reported later.

Out again in 1913 at the age of 30, Kürten took to robbing the homes of beer-hall owners on busy Saturday nights while they were serving their patrons. During one such foray, he later confessed, he committed his first murder since childhood, and it seemed to him to avenge his brutal past. Finding the barkeep's 10-year-old daughter asleep, he strangled her, then cut her throat. The next day he lounged in a café opposite the beer hall and overheard outraged discussions of his crime. He found the indignation very satisfying.

His marriage, in 1922, calmed him, and it was several years before he resumed killing. After four years of fire setting and vicious assaults, his final secret rampage of atrocities began in 1929. In February of that year, Kürten killed an eight-year-old girl, stabbing her 13 times, dousing her with kerosene, and setting her aflame.

Sometimes Kürten was satisfied to maim or frighten a victim, and let her live. It was one such survivor, 20-year-old Maria Büdlick, who at last led police to the man who was by now being called the Monster of Düsseldorf. After his arrest, certain details of his confession would gain him a new nickname. He said that one of his chief satisfactions in killing was to catch the blood spurting from a victim's wounds in his mouth and swallow it. He thus became known as the Vampire of Düsseldorf.

After a year's study, Germany's best psychiatric minds pronounced Kürten sane. At trial his defending counsel, summing up the experts' testimony, called Kürten "a concentrated complex of all sexual abnormalities known, a veritable king of sexual delinquents." Sadism, masochism, fetishism, and pyromania were listed among his disorders. Convicted of nine murders and sentenced to death, Kürten acknowledged no remorse and said he might kill again if he were free.

Peter Kürten was guillotined in Cologne, Germany, on July 2, 1931. In his last moments, he said he wondered if he would hear his own blood spurting after his neck was severed. ◆

CHRISTINE KLEIN

ROSA OHLINGER

GERTRUDE ALBERMANN

MARIA HAHN

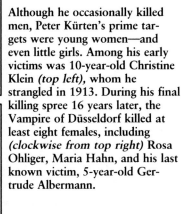

Although he occasionally killed men, Peter Kürten's prime targets were young women—and even little girls. Among his early victims was 10-year-old Christine Klein *(top left),* whom he strangled in 1913. During his final killing spree 16 years later, the Vampire of Düsseldorf killed at least eight females, including *(clockwise from top right)* Rosa Ohliger, Maria Hahn, and his last known victim, 5-year-old Gertrude Albermann.

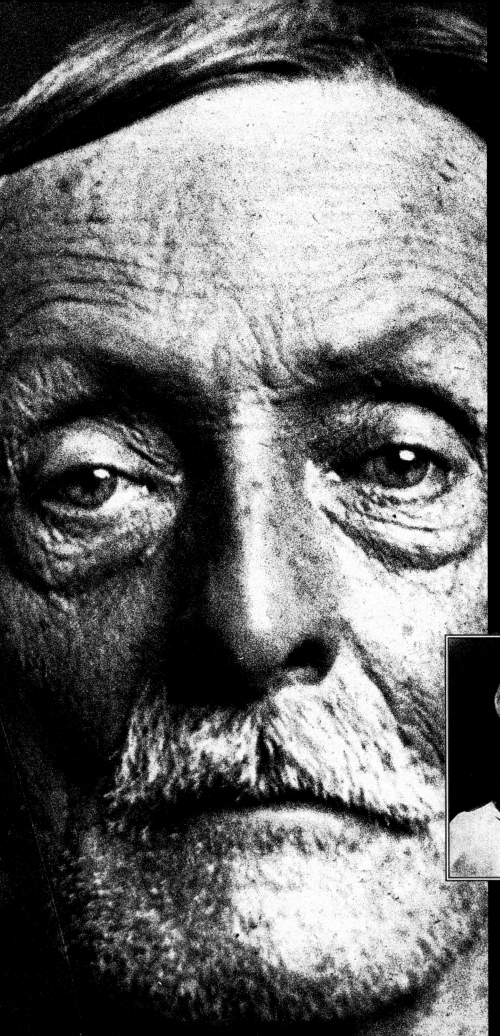

The Moon Maniac

Sadist, masochist, child molester, cannibal—Albert Fish compiled for himself a formidable résumé of sexual deviations. A psychiatrist who examined him declared, "There was no known perversion that he did not practice and practice frequently." Fish himself looked back over his 65 years and said, "I always seemed to enjoy everything that hurt."

Born in 1870, Fish was raised in an orphanage in Washington, D.C., and he blamed his later vices on the cruelties he experienced there. "Misery leads to Crime," he wrote; "I saw so many boys whipped, it took root in my head."

The adult Fish became an itinerant house painter, married, and sired six children. After his wife left him for another man in 1917, Fish became markedly strange. He took to dancing naked by moonlight, crying "I am Christ! I am Christ!" He also adopted uglier pastimes, burning himself with pokers, embedding

A mug shot *(left)* shows the watery-eyed Albert Fish after he was arrested for murder. A masochist as well as a sadist and cannibal, Fish enjoyed inflicting pain on himself. An x-ray *(above),* shows some of the 29 sewing needles he'd inserted into his groin.

needles in his groin, and flagellating himself with a nail-studded paddle. Seeking yet more abuse, he answered lonely-hearts ads from marriage-minded widows with obscene letters about paddling, punishment, and worse. (He bigamously married three women he located in this way.)

Somewhere along the line, his love of pain—receiving it and inflicting it—turned toward children. In 1928 the grandfatherly Fish befriended a Manhattan family named Budd and was given leave by trusting parents to take 10-year-old Grace Budd to his niece's birthday party. But there was no party, and Fish took Grace to an abandoned cottage in Westchester County. With him he carried a bundle containing what he called his "instruments of hell"—a butcher knife, a cleaver, and a saw. By his own later account, the aging pervert strangled the girl and dismembered her corpse. He then returned home with a wrapped package of her flesh, which he cooked in a stew with carrots and onions. He savored this concoction for nine days in a constant state of sexual excitement.

Although Grace was missing for six years, her family never gave up hope that she was still alive until 1934, when Fish wrote them an anonymous letter that revealed the horrible truth. After some rambling about cannibalism in famine-stricken China, he advised the Budds that he had killed and eaten their child—but, he primly noted, he had not molested her. Police feverishly traced the letter to Fish in a New York rooming house where he was arrested December 13, 1934.

Fish's trial was a field day for the tabloid press, which tagged the demented house painter variously as the Thrill Vulture, Vampire Man, and Moon Maniac. After a jury found him sane and guilty of first-degree murder, Fish confessed to several other crimes. He said he had killed eight-year-old Francis McDonnell on Staten Is-

land in 1924 and tortured, murdered, and cannibalized four-year-old William Gaffney in 1927. He recalled other assaults and mutilations going back 20 years, and reckoned he must have violated as many as 30 children a year in 23 states as he traveled in his work.

Though generally at a loss to explain his acts, Fish, who professed strong religious feeling, said he sometimes felt a need to make a sacrifice. He told a court psychiatrist he had killed Grace Budd "to save her from some future outrage" that he foresaw, and he had felt sure "an angel would stop him if he did the wrong thing."

Sentenced to electrocution in New York's Sing Sing Prison, Fish anticipated his demise with something akin to glee. "It will be the supreme thrill," he enthused— "the only one I haven't tried." He walked unassisted into the execution chamber on January 16, 1936, to become at 65 the oldest prisoner ever executed at Sing Sing. ◆

Police investigators search the cottage in Westchester County, New York, where Fish killed Grace Budd. After strangling the 10-year-old girl, Fish dismembered her and prepared a stew with her flesh.

JOE BALL

The Alligator Man

In the years after Prohibition was repealed, most rural counties in the American Southwest had their share of seedy roadside taverns. Many of them were tough, rowdy places, but for lowlife meanness few could match the Sociable Inn on Highway 181 outside Elmendorf, Texas. Glowering, potbellied Joe Ball was the proprietor, and he set the tone of the establishment with a surly "got-the-cash?" attitude toward customers. It was the landmark out back, however, that really gave the bar its nasty distinction.

Ball had built a cement pond that he stocked with a brood of full-grown alligators. Each night, as the saloon crowd hit its stride, he would duck out the rear exit with a gaggle of his regulars and toss chunks of horse meat to the hungry reptiles. His half-sloshed buddies would then gape in astonishment as a feeding frenzy ensued. As time wore on, Ball enlivened the spectacle by heaving live dogs and cats into the pond.

Local deputy sheriffs who frequented the tavern might have wondered about such cruel entertainment. But they said nothing, intimidated perhaps by the scowling, unapproachable barkeep. People around Elmendorf knew relatively little about Joe

Following the suicide of their hard-drinking master (inset), Joe Ball's alligators were trussed up and taken to a Texas zoo. A witness claimed that the gators ate some of the evidence of Ball's alleged murders.

Ball. He was clearly a heavy drinker and was said to have had his way with at least a few of the pretty waitresses who were endlessly cycling through his employ.

In September 1938, the anonymity surrounding this gloomy tavern keeper was abruptly swept away in the wake of inquiries about the unexplained disappearance of Hazel Brown, a popular new waitress at the Sociable Inn. Her absence was all the more alarming when coupled with rumors about a local laborer who claimed to have seen Ball dropping severed human limbs into the alligator pond. The Bexar County sheriff's office lacked hard leads that might shed light on these matters, but Hazel Brown's parents were pressing for action. So it was that two deputies confronted Ball with their concerns.

He reacted with stunning finality: Pulling a gun from the drawer beneath his cash register, he shot himself in the heart, ending his life in an instant.

At this point the Texas Rangers stepped in to investigate, but since they were under little pressure to convict a dead man, they never fully plumbed the case of Joe Ball. Most of what they did learn came from Clifford Wheeler, a longtime handyman at the Sociable Inn. Wheeler told a horrifying tale of slaughtered waitresses and gory dismemberings. The lone witness, apart from the laborer, who had since fled Texas, Wheeler was sent to prison as an accessory to murder — this despite his pleas that his longstanding silence was motivated purely by terror.

Investigators believed that Joe Ball may have killed as many as a dozen people, most of them women. Some victims, they speculated, were disposed of in the alligator pond; others, like the unfortunate Hazel Brown, were chopped up and buried at scattered locations in the sandy wastes of southern Texas. ◆

Joe Ball was the distinctly antisocial proprietor of the Sociable Inn, a seedy roadside bar outside Elmendorf, Texas. His alligators lived in a cement pond behind the building.

The Lipstick Killer

When William George Heirens was arrested for burglary on June 26, 1946, his classmates at the University of Chicago were shocked. The 17-year-old sophomore was a good student and regular churchgoer and, though shy and a bit prudish, fairly well liked. But with his arrest, police halted a one-man crime wave that included three murders on Chicago's North Side.

Josephine Alice Ross, a 43-year-old widow, had died of stab wounds to the neck, apparently after surprising a burglar in her home in June of 1945. In December, Frances Brown, 30, stabbed in the neck and shot twice, was found dead in her apartment. On Brown's living room wall the killer had scrawled in bright red lipstick, "For heavens sake catch me before I kill more I cannot control myself." But the best efforts of the police failed to find the so-called Lipstick Killer, and in January 1946 he struck again. Six-year-old Suzanne Degnan was murdered; parts of her dismembered body were stuffed into sewers near her home. In an odd twist, the bodies of all three victims had been carefully washed clean of blood. None was sexually assaulted.

Two other women had been wounded by shots fired through windows into their homes, and another was beaten and tied up by an intruder. The killings and attacks came amid a rash of burglaries in the area, near the University of Chicago campus. Heirens's undoing came when he was caught at the scene of one of the thefts. He resisted arrest fiercely until knocked unconscious by a policeman wielding flowerpots, but the only burglarized loot in his possession was a souvenir oversized dollar bill.

Stolen goods worth thousands of dollars were found in the suspect's dormitory room, however, and an incriminating note signed "George" pointed to a possible burglary ring. For three days Heirens refused to talk, until investigators took the unusual step of giving him sodium pentothal—a so-called truth serum. Under its influence, the

Girlfriends called him the "perfect gentleman" *(inset, top)*, but William Heirens, dazed after police questioning, looks like a different person. In his room police found surgical kits *(bottom)*, possibly used by Heirens to dismember one of his victims. Heirens blamed his crimes on an imaginary friend, George Murman. "George did it," he said. "I told him not to be such a bad boy."

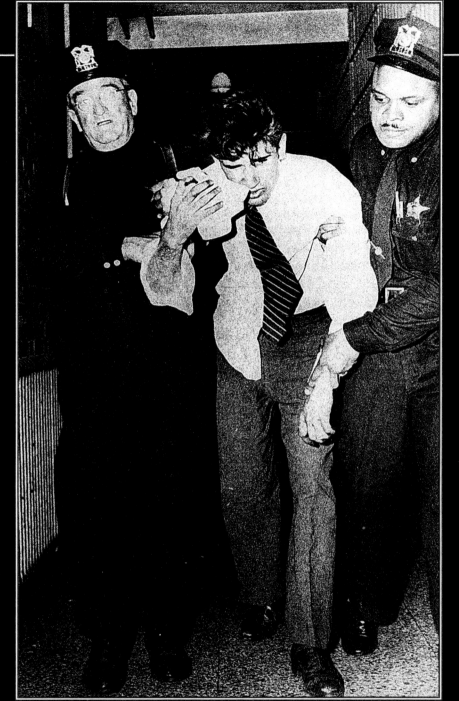

After hearing his bail set at $270,000, Heirens becomes ill and stumbles down a hallway at the Cook County jail.

suspect told the grisly details of the child's murder. But he blamed it all on an elusive friend, George Murman. An intensive search found no one by that name.

Under questioning, Heirens described feeling "hazy" or "vague" or even "blacking out" at the times of the crimes. He entered people's homes, he said, because burglary was his only source of sexual release. He guessed that he might have committed 500 burglaries.

The roots of Heirens's problems seemed to lie in his childhood, when he had been told that sexual contact was wrong and caused disease. Deeply ashamed of his own sexual impulses, he began sneaking into houses and stealing women's panties. He experienced orgasm when he put them on. He was already a practiced burglar and arsonist when he was arrested at 13 for carrying a loaded pistol. Sent to a special preparatory school where he did well academically, the boy entered the University of Chicago at 16. But he kept breaking into people's homes, even though he often left without taking anything but his own guilty pleasure.

Investigators quickly realized that George Murman was a fantasy, a second personality Heirens developed in childhood to do all the bad things Bill did not dare do. In his confession—a later session, without the use of sodium pentothal—Heirens acknowledged that George was "a concoction of my imagination. You can accept George as being me."

A court-appointed panel of three psychiatrists declared Heirens "a sexual psychopath with maniacal tendencies," but legally sane: At the time of the crimes, the panel judged, the prisoner knew right from wrong and knew that he was doing wrong.

Heirens was convicted of the three murders and 26 counts involving robbery, burglary, and assault. He was sentenced on September 5, 1946, to three consecutive life sentences for the murders, plus additional time for the lesser offenses. Once in prison, his condition deteriorated until authorities moved him briefly to the state prison for the criminally insane.

Heirens improved, however, so much that in 1977 he finally finished his interrupted college career. After 25 years of televised classes, correspondence courses, and prison education, he became the first Illinois prison inmate to be awarded a college degree. As of 1992, William Heirens remained behind bars at Vienna Correctional Center, the longest-tenured prisoner in the state of Illinois. ◆

The Butcher of Plainfield

In terms of numbers, Ed Gein was not much of a murderer, as serial killers go. But viewed through the lens of sheer, lunatic atrocity, he was one of the worst. So perverse and horrible were his crimes that they inspired two classic works of film and fiction: The Silence of the Lambs (in which Gein is the prototype for the ghoulish killer Buffalo Bill) and Psycho (as mad mama's boy Norman Bates).

Gein (pronounced "geen") grew up on an isolated farm outside Plainfield, Wisconsin, in the grip of an alcoholic, abusive father and a domineering mother. Augusta Gein, a woman who had little use for either men or sex, made sure that her sons Ed and Henry avoided temptations of the flesh. Neither son would ever marry. Nevertheless, Gein later recalled his rigid, fanatical mother as "good in every way."

Between 1940 and 1945, the father, then Henry, and then Augusta died, leaving Ed alone on the desolate farm, which was not even equipped with electricity. He was 39, reclusive, and ill-prepared to live in normal society. He boarded up his mother's bedroom and sitting room and never entered them again, preserving them as a shrine to her memory. A government subsidy freed him from farming, and he worked at odd jobs as a handyman and, appallingly, a baby-sitter. He devoted his free time to his psychotic experiments.

Ed Gein at first indulged his long-suppressed interest in women's bodies by poring over anatomical textbooks. To check their facts, he visited graveyards, dug up several female corpses, and took them home with him for study and clumsy dissection. He found special pleasure in handling the dead women's sex organs, but other parts of the bodies intrigued him too. He skinned some of his cadavers and wore the skins around the house, draped over his shoulders. He also kept heads, livers, hearts, and intestines scattered about. He later confessed a long-held secret wish to become a woman.

Alone in his hideaway, increasingly mad, Gein took to fashioning scraps of human hide into bracelets, lampshades, and even a coffee-can tom-tom. Sometimes he would

Its tranquil, snow-covered rural setting belies the horrors that police found inside Ed Gein's Wisconsin farmhouse *(below)*. After the death of his domineering mother, the "Butcher of Plainfield" boarded up the rooms she had used. Investigators found these rooms, including the one at left, in pristine condition. But Gein's living quarters *(right)* were another story. Veteran police were sickened by the sight of shrunken heads, human bones and organs, and preserved skin scattered among the filth.

dance around his kitchen and yard, naked except for an assortment of ghoulish treasures. Meanwhile, the simplest chores went unattended, and rotting garbage and filthy castoff clothing piled up in the corners of his dismal house. To his anatomy textbooks, Gein added horror comics and pornographic magazines.

The time came when corpses stolen from the graveyard were no longer enough. Gein set out to get a fresh one. He shot and killed 54-year-old Mary Hogan one night in 1954 as she was closing the saloon that she owned. For three years Hogan's murder went unsolved.

Then, in 1957, Gein killed his second known victim, Bernice Worden, when he found the 58-year-old woman alone in the hardware store she ran with her son. On his way out with the body, Gein picked up the store's cash register, but he left behind a sales slip that the dead woman had started writing out for his purchase. This evidence led police to the reclusive farmer, a man the townspeople considered "odd and shy but harmless."

The sight that greeted officers when they entered Gein's home was hard to accept. There were shrunken heads. There were skulls, some sawed in half for use as drinking cups. There were chair seats, a wastepaper basket, and a vest and leggings, all fashioned of human skin. A human heart was found in a saucepan on the stove. Police estimated that at least 15 bodies went to make up Gein's grisly collection. Bernice Worden's decapitated, disemboweled body hung upside down in a shed, dressed out like a dead deer's. Authorities identified one of the heads as that of the long-missing Mary Hogan.

Gein talked freely about the stolen cadavers and confessed to the murders of Mary Hogan and Bernice Worden. Police suspected him of at least three additional slayings, but he said he had not killed any

others. He discussed his mutilations as if commenting on the weather. He said he had killed both victims "while in a daze" and realized later that both reminded him of his mother.

One week after Bernice Worden's butchered body was discovered, Gein was con-

fined in a state mental hospital, where he was soon declared criminally insane. Ten years later, he was tried and found guilty of first-degree murder but again was declared mentally diseased. He spent the rest of his life institutionalized and died of natural causes in 1984. ◆

Ed Gein appears in court the day of his 1957 arrest. He was institutionalized for the last 27 years of his life.

ANNA SLESERS

HELEN BLAKE

IDA IRGA

SOPHIE CLARK

PATRICIA BISSETTE

MARY SULLIVAN

ALBERT DESALVO

The Boston Strangler

In December of 1962 Boston was a city of fear. In the previous six months, six women in and near the city had been strangled and assaulted in their homes by a killer who left no clues. The victims ranged in age from 20 to 75. As if to taunt police, the assailant, dubbed the Boston Strangler, left his victims propped up in lewd poses, decorated with bows made of their own stockings, scarfs, or sashes.

Almost 2,600 police officers—the greatest force ever assembled for any manhunt—worked doggedly to find the killer, but they reported no suspects and no leads. Fearful women all over greater Boston installed new locks and took to keeping dogs for protection. They refused to open their doors to telephone installers, meter readers, and salesmen. One woman, awaiting a friend, did admit a stranger—a harmless encyclopedia salesman—and in her fright dropped dead of a heart attack.

Meanwhile, Boston detectives were desperate for any clues. They puzzled over the peculiar combination of knots in the victims' grotesque neckwear and scanned taxicab logs to trace the victims' travels. They even called in psychics. The Massachusetts attorney general, responding to public cries for action, set up a Strangler Bureau to coordinate investigations.

But despite public caution and police scrutiny, the Strangler still managed to murder. Before 1962 ended, he killed again, and another year would pass before the last—the 13th—of his slayings. Among the six victims in 1963, the oldest one was 85, the youngest 19.

Then, in November of 1964, a 33-year-old house painter and handyman named Albert DeSalvo was arrested for rape and robbery. Diagnosed as schizophrenic and

Albert DeSalvo *(above)* claimed to be the Boston Strangler, but he was never charged with the 13 killings. As the pictures of the victims shown at top suggest, one of the case's many peculiarities was the broad age range among the women who died at his hands.

incompetent to stand trial, he was sent to a state mental hospital in 1965. There he boasted to a fellow inmate named George Nassar that he had killed 13 women. Albert DeSalvo was, it seemed, the Boston Strangler.

When news of these disclosures reached Boston police, they were surprised. DeSalvo had not been a suspect, even though he was certainly known to authorities: He had been convicted in 1962 of assault and battery and sentenced to two years in jail. The case was related to the sexual molestation of a number of young women, lured by DeSalvo with promises that he would get them work modeling. He was paroled in 1962 after serving 11 months of his sentence. His 1964 arrest involved a series of rapes. But whatever his predations against women, DeSalvo had never been accused of killing them. Initially, only his 1965 confessions to Nassar, who was institutionalized for psychological testing prior to being tried for murder, implicated DeSalvo in the sensational Strangler case.

Nassar's attorney, as it happened, was famed criminal lawyer F. Lee Bailey, who wound up representing DeSalvo as well. The supposed Strangler told his high-powered lawyer that he wanted "only to be found innocent by reason of insanity so I could go to a mental hospital" and find self-understanding.

During the ensuing seven months of questioning, DeSalvo confessed informally to the 13 Strangler killings. While refusing, on Bailey's advice, to give police a statement for the record, he nevertheless dis-

DeSalvo escaped from a state mental hospital in 1967 but was quickly recaptured. He was wearing a navy petty officer's uniform at the time. No one knows how he got it.

cussed the murders freely, giving scores of gruesome details known only to police and the killer. He even tied his shoelaces with the odd combination investigators had come to call the Strangler's Knot.

Moreover, there was much in the handyman's background that might have predicted severe sexual disturbance and homicidal tendencies. Born in 1931, he was one of six children of an abusive, alcoholic, thieving plumber. The family was desperately poor, and the father taught Albert to steal when the boy was five. During a stint in the army, DeSalvo met and married his proper, German-born wife, Irmgard. They had two children, but an unhappy marriage.

By his own account, DeSalvo had a huge sexual appetite that made him want intercourse five or six times a day. When his wife refused him, he called her frigid and looked elsewhere. He later told a reporter that when he worked at construction sites in Boston, he would sneak into apartments on coffee breaks and after work and rape the occupants. He estimated as many as 3,000 such conquests. In his choice of victims he had no pattern because he had only one concern: "It really was Woman that I wanted," he said—"not any special one, just Woman with what a woman has."

Ironically, after the public frenzy to catch the killer, DeSalvo was never tried for the Strangler crimes, or even charged with them: He was already institutionalized, probably for life, because of the previous rape charges. In the absence of absolute legal resolution of the case, however, not everyone was convinced that DeSalvo was the Strangler. One popular theory had it that, while in the mental institution, he overheard details from the real Strangler, then parroted them to police—either for attention, or as a by-product of his psychosis. As late as 1992, some Boston journalists still speculated that the real Strangler was George Nassar, DeSalvo's inmate confidante. A vicious but brilliant killer, Nassar theoretically could have taken advantage of DeSalvo's mental aberrations to prompt the confessions and thus deflect any chance of being tagged as the Strangler himself. This theory was based in part on the opinion of some psychiatrists that the Strangler crimes were far more suited to Nassar's psychological makeup than to DeSalvo's. After DeSalvo's confessions, Nassar was convicted of a murder unrelated to the Strangler killings. His death sentence was commuted to life when Massachusetts outlawed the death penalty.

Whatever the truth of the matter, it no longer matters to Albert DeSalvo. In 1973 he was stabbed to death in the hospital wing of a Massachusetts maximum security prison. No one was ever convicted of his murder. ◆

The Shoe-Fetish Slayer

Jerome Henry Brudos was the kind of serial killer experts now call a lust murderer. Murder was not his first crime, but he worked his way toward it in a crescendo of cruelties against women.

At five, young Jerry was fascinated by a pair of women's high-heeled shoes he found in the dump. When he took them home and clumped around the house in them, his cold, rejecting mother punished him harshly. At 16, he dug a tunnel in a hillside, hoping to capture a young woman, hide her in it, and make her do whatever he wanted. Still enthralled by high-heeled shoes, he began stealing them, along with delicate lingerie, from bedrooms where their owners slept; at home alone, he would fondle these prizes and try them on. In 1956 he was arrested for assault and battery after trying to force a young girl to take her clothes off.

When he was 23, Brudos married a 17-year-old who was pregnant with their child. By the time he started killing five years later, he was working as an electrician and was the father of two children.

In January 1968, in Portland, Oregon, Brudos killed a 19-year-old who had come to his door selling encyclopedias. He took her to his basement workshop and knocked her unconscious, then strangled her. When she was dead he undressed her and tried undergarments and spike-heeled shoes from his collection on her cooling corpse. Finally he severed her left foot, slipped it into a glamorous shoe, and stored it in his locked freezer. Then he tied a discarded automobile engine block to her body and disposed of it in the nearby Willamette River.

He killed his second victim 10 months later. This time he took photographs of the dressed-up cadaver and amputated one breast before dumping her body in the Willamette. By now his compulsion to kill

Oregon serial killer Jerry Brudos (in custody, above) indulged his fetish for women's high-heeled shoes by photographing his dead victims in footwear he kept for that purpose (right).

was stronger, and his next murder was in March 1969. He raped the attractive young victim before and after strangling her, and severed both her breasts before getting rid of the body. His last victim followed less than a month later; after the rape and murder, he applied electric shocks to the dead woman's rib cage to see if the body would jump.

A tip from a young woman who was suspicious of Brudos led police to the killer's home, where they found samples of special electricians' knots and twisted wire that matched those used in weighting the corpses. His stash of souvenirs also yielded a damning photograph. When he had snapped a portrait of a dead woman hanging from a hook in his garage, the camera caught his own demented likeness, reflected in a mirror at the victim's feet.

Charged with three of the four murders, Brudos pleaded guilty and drew three consecutive life sentences. He was scheduled to come up for parole no earlier than 1999. ◆

Machete Murderer

Juan Corona, a stocky Mexican national, was a labor contractor in the peach country of California's Sacramento valley, well regarded by ranchers around Yuba City. Devoutly religious, he lived quietly in his adopted country with his wife, Gloria, and their four young daughters. But on May 26, 1971, the 37-year-old Corona was arrested on suspicion of murder after the bodies of nine men were found in shallow graves in a peach orchard near his home. Each bore puncture wounds in the chest and deep gashes in the shape of a cross on the back of the head. All were stretched out face up, arms above the head, with their shirts pulled up over their faces. Some had their pants down and bore evidence of recent homosexual activity. All had been killed within the previous two months. All were farmworkers, drifters of the sort that Corona would round up in Yuba City's skid row for a few days' work at a neighboring orchard or farm.

The discovery touched off a 17-day search that quickly brought the total of bodies to 25. Although there were no eye-witnesses to the crimes, circumstantial evidence piled up around Corona. One of the bodies was that of an elderly man who had last been seen getting into Corona's van. In one grave police found two damning slips of paper—receipts from a butcher shop, made out to Corona. Another grave yielded two of his bank deposit slips. A search of his home turned up a machete, a pistol, two butcher knives, and a ledger containing the names of seven of the dead men.

Corona was tried on 25 counts of murder and, in January of 1973, convicted. Five years later, an appeals court threw out the decision and sent the case back to the lower court, finding that his attorney, Richard Hawk, had "failed to present any defense at all." Among other things, Hawk had produced not a single witness for the defense and had not raised the issue of insanity, even though his client had been diagnosed in 1956 as schizophrenic. The core of the defense case was the mere suggestion—without proof—that Juan's brother Natividad, an acknowledged homosexual with a violent temper, was the slayer.

Corona was retried in 1982 in an exhaustive seven-month proceeding and was again found guilty. Weighing heavily against him—and perhaps settling the case for good—was the testimony of a former Mexican consular official who had visited Corona in prison in 1978. The former mental patient had told him "Yes, I did it, but I'm a sick man and can't be judged by the standards of other men."

Corona was sentenced to 25 concurrent terms of 25 years to life in prison, and he was immediately eligible for parole. As of 1992, he was still in prison. ◆

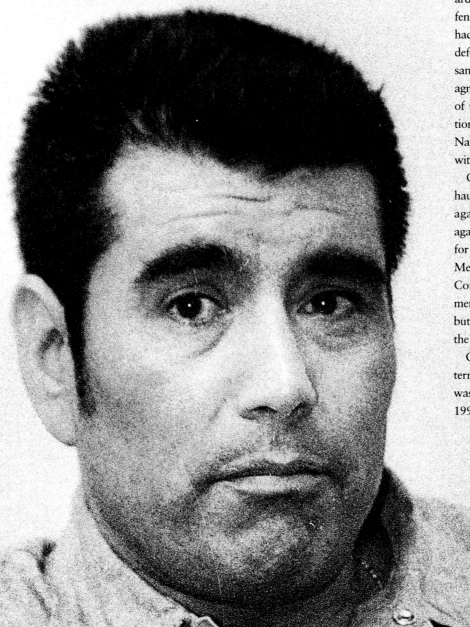

The Candy Man

When Dean Arnold Corll first displayed an interest in children, he was in his early twenties and—in retrospect—every parent's nightmare. He was the neighborhood man who won children's trust by giving them candy from his mother's store. Not that anyone minded at the time: Corll was, after all, polite, clean-cut, seemingly well-adjusted. People even knew his mother; she did indeed, run the local candy shop.

Corll never stopped making the good impression—not until the day he died, in 1973, pumped full of bullets by a greedy young friend who, at the time he killed him, also tore the wraps off Corll's bizarre double life of sexual sadism and murder. By then, the 33-year-old Corll and two teenage henchmen had snuffed out the lives of at least 27 adolescent boys, most of them from a tough Houston suburb called The Heights.

At the time of his death, Corll was employed as an electrician by the Houston Lighting & Power Company. Colleagues there generally regarded him as a man who, if something of a loner, was also warm and agreeable. Similar praise could be heard from former high-school classmates, friends, and family members. None knew about his secret life, which still involved handing out candy. Only now, the sweets came with death attached.

Corll knew from his own youth in The Heights that the existence of most teenage boys in that setting was marked by boredom and limited horizons. In 1970 he began luring youngsters to his home with the meager promise of a party or a little marijuana. Once there, Corll plied the boys, singly or in pairs, with that cheapest of abused substances—model airplane glue. The stuff wasn't elegant, but it was legal and thus carried little potential for attract-ing attention from the law. And it was potent enough to make the kids groggy, long enough for Corll to shackle them. After that, his victims could expect nothing better than sexual torture and murder.

Ever mindful of self-protection, Corll changed addresses frequently and had a pair of misguided boys do the dangerous job of hunting up victims for him. David Brooks and, later, Wayne Henley lured fellow youngsters—sometimes their own friends—into Corll's deadly trap. Henley was originally slated to be a victim himself, but Corll aborted that plan when he recognized the youth's potential as an aide in crime. Both Brooks and Henley eventually admitted to being Corll's lovers and were convicted for taking a hand in some of the killings. Henley was the one who eventually turned the gun on the boss. He killed Corll, then called police and revealed all the details of the gruesome serial slayings. ◆

Looking clean-cut in his army uniform in 1964, Dean Corll *(top)*, nevertheless became a notorious serial killer. He bribed Houston teenagers Wayne Henley and David Brooks *(above, left to right)*, to procure young victims for him with promises of parties and drugs.

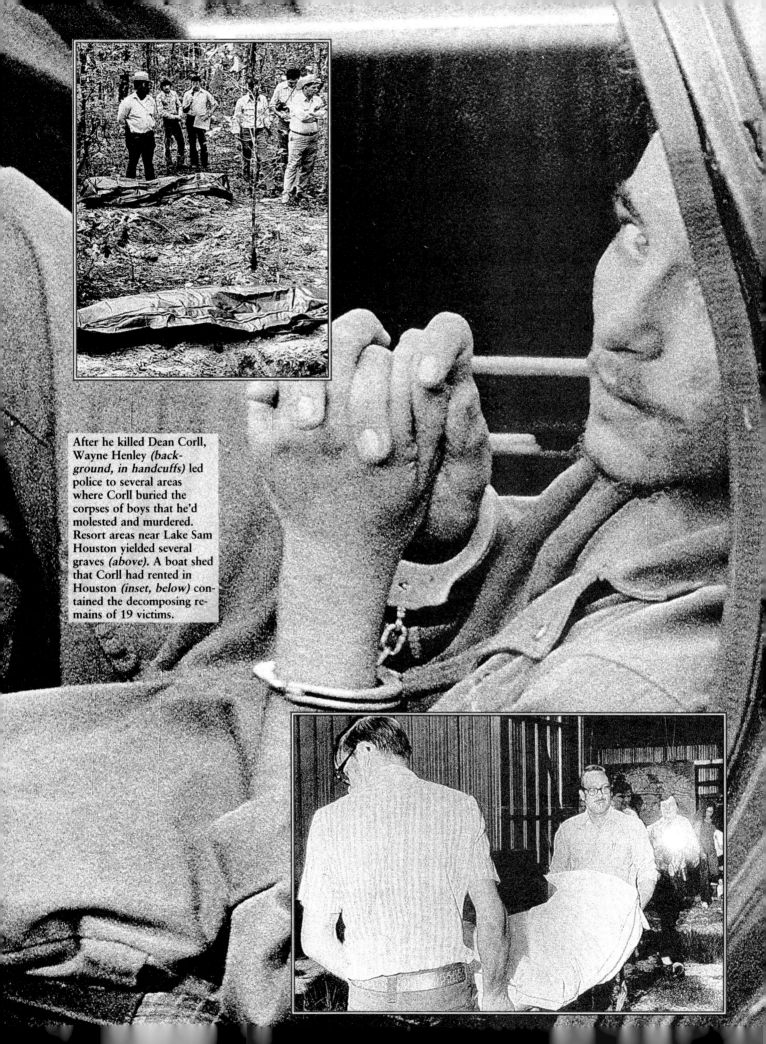

After he killed Dean Corll, Wayne Henley *(background, in handcuffs)* led police to several areas where Corll buried the corpses of boys that he'd molested and murdered. Resort areas near Lake Sam Houston yielded several graves *(above)*. A boat shed that Corll had rented in Houston *(inset, below)* contained the decomposing remains of 19 victims.

LARRY EYLER

The Interstate Killer

At 31, Larry Eyler was a sometime house painter and liquor-store clerk with a sadistic streak and a violent temper. In the summer of 1983, when police in Indiana and Illinois faced a string of murders involving bondage and the stabbing of young men, Eyler was a likely suspect. He had been arrested in 1978 for handcuffing and stabbing a young hitchhiker. Moreover, he commuted often among three places: the liquor store where he worked in Greencastle, Indiana; a friend's house in Terre Haute, where he often spent weekends; and Chicago, where he cruised gay bars and, during the week, lived with his lover and his lover's wife and children. This triangulation took Eyler over highways along which the violated corpses had been dumped.

Toward the end of the summer another victim was found; 28-year-old Chicagoan Ralph Calise had been handcuffed, stabbed 17 times, and thrown into a field. On September 30, Indiana state troopers detaining Eyler on a routine traffic violation found that his tire tracks and boot prints matched those found beside Calise's body. By October, circumstantial evidence had piled up against Eyler in the deaths of 18 other young men tortured, stabbed, and dumped on abandoned farms. One official told the press the suspect fit the FBI profile of the highway killer: "He is a macho-image, beer-drinking homosexual with a hatred for himself because he is homosexual."

Eyler was charged with the Calise murder, but the case all but dissolved over a judge's ruling that the police had obtained evidence illegally. The upshot was that on February 1, 1984, Eyler was freed on bond to await trial.

Seven months later, police had a call from an inquisitive janitor: Eight trash bags Eyler had heaved into a dumpster in Chicago held a teenage boy's dismembered body. Eyler was arrested and tried for the kidnapping and murder of 15-year-old Danny Bridges. This time investigators made it stick, with sophisticated chemical tests involving blood traces and latent fingerprints.

Like many serial killers, Larry Eyler had a rotten childhood. The battered son of an alcoholic father, he suffered abuse from two stepfathers and was sent by his mother to live with a succession of other families.

Convicted in the Bridges case, Eyler was sentenced in October 1986 to death by lethal injection. After four years on death row, he voluntarily confessed to another murder and offered to tell what he knew about 20 more killings if the state of Illinois would commute his death sentence to life without parole. The state refused. As of 1992, Larry Eyler was still on death row. ◆

The Night Stalker

In November 1989 Richard Ramirez began what was likely to be a lengthy stay on death row at California's San Quentin Prison. Dubbed the Night Stalker by the news media, he awaited execution for 13 murders and some 30 other assorted felonies, ranging from rape to robbery. At least three additional killings and numerous sexual assaults—some of them involving small children—were linked to this Texan turned California drifter, whose hallmark was random viciousness.

Even regarded side by side with other serial killers, Ramirez was bizarre. Whereas most repeat killers hew to some sort of pattern—slaying prostitutes, for instance, or coeds, or adolescent boys—Ramirez simply slipped into unlighted homes to randomly rape, murder, and pillage as the spirit moved him. His first victim was 79-year-old Jennie Vincow, whom he raped and then nearly decapitated in June 1984. Other victims that Ramirez was convicted of killing—nine women and four men—ranged in age from 30 to 83 years and cut across cultural and ethnic lines. The one thing they all had in common was that they died in their homes.

Richard Ramirez was born in El Paso, Texas, on February 28, 1960, the youngest of seven siblings in a working-class Catholic family. Friends remember him as a loner, even when he was a boy. He shunned

Richard Ramirez's trial dragged on for four years, partly because of his own disruptive antics. A rare calm moment (background, left) contrasts with a more typical outburst in which the Night Stalker flashes a satanic pentagram (inset). At times he was so unruly that he had to be shackled (opposite).

gangs but began sniffing glue and smoking marijuana by the time he was in the eighth grade. A high-school dropout, he was arrested twice on drug-possession charges before following a woman friend to California at the age of 22.

Things went from bad to worse for Ramirez in his adopted state: He began pocking his arms with injections of cocaine and subsisting on a diet of junk food. Before long his teeth were literally rotting in his head, and he was living out of a decrepit old backpack. If he slept indoors, it was generally in skid-row flophouses; more often, he simply curled up in unlocked cars or lay where he fell in alleys or doorways. His sole livelihood during 1982 and 1983 came from car theft and burglary, and once he wound up in a Los Angeles jail.

By the time Ramirez started to kill, he was spiraling remorselessly into a rampage of senseless destruction. Later, much would be made of his flirtations with Satanism, which he brought to the fore time and again in spontaneous courtroom tirades. But the law enforcement officials who brought him to justice placed little stock in his avowed devil worship. They viewed Ramirez as an antisocial deviant addicted to physical violence: He killed, they believed, because he enjoyed it.

Ramirez's capture marked a significant breakthrough in the field of computerized fingerprint identification. A state-of-the-art system in Sacramento had been up and running all of three minutes when it matched a print from a stolen car linked to the Night Stalker case with Ramirez's police record. Two days later the killer was apprehended in a Hispanic neighborhood in Los Angeles. ◆

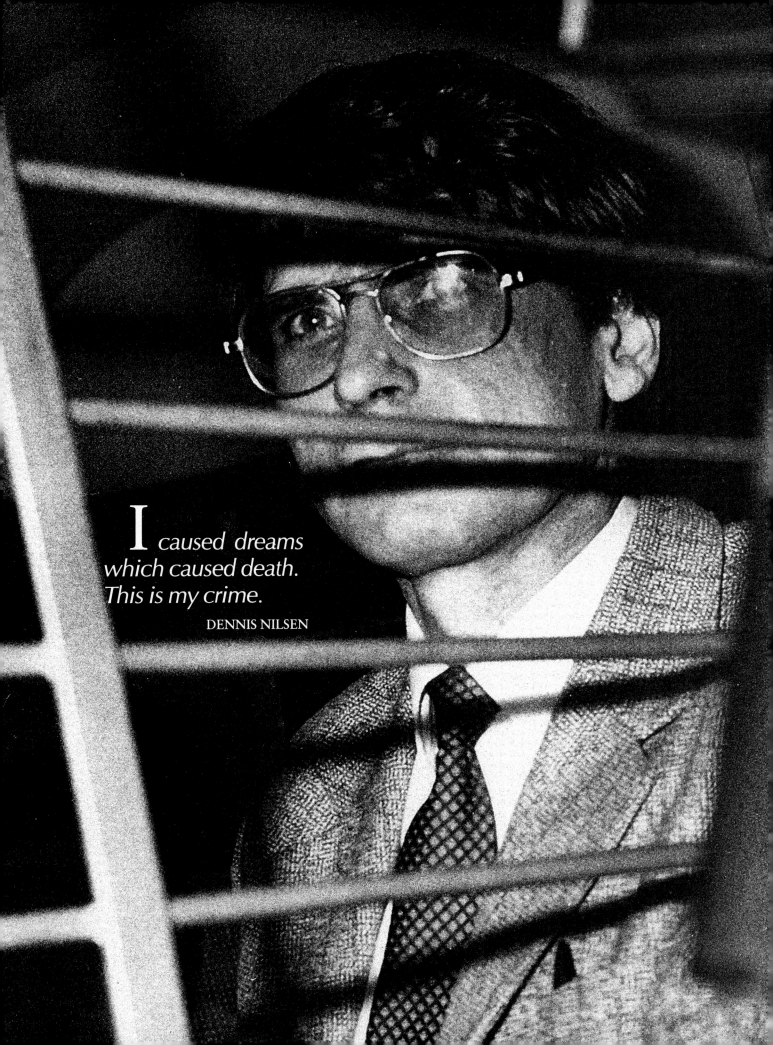

I caused dreams
which caused death.
This is my crime.

DENNIS NILSEN

3

Flatmates

Fiona Bridges was disgusted, and her patience was wearing thin. The toilet in the hall of her North London flat at 23 Cranley Gardens was out of commission and had been for 24 hours. When she tried the bowl in the adjoining cubicle it too failed to flush, and now backed-up sewage had the whole downstairs landing smelling awful.

Bridges' live-in boyfriend, Jim Allcock, had tried to clear the blockage with a hydrochloric acid compound. But that hadn't worked, and Bridges had informed the other downstairs tenants that the toilets would be off-limits until a plumber arrived. In the meantime, life in the building would be maddeningly inconvenient.

Early that evening — February 4, 1983 — Bridges had a rare encounter with her upstairs neighbor, Dennis Nilsen. She took the opportunity to ask the tall, stooped, 37-year-old government worker if he too was having trouble with the plumbing.

"No, no trouble," replied Nilsen in his usual taciturn fashion, and he wandered off without further comment.

Dennis Nilsen — Des, as he seemed to prefer — was a thoroughgoing recluse, as far as his neighbors could tell. They heard him coming and going often enough, taking his little dog, Bleep, for walks. But he was jealous of his privacy and rarely offered more than a polite nod in passing. For a man who seemed to treasure his solitude, Nilsen was fortunate: He had the attic floor of the building to himself, and the floor beneath him was vacant.

The next morning, a Saturday, plumber Mike Welch visited 23 Cranley Gardens and tried his hand at clearing the pipes. He too met with frustration, finding that his tools could not reach the blockage. He advised Bridges and Allcock to telephone an outfit called Dyno-Rod that would send heavy-duty equipment. Dyno-Rod was ready to take on the job, but still there was a hitch: The apartment building's management couldn't authorize such a major repair until Monday morning. Allcock stuck a note on Nilsen's door telling him not to flush the toilet.

Later that day, Fiona Bridges bumped into the aloof Mr.

Nilsen once again, and this time she offered to let him know when the plumbing had been fixed. She warned that it would probably be Monday at the earliest. Nilsen seemed to take the news with characteristic detachment.

As things turned out, the Dyno-Rod engineer didn't show up until 6:15 Tuesday evening. Michael Cattran, 30 years old and relatively new to his job, quickly surmised that the blockage was underground. It was dark by then, and the repair would require daylight, but Cattran dutifully walked to the side of the house to have a quick look in the sewer. With Allcock holding a flashlight, he lifted the cover.

It was 12 feet down to the sewer floor, and a built-in ladder made the descent simple. But a horrible stench was rising from the hole, a smell that gave even a sewer worker pause. Cattran climbed down anyway — and in the semi-gloom he encountered a scene that surpassed his darkest fears. The smell was coming from a pool of putrifying flesh: Perhaps 30 or 40 grayish white pieces of the stuff mixed with knuckles, slivers of bone, and the wastes more commonly found in a sewer. As Cattran stared in horror at the reeking, glutinous porridge, more chunks of flesh plopped out of the drainpipe from the house. It occurred to him that it might be human flesh.

The repairman struggled to trust his own senses as he went back to the house and telephoned his manager, who also had a hard time believing that bits of human bodies had turned up in a sewer. Cattran's boss advised him to leave the matter till morning. When the sun came up, he said, they could have a better look and inform the police, if necessary.

As Cattran talked on the phone, all the tenants nervously gathered round. When he finished reporting to his boss, the repairman turned to Des Nilsen. "You've got a dog, haven't you?" he asked. "Do you put dog meat down the toilet?" Nilsen impatiently shrugged off the question, and eventually the neighbors, puzzled and distressed, went their separate ways. Nilsen returned to his flat and pondered the situation. He also was distressed — but not puzzled. He was pretty sure he knew what was causing the plumbing problem.

The top floor of this London apartment building was home to Dennis Nilsen until plumber Mike Cattran *(right)* discovered human remains in the sewer.

Around midnight Nilsen sneaked out to the manhole, clutching a flashlight and a plastic bag. He dragged off the cover and climbed down into the sewer. Then he rolled up his sleeves and reached his bare hand into the sewage to extract, one by one, the chunks of putrid flesh. When the bag was full he climbed back up the ladder and walked to the rear of the lot. There he matter-of-factly lobbed his collection of human remains over the back-garden hedge.

But his errand had not gone unnoticed. Fiona Bridges and Jim Allcock had been listening. They'd heard his footsteps and the scraping of the manhole cover. Allcock investigated and came face-to-face with Nilsen, just as the reclusive neighbor was returning to the building.

"Just went out to have a pee," he explained. Allcock didn't believe him, but he let it pass.

The next day, while Nilsen was away at work, Mike Cattran returned to 23 Cranley Gardens with his Dyno-Rod manager, Gary Wheeler. When Cattran set about reexamining his discovery, he was astonished to see that conditions in the sewer had changed. Shocked and angry, he resolved to find out what was going on. With Wheeler looking on, he clambered down the ladder and stuck his hand down by the drain. Almost immediately, he produced a wrinkled hunk of grayish yellow flesh. Hurrying back aboveground, he placed the dripping evidence on the walk, then descended again, this time to return with four small pieces of bone.

The two men gaped at the bones, unable to shake the sinking feeling that they were examining the remains of a human hand. The horror of the situation was still settling on the repairmen when Fiona Bridges approached to tell of the noises she'd heard the night before and of Allcock's encounter with Nilsen.

It was time to call the police.

Detective Chief Inspector Peter Jay, a seasoned, 26-year veteran of the London police force, arrived at the apartment house around 11 a.m. and picked up the samples from the drain. By about 3:30 p.m. he had forensic confirmation that the bones and flesh were indeed human. He returned to 23 Cranley Gardens with two other police officers. Nilsen met them at the front door. After brief expressions of surprise over the visit, he meekly led the chief inspector and two other officers up the stairs to his flat.

Nilsen was highly agitated; he knew full well what was coming. Cloying, fetid air greeted the visitors as they opened the door to his flat. The stench grew worse as they moved farther into the apartment. Nilsen offered no explanation for the odor. Perhaps he didn't notice it; he was, after all, accustomed to it.

When Jay told Nilsen that material taken from the sewer had turned out to be human remains, the suspect briefly feigned shock and bewilderment. But the chief inspector bluntly pressed the matter: Where, he wanted to know, was the rest of the body?

"In two plastic bags in the wardrobe next door," Nilsen replied. "I'll show you." From that moment on, his surrender was unreserved. He led Jay to the front room and pointed to a large cabinet, handing over a set of keys. Jay declined to open the wardrobe; he didn't need his eyes to confirm what his nose already told him.

Nilsen was ushered into a police car with Jay and Inspector Stephen McCusker. On the way to the station house, McCusker asked, "Are we talking about one body or two?"

Nilsen stared out the window. The apartment buildings and shops of North London flashed by. Not much to look at, perhaps, but a far cry more than he would be seeing for quite some time to come.

"Fifteen or sixteen," Nilsen said, "since 1978. I'll tell you everything."

And he began to talk, nonstop, almost obsessively—less to inform the police, it seemed, than to find for himself some explanation for the terrible things that he'd done. There was so much to tell.

The nightmarish existence that Nilsen described for his captors was a study in contrasts, in outward normalcy and hidden stresses. The killer was gainfully employed; he was socially aware and contributing to the betterment of his fellow Londoners. But he was also encumbered by a creeping tide of young male corpses and felt utterly powerless to stem the accumulation of bodies. He was chafing under a life of soul-withering loneliness, drinking himself senseless nearly every evening, and caught up in a self-perpetuating cycle of violent and random murders. Nilsen's living hell had persisted for more than five years, and its roots stretched back further still to a boyhood in a remote Scottish fishing village—a place where love and death first came to be linked for him, fatally and forever.

It would be extravagant to ascribe too much significance to the buffetings of the North Sea. But harsh weather and the arduous demands of a life dependent on wild and frigid waters did go far toward shaping personalities in the town of Fraserburgh, Scotland, where Dennis Andrew Nilsen was born on November 23, 1945.

Fraserburgh perches on a rocky headland at the far northeast tip of Aberdeenshire. The weather there is severe and unforgiving, and it has been said to foster a deep streak of pessimism among the local herring fishermen and their dependents. Death has visited this community with appalling swiftness and caprice: Women are not surprised when their fathers, husbands, brothers, and sons are lost to the sea. Historically, this hard way of life and the unpredictability that is such an integral part of its fabric has bred among the Buchans, as the people of the region are called, a fatalism as bleak and deep as the sea that both sustains and threatens them. They are a prickly people, tough and self-reliant, wary of outsiders. Having faced the worst that nature can bestow, they have never been reluctant to defy governmental authority. They have a characteristic aversion to compromise or to any form of diplomacy. They often express themselves with the same gloomy bluntness that came to be a distinctive feature of Dennis Nilsen's adult personality.

In keeping with this legacy of noncompliance, the people of Fraserburgh have also often defied the usual social prohibitions against marriage between close relatives. Centuries of inbreeding have led to a high incidence of mental and physical infirmities. Since long before the 1940s, Fraserburgh has been populated by what amounts to one big extended family—although not a particularly happy one.

All this said, it should be noted that the name Nilsen is neither Scottish nor English. It is Norwegian. Dennis Nilsen's father, Olav, came to Scotland during World War II as a soldier in the Free Norwegian Forces. The armies of conquered Norway were training on foreign shores while awaiting the opportunity to reclaim their homeland from the Germans. During this period of involuntary exile, Olav Nilsen won the affection of a Fraserburgh beauty named Betty Whyte. The two young people were married in May 1942, but Olav was—almost from the start—absent more often than not. Soon after Dennis's younger sister was born, the absenteeism became total and permanent.

Dennis had little or no memory of his father, and his mother seldom mentioned him. Thus, other than having imparted the clear, cruel message of abandonment, Olav Nilsen could have exerted scant influence on his son.

Two days after his arrest, a bespectacled Dennis Nilsen is led away from Highgate Court in North London, having listened to charges of murder brought against him. The profoundly alienated British civil servant provided his captors with a disturbingly detailed confession.

Norwegian soldier Olav Nilsen stands with his Scottish bride, Betty Whyte, in May 1942. By the time Nilsen's six-year-old son Dennis posed for the picture at bottom, the father had deserted the family.

The only truly untroubled time of the boy's life must have been his first five years. His grandfather, Andrew Whyte, took the child under his wing as a sort of adoring mascot. Whyte was a hardworking fisherman, but his skill and industry were not always enough to persuade his employers to overlook certain unattractive features of his personality—in particular, a sullen pride and rebelliousness. Despite his crotchety nature, however, Whyte seemed to find real joy and contentment in his relationship with little Dennis.

The two of them, gruff old man and impressionable child, spent hours together walking the harbor, strolling the beach, and climbing the stony heights beyond the village. Andrew Whyte's periodic homecomings from the sea were magical times for the small boy. Nilsen later recalled "being borne aloft on the tall strong shoulders of my great hero and protector."

The grandfather enchanted the boy with gripping tales of danger and adventure at sea, not worrying overly about stretching the truth when it suited his narratives. The grandson thrilled to the old man's stories, and the bond between them grew stronger. But this healthful relationship was not to last. Andrew Whyte was found dead in a fishing boat on Halloween day, 1951. He was 62 years old; his grandson was three weeks shy of six.

There were tears and lamentations when the body arrived home, but nobody saw fit to communicate the news of death in so many words to Dennis or his brother and sister. An open coffin was set in the room where the children had been born. Dennis was lifted up for a moment or two so that he could have a look at the body. But his mother couldn't bear to tell him the truth and claimed that Granddad was only sleeping.

The next day the coffin was gone. Dennis spied the funeral procession gathering outside the house, but, still, no one explained to him the significance of the events that were unfolding. In the boy's mind, Andrew Whyte had simply gone away again, and it was little more than a nagging worry that the grandfather's name was no longer mentioned in the home.

For several expectant months, Dennis waited for his idol to return. When this failed to happen, and the boy realized belatedly that Whyte would never reappear, he was desolate. So awful were the feelings of loss and despair that Dennis could hardly acknowledge them. Looking back on this experience from the perspective of his prison cell, he would theorize that all of his destructive tendencies had sprung from the childhood trauma. "It blighted my personality, permanently," he recorded in a journal. "I have spent all my emotional life searching for my grandfather."

From the time of Andrew Whyte's death, Nilsen's childhood was a woefully lonely one. He would never again love another person healthily or wholeheartedly; he would never again have a whole heart to give.

Apart from a tendency toward solitude, however, Nilsen's boyhood was not without certain trappings of ordinariness. Whatever her failings at the time of her father's death, Dennis's mother did her utmost to give her offspring a secure home and a supportive upbringing. And Dennis discovered his own boyish diversions, taking great pleasure in animals, for one thing. His mother didn't allow pets in the house, but Dennis and two other boys contrived to keep a flock of pigeons in boxes on an old air-raid shelter. Dennis became particularly attached to two birds named Tufty and Jockey. He visited them twice daily and even taught the pets to come to his arm when he called their names. This attachment led to a new sorrow, however, when another boy killed the pigeons in an act of senseless cruelty. Dennis sobbed inconsolably, and his sense of loss went beyond a purely emotional response: The death of the birds seemed to snatch from him the feeling that he was doing something useful in the world.

Through animals Dennis experienced a closeness to nature, and he was appalled to find that others sometimes lacked this

sensitivity. He was shocked by the notion of hunting small creatures, and he felt so sorry for sick animals that he sometimes took it upon himself to put an end to their suffering. He would later claim similar motives in the killing of some of his human victims.

If young Dennis Nilsen was captivated by animals, he was virtually obsessed by the sea. This passion he related to his grandfather, recalling a sense of oneness with nature that still continued to move him in the later years of his life: "On the rocks I stood gazing at the all-powerful restless sea. I felt very akin to that great force, we reciprocated in a spiritual affinity of great love and great fear. I would stand for some time with a tear-filled face look-

A certificate records the birth of Dennis Andrew Nilsen on November 23, 1945. For the first 10 years of his life the youngster would share a single room of his grandparents' house with his mother and two siblings.

The rocky shores and seemingly limitless horizons of the North Sea held tremendous fascination for Nilsen. A loner from an early age, he spent many hours staring out over the waters, as if mesmerized by the powers of the sea. In the aftermath of his grandfather's death, he found his meditations on nature far more comforting than any human relationship.

Two fixtures of Nilsen's troubled youth were a solitary ruin called the Hunter's Lodge *(right)*, outside the village of Strichen, and the tidy brick home of his grandparents in nearby Fraserburgh *(below)*. The Hunter's Lodge became a favored retreat during Nilsen's adolescence. By then, an early trauma in the Fraserburgh house had been seared into his memory: It was there that he struggled to adjust to the loss of his beloved grandfather.

ing out there for Andrew Whyte to come and comfort me."

In less rapturous moments, the boy sometimes fantasized about drowning—daydreams that were at once morbid and somehow satisfying. As an adult, he would vividly recall one event, real or imagined, that had affected him deeply: He wrote of wading into the waves while an older boy on the shore poked at the sand with a stick. Suddenly and without warning, Dennis lost his footing and was swept into deep water by the currents. Panicking and struggling for air, he called out wildly to shore. But exhaustion overtook him in the choppy surf, and he was on the verge of drowning.

Somehow, Nilsen awoke on the beach, a bright blue sky above him. He was naked; his clothes were strewn on the ground around him. It appeared that the boy on the shore had saved him. But there was also evidence that the older boy had been sexually aroused by Dennis's helpless condition. Some psychiatrists who listened to this tale following Nilsen's arrest believed that he might have played a three-part role in the drama—as victim, rescuer, and defiler. Real or not, the remembered incident exemplified the flaw at the core of Nilsen's emotional makeup—the entwining of extinction and fulfillment.

That peculiar incident aside, Nilsen remained sexually uninitiated throughout his years at school, although he did from time to time feel stirrings of attraction for other boys. At one point he became infatuated with the son of a local minister, but a keen sense of his own social awkwardness kept him from making any stronger advance than to fix longing stares on the boy. He also built fantasies, for a time, around a picture of a boy in his French grammar book. This obsession seemed all the more urgent because the youth in the illustration was inanimate and unattainable.

Thus, when Nilsen enlisted in the army at the age of 15, he was interested in sex but entirely innocent of it, a situation not uncommon among his contemporaries, although few were likely to admit to being virgins. At the same time, the new recruit seemed clearly on a track that would lead to a life of homosexuality.

For the next three years, Nilsen received military training at Aldershot in southern England. It was an unusually happy time for him. He took well to the structure of army discipline, and the rigorous regime of hard work and training left little space for morbid introspection. He found genuine satisfaction in the grueling Ten Tors marches, 60 miles of trekking across the rugged hills of Dartmoor. He looked back on these exercises as "a boy's dream of high adventure." He also liked the warmer climate of Cornwall better than the blustery cold of Aberdeenshire, and the change seemed to warm his soul.

Nilsen got along well with the other young soldiers and he reveled in the feeling—however transient—that he was like everybody else. By the time he celebrated his 18th birthday, he seemed to have within his grasp at least the prospects of social and material security. Before him lay a potentially successful military career.

Yet, even in these seemingly lighthearted years, a troubling undercurrent was flowing through his life. Nilsen could not escape the fact that he felt physically attracted to his comrades. He worked hard to repress his emotions, but still they left him feeling guilty and out of place. The best he could do to ease his private concerns was to cling to the reassuring idea that he probably was bisexual.

At Aldershot, Nilsen mastered a skill that would provide fodder for sensational speculation following his arrest more than 18 years later. As a member of the Army Catering Corps, he learned the art of butchery. He didn't ordinarily kill animals as part of this training; the only creature he ever slaughtered for food was a Christmas goose one year. But he did learn to cut meat from the bone and, in the process, he acquired a working knowledge of animal anatomy. He would put this learning to terrible use during his later career as a murderer, and—as a consequence—he would become a figure of grisly fascination for the tabloid press.

Nilsen's eagerness to please with his kitchen skills made him popular with his fellow soldiers. At a two-month ski-training school in Bavaria, he cooked seven days a week for 32 British soldiers. He took special pride in providing hot, nourishing breakfasts, and he felt that no one else associated with the program could so powerfully boost the morale of his comrades. Nights, he stayed up drinking with the other lads—overjoyed to be one of the crowd.

But contentment was always short-lived for Nilsen, and he could never escape his conflicting feelings about sex and his place in the world. In spite of what he called the "wonderful shock of ejaculation" with a prostitute in Berlin, he remained unmoved by women. He later described his experience with the prostitute as "over-rated and depressing." There were also, apparently, several unsatisfactory encounters with anonymous German men. And Nilsen's prison journals recall as well the experience of bedding down with an opportunistic Arab boy during a posting in the British protectorate of Aden. All the while, however, the young soldier was making every effort to conceal his homosexuality, with two results: His erotic yearnings went largely unfilled, and the guilt he felt over hungers that he could neither fully admit nor express grew, compounded, and fed on itself. "If the guilty feel like criminals," he would write years later, "then I have been all my life a criminal."

The most noteworthy exception to the sexual emptiness of his life was a disturbing fascination with the image of his own body—a fetish that began to make itself felt during Nilsen's stay in the Middle East. Many people have, at one time or another, indulged in narcissistic fantasies. But Nilsen's activities were decidedly different in that he preferred to see himself in the glass not as a vibrant, desirable person, but as a dead body. In private moments he would arouse himself by lying very still in front of the mirror with his head outside the scope of the reflection. Gazing at this view of his motionless body, he would pretend the lifeless figure was someone else, or call up images of his grandfather in the coffin. And—as when he was five—love and death overlapped in his mind to become nearly indistinguishable.

Toward the end of his army career, Nilsen was posted to the Shetland Islands, just off the north coast of Scotland. There, in the summer of 1972, he fell in love with an 18-year-old private. The young man was receptive to Nilsen's affection and seemed to value the companionship that it offered. But if Nilsen harbored any hopes of escalating the friendship to a full-fledged romance, the closest he ever came was one evanescent moment of holding hands. The memory would linger in his mind for many months.

The corporal and the private spent a lot of time indulging Nilsen's interest in making movies. They exposed reel after reel of home-movie film, playing out brief, original dramas. Not surprisingly, in light of later revelations, the scenes that Nilsen treasured most were those in which his friend would playact the role of a dead man. On Nilsen's last night in the Shetland Islands, however, he burned every last one of these collaborative works. He was devastated by the hopelessness of a love undeclared and unreturned, and he believed he would never see his friend again.

Dennis Nilsen spent 11 years and three months in the army. His conduct was recorded as "exemplary," and he could have been a career man, a valued noncommissioned officer. Yet, as the 1960s gave way to the 1970s, he fell in

A bony 15-year-old, newly enlisted in the British army, Nilsen scarcely conceals his pride over his Junior Leaders' Regiment uniform.

An 11-year army career included some of Nilsen's happiest times. He gained confidence from his culinary training and welcomed the camaraderie of his fellow soldiers, but he also began a lifelong habit of abusing alcohol.

Nilsen developed a passion for filmmaking, which led him to study cameras
and the other apparatus of the cinematic craft. He also spent many solitary hours
wandering in search of seascapes and other natural settings to film.

step with the widespread antimilitary bias of the era. Nilsen developed an aversion to the military mind and to regimentation in general. He was especially galled by England's involvement in Northern Ireland, and he bridled at the requirement that soldiers be prepared to follow orders to kill. He couldn't countenance that, he claimed.

After he left the army in late 1972, Nilsen spent about five weeks in Strichen, Aberdeenshire, where his mother now lived with her second husband, Adam Scott. It was not a warm homecoming for the disgruntled soldier. Among the problems was a serious row with his older brother, Olav, over the brother's contempt for homosexuals. One evening Dennis and several other guests at Olav's house watched a television movie depicting gays in a relatively sympathetic, straightforward way. Some of the guests hooted with derision at the characterizations. Nilsen was outraged, and his fury turned into a fight with his brother, who saw a defense of the film as evidence that Dennis himself was homosexual. The brothers never spoke again.

Feeling uprooted from his stony native soil, Nilsen decided to seek his future in the city: In December 1972 he enrolled in the Metropolitan Police Training School in North London. There he hoped to find something of the camaraderie he'd enjoyed in the army; although he'd grown uncomfortable with life in a uniform, he was even more uneasy in his anonymous civilian clothes.

Nilsen learned quickly enough that the fraternal feeling among policemen was only a pallid substitute for the closer bonding of army life. In the military, he'd not only lived with his fellow soldiers but had spent most of his spare time in their company. As a police constable, by contrast, he was left on his own during off hours. Other men might have preferred such freedom, but Nilsen did not; however much he sometimes seemed to seek solitude, he never fared well when he had it. During his brief career as a police constable, he had far too much time on his hands—time to brood, time for self-doubt and self-loathing.

English biographer Brian Masters befriended Nilsen after his arrest, elicited a detailed account of his life, and wrote the definitive book on him, *Killing for Company,* from which this chapter was adapted. Masters, who came to know Nilsen perhaps better than anyone else ever had, believed this of his subject: Nilsen was fully engaged by only one narrow topic, and that was himself. For most people,

a certain amount of introspection is healthy; for Nilsen, it was utterly destructive.

The rookie constable had no luck establishing friendships in London. Inevitably, it seemed, he gravitated to places that a London policeman more mindful of his career would have shunned: He became a regular in gay bars.

To believe Nilsen's markedly sour accounts of his life during this period is to accept that a night spent in any one of the homosexual pubs—the King William IV, the Coleherne, the Golden Lion, the Cricklewood Arms, the Black Cap, the Salisbury—was a night squandered. The scenario was always the same: up to the bar for the first pint, survey the clientele, establish eye contact, and chat up a prospect— all the while engulfed in cigarette smoke and deafening conversation. At best, this joyless socializing would lead to a little furtive sex, followed by empty good-byes muttered by the parting lovers.

For Nilsen—who craved companionship far more than casual sex—the anonymity and the lack of true emotional commerce in these transactions was almost unendurable.

"I was left," he wrote, "with an endless search through the soul-destroying pub scene and its resulting one-night stands, passing faces and bodies the unfulfilled tokens of an empty life." Dispiriting as this existence was, it at least afforded Nilsen one cold nugget of self-knowledge: He at last largely recognized—even if he did not embrace—his true sexual orientation. He admitted to himself that homosexual love was what he sought.

To lead a double life, with one foot planted in the gay-pub scene, would have been troubling enough for a bank clerk or a salesman. For a policeman, the contradictions were simply unacceptable. Looking back, Nilsen recalled an episode in which he chanced upon a gay couple having sex in a car. He couldn't bring himself to make an arrest, which, strictly speaking, was required by law. He resigned in December 1973 after one year on the force. Apparently, he'd been a reasonably competent rookie cop: His performance report was acceptable, and his file held no complaints.

For several months he lived on the edge of poverty. He took work where he could find it, as a security guard, earning meager wages that barely paid the rent and kept him fed. He stood watch at various government buildings, including some that belonged to the Parliament, the Admiralty, or the Ministry of Defence. Working in these places, he felt like a tick lodged anonymously in the scalp of the Establishment.

Police Constable Dennis Nilsen served a one-year stint with the London Metropolitan Police Force. The young bobby penned an ironic warning inside the front cover of his standard-issue handbook, *Moriarty's Police Law*—the page reference leads to a legal discussion of theft.

In his heart, he knew that he was not genuinely a part of anything.

With little pride in the past and even less hope for the future, Nilsen applied for unemployment compensation. It was a humiliating experience, and he worried that he was really skidding toward complete destitution. For once, however, the young man's résumé was a little brighter than his crippled morale, and he was offered a job in the very bureaucracy that he'd approached for charity. Nilsen was sent to one of the many government-run Jobcentres scattered throughout London. His employer was the Manpower Services Commission, and he became a member of the English Civil Service.

In May 1974 unemployment was rife in Britain, and the Jobcentres were on the front lines of a national effort to put people back to work. Of all London's jobless, those willing and able to labor as busboys, janitors, dishwashers, and hotel maids were the easiest to place in jobs. But they were also likely to be the worst paid, and—because many of them were illegal aliens—the most likely to be exploited.

The reviewing board at Manpower Services had perceived that Nilsen's experience in the Army Catering Corps would aid him in helping job applicants for the hotel and restaurant trades. Accordingly, he was assigned to the Denmark Street Jobcentre near Charing Cross Road in London's West End. There were a great many hotels and eating establishments nearby, and an extremely high turnover of personnel, so it was a strategic location for Nilsen's designated specialty. For his part, the new bureaucrat believed that he was beautifully suited for his position. Still, he went about the work with a bit of a chip on his shoulder. He was, after all, a Buchan, and thus naturally disposed toward contempt for the inequities of England's economic system. Thrown into daily contact with those inequities, he came quickly to envision himself as a savior of the downtrodden.

By all rights, the young man should have found a rewarding niche in his new profession; and he did, in fact, work hard at the job for the eight years to follow. There is little doubt that he helped many people in the lower stratum of society, but his instinctive radicalism led him to ardent involvement in activities that put him at odds with his government employers. Nilsen aligned himself with labor organizing, but even the union leaders considered him something of a reckless fool, given his position. Beyond these political problems, his self-righteous posturing made him unpopular with many of his coworkers. It was not, necessarily, that they disagreed with his ideals; what put off Nilsen's officemates was his tendency to be long-winded and boring. Even when his colleagues sighed, grew silent, or pointedly barricaded themselves behind open newspapers, he plunged relentlessly on with his indignant harangues.

It's likely that Nilsen's coworkers wouldn't have found him nearly so dull if they had known about the exotic secret side of his life. For although he'd changed occupations, he still lived with feet in two worlds. Not long after he went to work at Denmark Street, his clandestine social habits took a dangerous turn.

One evening in June 1974 the pedantic civil servant brought home a 17-year-old boy named David Painter. In Nilsen's tiny rented room, the two shared a few drinks and the boy crawled into bed. When Nilsen followed, Painter rebuffed his host's sexual advances and soon fell fast asleep. Nilsen decided to make the most of the situation by taking some photographs of the slumbering youth, but this plan went horribly awry. Painter awoke and, spying the camera, became hysterical. Thrashing around and screaming, he smashed his arm through a glass partition. The boy was cut, bleeding, and totally out of control.

Nilsen himself must also have panicked, for, putting aside all thought of his compromising position, he called the police and summoned an ambulance. In the process, he exposed himself to the humiliation of being interrogated at the same police station where he'd served as a constable just 18 months earlier. The authorities kept him at the station until they got assurances from a hospital that the boy had not been sexually molested. Painter's parents might still have pressed charges, but they decided in the end to let the matter drop, sparing their son further stress.

In the wake of this episode, Nilsen's fragile self-esteem plunged to new depths. Totally absorbed in his own troubles, he wallowed in self-pity and worried that perhaps he deserved nothing better than to stay forever friendless and socially detached. He became more wary of the people he met in the pubs, and his evenings there became more sordid and aggressive. His personal life was thus filled with sorrow and ugliness even before he began to kill.

Before that happened, Nilsen made one last stab at achieving some sort of domestic equilibrium. One night in a pub he went to the rescue of a flamboyant young man

named David Gallichan, who was being harassed by two other admirers. As was his habit when he picked up men in the bars, Nilsen escorted the heavily made-up and bejeweled Gallichan back to his room. This time, however, something joyous and totally unexpected happened: Gallichan consented to an out-of-the-blue proposal that they set up housekeeping together. It was the romantic breakthrough that lonely Des Nilsen had sought for years.

Gallichan had been sleeping in a hostel, Nilsen in a one-room flat. To establish a joint household, they needed roomier accomodations, and their search led to a cheery ground-floor apartment in the Muswell Hill area of North London. The address was 195 Melrose Avenue.

A charming feature of this flat was a set of French doors that opened onto a sizable garden at the rear of the building. At the time that the two men moved in, the plot out back was overgrown with weeds and littered with years of accumulated debris. But Nilsen and Gallichan worked hard to make the garden presentable. They planted fruit trees and ornamental shrubs and even sowed a small vegetable garden. In return for these improvements, the landlord gave them permission to put up a fence around the garden and to claim the space for their private use.

Nilsen's relationship with Gallichan lasted two years, long enough for the younger, more passive partner to acquire the affectionate nickname of Twinkle. The capricious Gallichan was not all his lover might have hoped, but he did ease Nilsen's loneliness in two ways: with his own presence and by persuading his flatmate to get a dog. The mongrel puppy Bleep would prove a far more faithful and enduring companion than Twinkle himself; if Nilsen was looking for stability in his friendship with David Gallichan, there was little to be had after the first few weeks. Twinkle remained emotionally remote and continually went off with other men, mindless of the hurt that he caused his benefactor. In spite of these provocations, Nilsen continued to cherish the younger man and—more important to Twinkle—kept on paying the bills. One year Nilsen even took his outlandish-looking friend to the office Christmas party, thus ending any lingering doubts his colleagues might have had regarding his sexual preference.

The futility of the romance became obvious to Nilsen when he wound up in the hospital for a week and a half following a gallstone operation. Twinkle only visited him once—and then only because Nilsen insisted on the cour-

Hoping desperately for a stable relationship, Nilsen set up house-keeping with David Gallichan *(inset)* at 195 Melrose Avenue. The affair proved short-lived and left Nilsen all the more emotionally bereft and dependent on the comforts of alcohol.

133

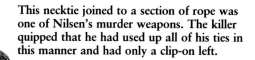

This necktie joined to a section of rope was one of Nilsen's murder weapons. The killer quipped that he had used up all of his ties in this manner and had only a clip-on left.

tesy. Relations between the two already were deteriorating, but now things went from bad to worse. Nilsen adopted an increasingly harsh attitude toward his roommate, and Gallichan retaliated by dropping all pretense of loyalty and bringing his lovers right to the apartment. When Nilsen responded in kind, an end to the relationship became inevitable.

During the acrimonious period leading up to a final split, Nilsen shocked Gallichan—and probably himself—by bringing home a woman. The affair was only a one-night stand, but Nilsen took pride in his conquest, even bragging about it at the office. The dalliance seemed to renew his conviction that his social and sexual interests were broad, and not limited strictly to men. Even after all his many months of cruising London's gay nightspots, he remained conflicted over his sexuality. The distinction between being homosexual and bisexual was still terribly important to him.

When the break with Twinkle did come, it was abrupt and jarring—and had nothing to do with the female visitor. Nilsen simply had too much to drink one night and insisted angrily that Twinkle must leave. The theatrical younger partner made a big show of being all too glad to be rid of the entanglement; he packed off immediately with his meager belongings.

Gallichan would latch on quickly to a new benefactor, but Nilsen was not so resilient. Bereft, his only attempt at a stable relationship come to nothing, he tried to obliterate his loneliness with an obsessive dedication to work. Once again he threw himself headlong into union organiz-

ing, further raising the hackles of his supervisors. He also made an effort to resume his rounds of the bars, but his heart wasn't in it. More often he simply stayed home in the evenings to drown his sorrows in rum and loud music. Nilsen had always gotten an emotional lift from pop music; now he spent hours with earphones clamped on his head, drinking his way toward stupor.

As 1978 wound to a close, Nilsen passed the Christmas holiday alone in his rooms with only his dog, his music, and a bottle for solace. He sank into a deep depression, believing there was no one he could turn to for help. In his desolation he took up once again the old autoerotic rituals with the mirror, adding a new and deeply ominous twist: Before lying down to contemplate his own inert form, he powdered his body to a deathly pallor and applied makeup to simulate gunshot wounds. He had a platform built for his bed so that it sat high above the floor, at once an altar and a bier. In his isolation, the sickly love/death fantasy took tighter hold on his mind, and soon its implications would be lethal. Nilsen was about to embark on a course that he would one day analyze with poetic precision. "I caused dreams which caused death," he said. "This is my crime."

By December 30 Nilsen was desperate for companionship and he rallied from his morbid state of mind to go out on the town for the evening. When he returned, he brought with him a boy no older than 18, a short Irishman with curly brown hair and rough hands. By the time the events of this night came to light years later, Nilsen could no longer remember the youth's name. But he knew that they'd met at the Cricklewood Arms, and certain other recollections of the evening's activities were understandably vivid.

Nilsen and the Irish youth drank themselves to a slow crawl, then collapsed on the bed together, falling sound asleep. The slumber didn't last long for Nilsen, however. He awoke perhaps two or three hours later, and the usual anxieties swept over him. Pulling back the blankets, he stared at the boy sleeping by his side and realized that, within a few hours, this new friend would disappear forever. "I remember thinking that I wanted him to stay with me over the New Year whether he wanted to or not," Nilsen would later write in a jailhouse journal. And he took steps to make his wish come true. Many times in the past, he'd watched helplessly as his dreams of friendship or love came to nothing. This time would be different.

He reached for his necktie, which had fallen close at hand the night before. Looping it around the teenager's neck, he straddled the motionless body and pulled on the tie with all his strength. The sleeper sprang instantly to life and struggled desperately, falling to the floor and flailing spasmodically across the carpet. But Des Nilsen stayed on top of him, tightening his grip at every opportunity. In less than a minute the boy's body went limp, and the attacker was able to stand upright, shuddering with fright and exhaustion. The struggle was not entirely over, however. The victim was unconscious, but he'd resumed a sort of tortured breathing.

A bucket of water carried in from the kitchen finished off the assault. Draping the incapacitated boy over a chair, Nilsen grasped him by the hair and forced his head to the bottom of the bucket, holding it there until air bubbles stopped rising. And with that, he possessed at last his perverse dream come true: a wholly compliant companion, one who would never betray him, never leave him. Nilsen lifted the body upright and placed it in a comfortable armchair.

The murderer drank coffee and smoked half a pack of cigarettes, but still his hands trembled. He stared at the dead youth for a long time, then walked into the bathroom to fill the tub. Covering the window with a towel, he returned to fetch the body, which he hoisted over his shoulder and carried to the bath. He used dishwashing soap to tenderly scrub his victim clean and shampoo the hair. Getting the wet, slippery corpse out of the tub was no simple matter, but when Nilsen had accomplished the task he seated his docile guest on the toilet and patted him dry with towels. Later he placed the body on the bed.

In retrospect, Nilsen had no illusions about what this first murder meant. It was, he wrote in his prison journal, "the beginning of the end of my life as I had known it. I had started down the avenue of death and possession of a new kind of flatmate."

Examining the face of this first dead flatmate closely, he saw that the complexion was a little pinker than normal and that the lips were slightly blue and puffy. Otherwise his victim seemed not much the worse for wear and was still warm to the touch. By this time, however, Nilsen was growing fearful; he almost expected the police to appear, searching for the missing Irishman. Caught up in this new concern, he lost all interest in keeping the boy with him for the New

Nilsen's beloved pet, Bleep, was brought to the police station for a final good-bye, but the prisoner declined to see the dog for fear of causing her further distress.

Year and began to focus on finding a way to dispose of him.

With only the vaguest notion of how to proceed, Nilsen walked to a hardware store and bought an over-size cooking pot and an electric knife. In the months to come, he would find multiple uses for the pot, but he had second thoughts about using the knife on a human being. Not that his reasoning was terribly acute by this juncture, for he was suffering from a vicious hangover. He knew only that he had to do something with the Irish boy, and do it soon.

Returning to the flat, he dressed the youth's body and climbed into bed to snuggle with it, hoping to calm his fears. He considered having sex with the corpse but changed his mind when he realized that the body was already growing cold. Instead, he lifted it onto the floor, gave way to his own exhaustion, and slept soundly until evening.

As he ate his supper that night, Nilsen watched a little television. The young man's body was still lying on the floor where he'd left it. The killer then hit on an idea that would serve him well for many months to come. He pried up a few of the floorboards and pulled the boy over to the opening. Nilsen tried to stuff the body under the floor, but there was a glitch in his plan. The corpse was stiff with rigor mortis, and try as he might, Nilsen couldn't make the limbs fit into the hole.

He wasn't overly concerned; he'd heard somewhere that the muscles of the dead loosen up after a period of stiffness. So he leaned the body against a wall and went about his business. When he woke the next morning, the problem had resolved itself. The unfortunate Irish boy was still leaning against the wall, but his joints had loosened enough for Nilsen to stuff him under the floorboards.

A week passed, and the killer's curiosity was piqued. He pried up the floorboards again and brought his victim out of hiding. Finding that the body had gotten rather dirty, Nilsen stripped its clothes off and gave it another good cleaning. He then enjoyed a leisurely bath himself before settling in to examine his prize more minutely. He discovered that the body had turned very pale but was not showing any pronounced discoloration. The limbs, by then, had become more or less relaxed. Nilsen carried the dripping

I had started down the avenue of death and possession of a new kind of flatmate.

corpse into the next room and placed it on the carpet.

For the next 24 hours or so, he treated the body alternately as a sort of mute companion and unrespon-sive love slave. For much of the time he kept the corpse suspended by its ankles from the platform of his bed. Occasionally the sight of it inspired in him a sad and solitary lust. Eventu-ally Nilsen had second thoughts about his behavior and prepared to cut the body up for disposal. Again his nerve failed him. "I just couldn't do anything to spoil that marvellous body," he later wrote.

Nilsen put the corpse back under the floorboards and nailed them down. It would stay there for the next seven and a half months—long past the time when even the most diligent bacteria had lost interest in the withered flesh.

With his first murder, Nilsen had initiated a three-stage procedure he would adhere to in most of the 14 killings yet to come: First came the snuffing out of life, usually with the help of a tie or some combination of stran-gulation and drowning. Then followed a ritual of bathing and pampering the victim's body and using it as a sort of prop, like a ventriloquist's dummy. Often, during this phase, Nilsen would play out little scenes of domesticity—watching television with the corpse, listening to music with it, or dining in its presence. On occasion the bodies served as inspiration for private acts of sex. But sex was far less important to the killer than the illusion of companionship the bodies provided. He cared for them and cherished them, for their presence fulfilled for him a fantasy far more com-pelling than any erotic fancy. They were, at last, embodi-ments of his old dream: love and death, united and perfect.

The third stage of the routine, disposal of the body, was an event that Nilsen tended to put off at all costs, until necessity ruled out any further procrastination.

A pattern was set, but it hadn't yet revealed itself to the killer. Nilsen clutched at the hope that the murder of the Irish boy would prove to be an aberration, the first and last. It seemed likely to him that he would never kill again. And, it seemed, he wouldn't be called to account for the initial crime. Months passed, and no one came around asking questions about the missing teenager. Nilsen's fears of discovery dissipated. On August 11, 1979, more than seven months after the killing, he bagged up the body and carried it out to the garden, where he kindled a bonfire. The ashes he scattered and raked into the ground. Having done so, Nilsen felt vastly relieved. He'd cast off a burden that had put him at risk for many weeks.

Unfortunately, however, he hadn't escaped the problems that had made him a killer in the first place. On October 13, 1979, nearly 10 months after the first murder, he invited to his flat a young Chinese man named Andrew Ho, another casual acquaintance from the pubs. A chaotic struggle ensued in which Nilsen partially bound the other man and was on the verge of strangling him when Ho battled back. The smaller man smashed Nilsen over the head with a brass candlestick, then fled. Within 30 minutes, police were knocking at Nilsen's door, responding to Andrew Ho's complaints. In the end, however, no charges were filed because the victim declined to press the matter, and Nilsen steadfastly denied any attempt at strangulation. But the episode was not without consequences. It made Nilsen aware, he would claim later, that he would murder again.

The premonition was on the mark. Between December 1979 and February 1983, he murdered 14 young men and attempted to kill seven others. About six weeks after the assault on Andrew Ho, nearly one year after the first murder, Nilsen took a second life, and there would be no more extended respites from the violence.

Nilsen's second victim was a young Canadian tourist named Kenneth Ockenden. He was the only one of the slain men whose disappearance was noted in the British press. Ockenden was also unusual in that he was not a homosexual and thus may have been oblivious to the sexual dimension of Nilsen's come-on in the bar where they met.

The two men crossed paths at the Princess Louise pub on December 3, 1979. They bought each other drinks and had an amiable chat before Nilsen escorted the eager, outgoing Canadian on a private tour of central London. Later they retired to Nilsen's flat for supper, watched a little television, and got down to serious drinking.

Nilsen was soaking up Bacardi and Coke while Ockenden was downing whiskey mixed with ginger ale. According to Nilsen's later account, Ockenden was having a fine time and was quite a pleasant guest. The Canadian drank his way into the wee hours and became more and more engrossed in the music he was enjoying through Nilsen's stereo earphones. Then, according to Nilsen, he insisted on his own turn with the earphones and dragged Ockenden across the floor by the neck, the stereo cord twisted tight around his windpipe.

The Canadian didn't put up much of a struggle, although Nilsen's dog barked frantically and caused a bit of a commotion. As the killer recalled the event, he simply untwined the cord and walked away from the body, once he was sure that his guest was dead. Nilsen went on drinking and listening to music for a time, then dragged Ockenden over to the bed and curled up with him for the rest of the night.

In the morning the stereo turntable was still spinning and the dog needed reassuring. But Nilsen, no longer a novice at murder, seemed to carry on quite well. He'd liked the living Kenneth Ockenden, and the Canadian became the most favored of the dead companions. Over the next two weeks, Ockenden's corpse was in and out from under the floorboards on four separate occasions. Nilsen dressed his new silent companion in clean socks and underwear. When necessary he would dab makeup on the face to disguise any signs of puffiness or changes in skin coloration. The day after the murder, Nilsen ran out and bought a cheap Polaroid camera. He was then able to pass the time arranging the body in poses and snapping photographs.

Often he would cozy up to the body in a chair or drape its spread-eagled limbs over his own while sharing his reflections on the day or watching his usual television shows. Nilsen's feelings toward Ockenden, although twisted and self-centered, were also deeply tender: "I thought that his body and skin were very beautiful, a sight that almost brought me to tears." This affection did not, however, prevent the time-pressed civil servant from stuffing the body into a cupboard when he had to run off to work.

Martyn Duffey was Victim Number 3, a sensitive young man from Merseyside who had, in the months leading up to his death, shown promise of pulling his life together. Once a deeply troubled adolescent, Duffey had recently completed a course in catering and seemed to be on the verge of pursuing practical vocational goals. Nevertheless, he left Merseyside without explanation and went off to London, a city in which he had no known ties. Duffey had lived by his wits before, and he probably thought nothing of sharing a few beers with Des Nilsen and accepting free lodging for the night.

Surviving Dennis Nilsen

Fifteen young men went home with Dennis Nilsen and died at his hands. But there were other visitors to Nilsen's flat who encountered nothing but hospitality. There were even a few guests who, in the space of a single night, saw both the murderous Nilsen and the genial one. Among those were Paul Nobbs and Carl Stottor. Both survived Nilsen's attempts to kill them, and, remarkably, neither one of them seemed fully aware at the time how close he'd come to death.

Nobbs was a 19-year-old student when he ran into Nilsen at the Golden Lion pub. After chatting amiably for a while, the two men went to Nilsen's flat and spent the evening drinking and watching television. When they went to bed there was some tentative sexual activity, but they both quickly fell asleep. Between 2 and 3 a.m. Nobbs awoke with a splitting headache. He drank some water and returned to bed.

The next morning Nobbs looked into the mirror to find his eyes badly bloodshot and his face sore and red. There was an ugly welt on his neck. Nilsen remarked with concern that his companion looked "bloody awful" and should see a doctor. Nobbs took this advice and was told that he had injuries consistent with strangulation.

Like Nobbs, 21-year-old Carl Stottor met Nilsen at a pub and went home with him. At Nilsen's flat Stottor went straight to bed. His host crawled in beside him and pulled up a sleeping bag that he used as a blanket. He warned his guest to be careful of the bag's zipper. If Stottor thought the comment odd, he was too tired and drunk to mention it; he fell asleep at once.

He awoke to find the zipper wrapped around his neck. Struggling for breath, Stottor sensed that Nilsen might be trying to kill him, but he was too foggy mentally to offer much of a fight. He phased in and out of consciousness, realizing at one point that he was being held underwater.

His next recollections were gentler. There was Nilsen's dog, Bleep, licking at Stottor's face. Then there was a warming embrace, probably from Nilsen. Despite the gesture of affection, Stottor soon found that he'd suffered the same physical damage as Nobbs. Nilsen explained that his guest was having a bad dream and that Nilsen had to throw water on him to wake him. Stottor accepted this lame excuse, possibly because he found it almost impossible to believe that his gentle host had tried to hurt him. Indeed, amiable to the end, Nilsen walked with Stottor to the subway and bade him farewell with the wish that they might meet again.

How Nilsen could shift from hospitality to homicide so quickly and inexplicably remains an abiding riddle of his complex personality. The killer himself theorized that he was a psychopath who became violent when he drank too much. If he considered alcohol partly to blame for his deeds, however, the British courts apparently did not. They held him fully responsible for the murders he'd committed. It's possible that no one—including Nilsen himself—will ever understand fully the triggers that caused him to kill.

GOLDEN LION

Douglas Stewart *(above)* survived an attack by Dennis Nilsen, escaping by talking Nilsen out of using a knife on him. Unlike Paul Nobbs *(left)* and Carl Stottor *(right)*, Stewart had no doubt at the time that Nilsen was trying to kill him. All three men testified at Nilsen's trial.

Strangling didn't get the job done with this particular visitor, so Nilsen had to finish him off by submerging Duffey's head in the kitchen sink. After two days of haphazard storage in a cupboard, the corpse became bloated, so Nilsen shoved it under the floorboards along with the remains of Kenneth Ockenden. In one of Duffey's pockets Nilsen discovered a luggage ticket, and he took the trouble to fetch the bag so no suspicion would be raised by the unclaimed gear. The murderer discarded most of Duffey's belongings, but for a time he kept a collection of kitchen knives that were engraved with Duffey's name. When he did get around to disposing of them, he had the presence of mind to let them rust in the garden first, reasoning that it might seem odd for perfectly good cutlery to end up in the trash.

Nilsen also used Duffey's body to play out his fantasies. He kissed and hugged his new companion and showered him with compliments for having the youngest-looking body he'd ever seen.

By this time Nilsen knew that the murders were not aberrations; they were likely to continue. He had begun to think of killing as a sad but inevitable part of his fate, and he knew that he would eventually be called to answer for his crimes. Still, he would from time to time give serious consideration to mending his ways, and he decided at this juncture to once again dispose of the evidence.

Nilsen hauled Duffey and Ockenden up onto the stone floor of the kitchen and began to cut them into pieces. After filling two suitcases that he'd set aside for this purpose, he hid the luggage in an unlocked shed in the garden. There the bags would remain for the length of the summer. The neighbors never complained about the smell, at least not directly to Nilsen. But he took the precaution of dousing his cache, every so often, with a disinfectant solution.

Nilsen recalled that Victim Number 4, Billy Sutherland, may have put up a struggle. He apparently wasn't quite drunk enough to submit meekly to death. After two days of companionship with Sutherland's body, Nilsen pulled up the floorboards again.

Of Number 5, the murderer remembered the pub where they'd met and certain characteristics of the man's body. But Nilsen claimed to be utterly blank on most other details. "It's academic," he stated. "I must have put the body under the floorboards." He did remember cutting up the body, and he also recalled that when he transferred the limbs, head, and torso to the shed there were a lot of pesky flies.

Number 6 was another Irishman. Perhaps they'd met at the Cricklewood Arms. Perhaps not. By then Nilsen had learned quite a lot about the handling of dead bodies. He'd seen enough of rigor mortis to know that he had to put his lifeless flatmates under the floorboards right after killing them. The alternative was to wait patiently, sometimes for days, until the bodies loosened up a bit.

Many of Nilsen's victims he remembered mainly for

A poster was issued in the weeks following Kenneth Ockenden's disappearance. Nilsen slew the young Canadian tourist just hours before he was scheduled to fly home.

METROPOLITAN POLICE
Appeal for Assistance
MISSING
Kenneth OCKENDEN, aged 26, a visitor from Canada, vanished from his central London hotel in very suspicious circumstances in December 1979.
He was looking forward to returning to his family in Canada for Christmas 1979.
He left most of his personal property in his hotel room but took his camera and lenses. These could provide a vital clue :-
Canon Single Lens Reflex Camera - Serial No :- 315448TX
Lens - Serial No :- 1210427FD50 - F18
Telephoto Lens - Serial No :- 171431FD28 - F28
DO YOU KNOW WHERE HE IS?
HAS HE BEEN MURDERED?
HAVE YOU SEEN OR BOUGHT THE EQUIPMENT?
Please contact the Police on
01-230 1212
or your nearest Police Station.
All information treated as strictly confidential

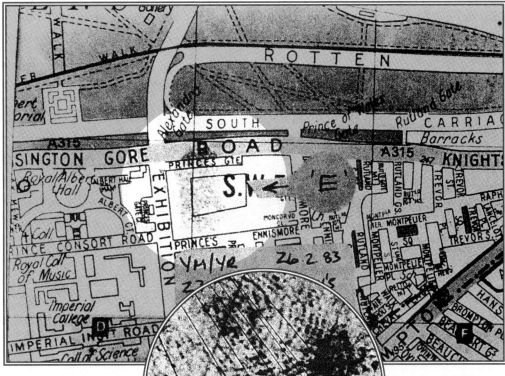

some particular characteristic in their person or some odd circumstance of their dying. Number 7, for example, struggled soundlessly, his legs churning in a circular motion, as if he were riding a bicycle. Of this one Nilsen said, "It was as easy as taking candy from a baby."

The need for dismemberment grew apace as the bodies accumulated. For one thing, flies were reproducing industriously underneath the floor, generating great quantities of maggots. By the end of 1980, an inventory of Nilsen's premises, including the garden shed, would have revealed six corpses, some of them with pieces scattered about in various hiding places in the flat itself. The killer had successfully burned his first victim many months before, but now the space under the floor was crammed to overflowing.

Even more worrisome, Nilsen's state of mind had so deteriorated that he would actually forget, at times, where

Three years after Kenneth Ockenden's death, investigators searching Nilsen's apartment turned up this London street map. It bore the Canadian's fingerprints *(inset)* and served as proof of a fateful meeting with the killer. The map shows the Kensington section of London.

he'd last left his victims: On one occasion he opened a cupboard door, and a pair of naked legs tumbled out on him. Such grim reminders would abruptly ground his flights from reality. All too real, for instance, was the ooze from the suitcases in the shed. It was time for another bonfire.

The risk of carting whole bodies to a blaze was too great even to contemplate. Nilsen calculated that smaller pieces would be easier to disguise and would make the task more manageable. So he girded himself for the horrifying job of dismembering the remaining uncut bodies, most of which were in advanced stages of decay.

Once again he took up the floorboards—the nails had by now become conveniently loose—and he grabbed the nearest body by the ankles, dragging it onto plastic sheets spread across the kitchen floor. Nilsen equipped himself with a bowl of water, paper towels, plastic bags, and a sharp kitchen knife. He would later relate with a glimmer of pride that no saws or power tools had ever proved necessary. After steeling his nerves with rum, he removed the underclothes from the corpse and stripped off his own garments to avoid soiling them.

He began by cutting the head from the body, carrying it to the kitchen sink to be washed and placed in a plastic bag. Next came the hands and feet, each piece washed and dried, then wrapped in paper towels. A major incision from the navel to the breastbone allowed the removal of the stomach, kidneys, liver, and intestines, but the diaphragm had to be breached before Nilsen could get at the heart and lungs. The internal organs went as a unit into their own plastic bag.

The gruesome labor continued in this fashion with Nilsen gradually breaking down the entire corpse into suitably small pieces, then moving on to a second set of remains. He dispatched the maggots from this body by pouring on handfuls of salt and brushing them away.

Needless to say, the work was exceedingly vile, even for someone as accustomed to carnage as Dennis Nilsen. The killer recalled retching violently during the course of his work and stopping from time to time to drink more rum. By the time he was well into the second corpse, he was more than a little drunk. He saw the job to completion, however, butchering four bodies before taking a bath and losing himself in music and more liquor. Bleep, the dog, had been nervous and fearful of the butchery, and she instinctively kept to the garden while her master was wielding the knife. Now she came back inside, eager for attention.

In the vacant lot beyond the garden lay large sections of an old poplar tree that had been cut down several months before. Using these for a base, Nilsen stacked up fragments of abandoned furniture that he'd been collecting from around the neighborhood. He built his pile of wood about five feet high and left an opening in the center.

Before first light the following morning, a cold day in early December, Nilsen reconnoitered to make sure nobody was around. Then he began preparing the pyre in earnest.

First he dragged out the parcels from inside the flat, bound in sections of old carpeting. Then came the contents of the garden shed, beginning with the suitcases full of human debris. The bags on the bottom had been crushed by the weight of those above them, and this, combined with the fluids of decomposition, made the suitcases impossible to carry without spilling bones and rotting flesh. Countless generations of dead flies had piled up, but maggots were still chewing away.

All the human heads were still in their shopping bags, and these Nilsen stuffed into the center of the pyre along with the other body parts. He topped off the eerie structure with an old tire, hoping that the fumes of burning rubber would conceal the odor of burning flesh. Newspapers and lighter fluid were tinder enough to set the pyre roaring to life.

Nilsen kept vigil throughout the day, poking the remains of six human beings into the hottest parts of the fire and, from time to time, throwing more wood on the conflagration to keep it burning intensely. Not surprisingly, children from the neighborhood were attracted to the blaze. Nilsen's recollections of the scene are infused with a sense of pagan ritual.

"The large bonfire is blazing fiercely while I stand near, stone cold and in a nervous sweat," he wrote. "Three neighbourhood kids are gathered and it would seem in order if they danced around it. The devilish purity and innocence of children dancing around a mass funeral pyre would have a simple and solemn grandeur beyond the most empty and formally garish State funeral. The sparks, heat, hot air, smoke and energy of life arrowing skywards in a great visual display of living natural forces."

At least for a few moments that day, the killer was able to convince himself that he'd done his victims an enormous favor. If nothing else, he'd given them a fitting send-off from this earth, a "mixing of flesh in a common flame and a single unity of ashes." After the fire died down, Nilsen raked the ashes and tried to make the place look like the residue of an ordinary bonfire. When he saw that a skull had survived the flames he smashed it to pieces with his rake.

I *am damned and damned and damned. How in heaven's name could I have done any of it?*

Both Malcolm Barlow and Billy Sutherland died because they caused Nilsen inconvenience. Barlow was killed because he needed medical attention; Sutherland became a nuisance when he followed Nilsen home.

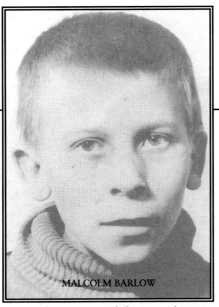

MALCOLM BARLOW

BILLY SUTHERLAND

Later that evening Nilsen bathed and put on fresh clothes. He strolled to a pub and brought a young man home with him. The two had sex and enjoyed a sound night's sleep. The next morning Nilsen walked with his overnight guest to the Underground station and bade him a cordial farewell.

The young man had no idea how lucky he was. As for Nilsen, he'd been stretching his luck far longer than it could reasonably be expected to hold. This might have been a day for congratulating himself on getting away with seven murders. He might have pledged himself to a fresh start and put his life on a new tack. But new beginnings were beyond his power. His sails were set and his rudder was jammed.

Within six weeks, new bodies would begin to accumulate again at 195 Melrose Avenue. The only fresh start Nilsen took away from his bonfire was renewed storage space.

Victims Number 8, 9, and 10 went to their fate, doomed to remain among the nameless. "Floorboards back, carpet replaced, and back to work at Denmark Street," as Nilsen tersely and callously put it. But if his written reflections on his crimes were sometimes brutal in their passionless objectivity, they could alternately be heartrending in their profound despair and remorse. The same bureaucrat who skipped back to the office after murdering wrote: "I am damned and damned and damned. How in heaven's name could I have done any of it?"

An English skinhead distinguished by a "CUT HERE" tattoo around his neck was Victim Number 11. "After killing him I went to bed," wrote Nilsen. "End of the day, end of a drink, end of a person." Nilsen later followed the directions spelled out in the man's tattoo.

Number 12, the last man to be murdered at 195 Melrose Avenue, had a name: Malcolm Barlow. Mentally retarded and epileptic, Barlow had fallen into a deep sleep after consuming two drinks on top of his usual prescription drugs—this despite Nilsen's warnings about the dangers of mixing alcohol and pharmaceuticals. When the host couldn't wake his guest, he realized that Barlow urgently needed to go to a hospital. Nilsen chose to murder him instead. As he later explained, he "didn't want to deal with ambulance men asking silly questions." By this time the killer had grown so jaded with the business of death that he preferred murder to the bother of calling a doctor.

While a new harvest of bodies was finding its way under his floorboards, Nilsen was working hard at the Denmark Street Jobcentre. He was taking good care of trusty old Bleep, and he was even entertaining visitors from time to time—visitors who came to no harm. At the same time, his life was spiraling down into desperation. It was as if the guilt lodged in his heart was drawing ill fortune Nilsen's way. He was robbed on several occasions, once losing an entire month's salary and having to turn to a relief agency for assistance. Even more devastating—in the long run—he let a long-standing tension between himself and his landlords boil over into a major dispute.

The landlords had always considered Nilsen a demanding and troublesome tenant, and indeed he'd never been slow to fire off indignant letters disputing any changes that they might propose. He made a point of knowing the statutes protecting tenants' rights, and he let the owners get away with nothing. Considering him a nuisance, the landlords had been trying for months to get Nilsen out of the building when he came home one day to find his living quarters ransacked by vandals. Practically everything he owned had been destroyed. Police were called in to investigate, but their inquiries led nowhere. Although the destruction undermined Nilsen's morale, he must have felt at least a little fortunate: If investigators didn't find leads to help them catch the vandals, neither did they form suspicions about what lay under the floors they were walking on.

After the break-in, agents for the landlords came forward with a proposition offering Nilsen a new apartment at 23 Cranley Gardens. In exchange for his troubles in relocating he'd be given a sum of £1,000. It was a reasonable offer, and one that held great appeal to Nilsen for reasons the landlords couldn't begin to imagine.

Since his second bonfire, Nilsen had concluded that rotting internal organs were the primary cause of the deathly smell that filled his apartment like a cloud. So he'd taken to routinely relieving his corpses of the lungs, hearts, kidneys, and other organs, all of which he would spill into a gap between the double fences on one side of his garden. He credited "beasties in the night" with devouring the organs. Nilsen had also become more systematic in keeping up with his dissections, so that all of his bodies through Victim Number 11 were neatly chopped, wrapped in little parcels, and carefully stowed beneath the floorboards. There was no room for Victim Number 12, however, and by the time Nilsen received his landlords' offer of cash, he'd been living for some time with Malcolm Barlow's body stashed in a kitchen cabinet. He leaped at the prospect of a move.

By now, Nilsen was almost cadaverously cool under pressure. He took his time in assembling a last funeral pyre and waited until his final day at 195 Melrose Avenue before carrying out the cremation. "The fire burned fiercely, extraordinarily fiercely," he wrote. "There were spurts, bangs, cracks and hisses." Afterward, a last-minute search for incriminating evidence brought to mind a neglected detail. Malcolm Barlow's hands and arms were concealed in a hole just outside the flat. Nilsen did his best to break up the bones, which he heaved into the common ground beyond the back of the garden. The flesh he simply buried. A moving van was due any moment.

After Nilsen moved to the attic flat at 23 Cranley Gardens, it became dramatically more reckless for him to keep killing. Not only was he now without a convenient place for burning his victims, but since his new floors would not accommodate bodies, he no longer even had suitable short-term storage. Nevertheless, he was apparently beyond the point where he could live very long without murdering. Within six months he was at it again, strangling a man named John Howlett, a London ne'er-do-well whom he'd befriended in a bar. Howlett's murder was marked by a ferocious struggle in which the victim amazed his assailant by appearing to come back to life over and over again. Nilsen finally drowned the luckless Howlett in the bathtub.

Howlett was followed within a few months by Graham Allen, who was garroted while eating an omelet Nilsen had prepared. The new bodies would be disposed of in a way that was even more degrading than the methods used by the killer at his previous address. After storing the corpses for several days in either the wardrobe or the bathtub, Nilsen cut them into small chunks and flushed them down the toilet—the practice that eventually led to his arrest.

To facilitate this messy and time-consuming process, Nilsen boiled certain sections of the bodies on top of the stove, using the big soup pot that he'd acquired after his first murder. The heads Nilsen boiled for hours on end, trying to render them down to mere bone. Skulls and sections of the bodies proved too formidable to be hacked into fragments and discarded with the trash. These Nilsen hid here and there about the flat. Among the hiding places was a wooden tea chest draped with a red curtain. Apparently, he also discarded a few bags of human remains along the route of his nightly walks with Bleep. He might have been drunk when he used this last method; he later claimed not to remember it.

In June 1982, after having been stuck in the same job for nearly eight years, Nilsen won a promotion and was transferred to the Kentish Town Jobcentre. He was elated at this shift in his professional fortunes, and he threw himself into his new responsibilities with fresh vigor. But his private life had deteriorated beyond the point where he could harbor any serious illusions about putting things permanently on an even keel. Already the dedicated civil servant was in the awkward predicament of having to regularly replenish the supply of deodorant sticks hidden about his apartment, and he knew that the stench of his partially discarded trophies might someday bring about his downfall. Besides, one last murder awaited him.

Stephen Sinclair was the 15th man for whom a friendly invitation to Des Nilsen's apartment was a summons to death. A drug addict, Sinclair had passed out from a dose of narcotics, providing Nilsen with the opportunity to slip a cord around his neck and—without much effort—cut off the supply of oxygen. Afterward, the killer bathed Sinclair's body and used it for his usual forlorn socializing. Then he stashed this last flatmate in the wardrobe for a week. He'd begun the weary business of disposing of the corpse when the plumbers started poking about at the apartment house, and Nilsen realized with mixed dread and relief that his life of crime was finally ending.

The morning of his arrest Nilsen put on his customary gray coat and dark trousers, then set off on the Underground to go to his office in Kentish Town. The only

The well-worn staircase to the attic of 23 Cranley Gardens carried three of Nilsen's victims to their death. The stairs were the only way in or out of his quarters, and this proved to be the civil servant's undoing. Discreet disposal of bodies was very difficult because of the limited access.

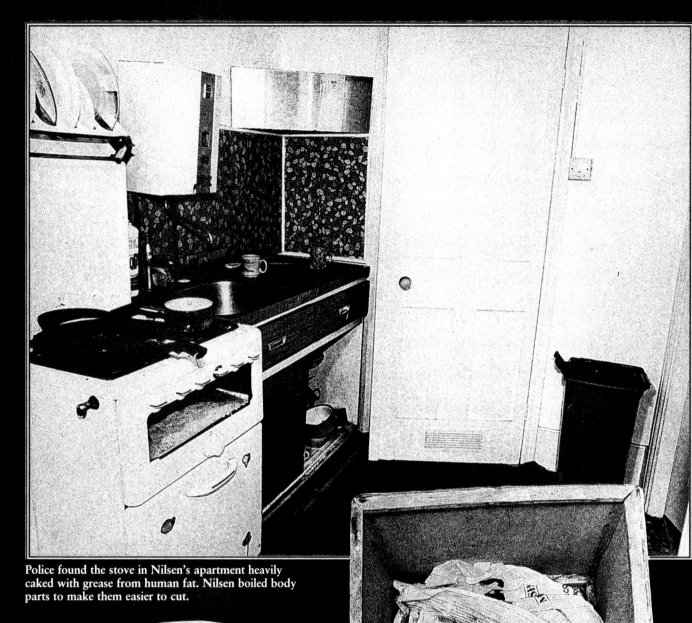

Police found the stove in Nilsen's apartment heavily caked with grease from human fat. Nilsen boiled body parts to make them easier to cut.

A tea chest provided unceremonious storage for the remains of Nilsen's last victims.

Nilsen simmered heads overnight in this covered pot.

146

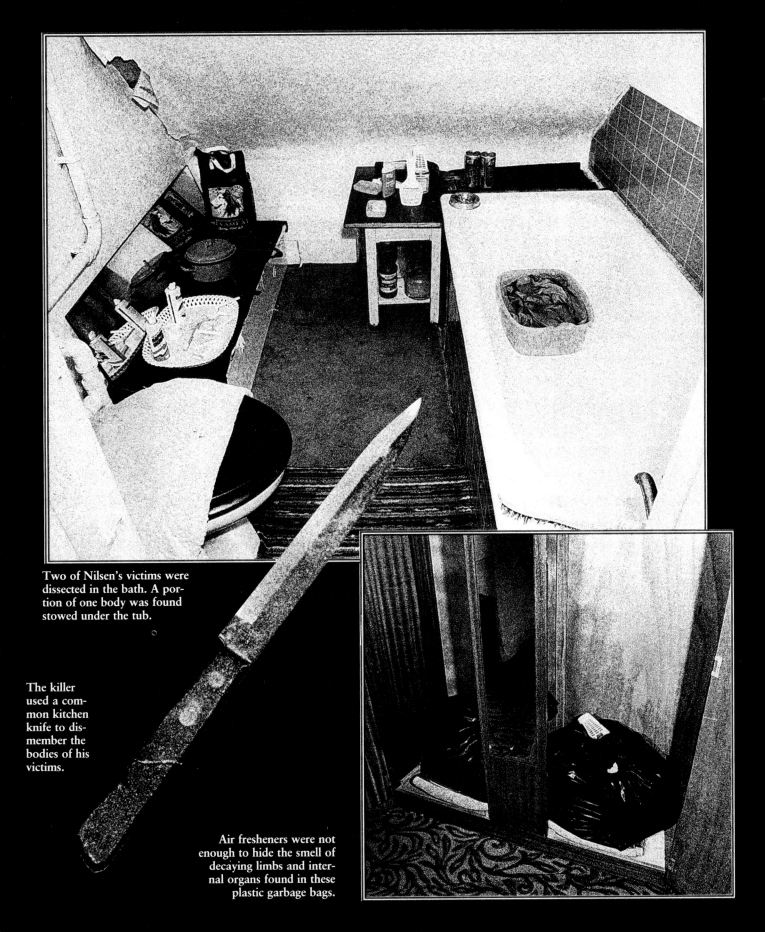

Two of Nilsen's victims were dissected in the bath. A portion of one body was found stowed under the tub.

The killer used a common kitchen knife to dismember the bodies of his victims.

Air fresheners were not enough to hide the smell of decaying limbs and internal organs found in these plastic garbage bags.

thing that was unusual about his attire that day was a blue-and-white football scarf that he had usurped from the dead Stephen Sinclair.

Knowing that this would probably be his last day at the office, Nilsen took pains to leave things tidy. In the back of his desk drawer he left a note advising his coworkers that if they should ever hear that he'd committed suicide in a jail cell, the report would be untrue. The killer knew that he would never do such a thing.

The stress of his situation, of knowing that the inevitable reckoning would soon begin, had left him exhausted. He'd been unable to summon the energy to complete the disposal of Stephen Sinclair's body, but the incriminating evidence of that murder and two others awaited the police back at his

flat. Beyond his desperate nocturnal visit to the sewer, he'd made no special effort to conceal the remains of his guests. He was worried, more than anything else, about what would happen to Bleep. This sad concern was well-founded. Soon after her master's arrest, the grieving little dog fell ill and was disposed of by lethal injection.

When the story of Nilsen's arrest was made public, London's tabloid press had no need to be inventive; the gory truth was sensational enough. Nevertheless, the newspapers churned out banner headlines about the chopped-up bodies and orgies of murder. The more restrained and solemn *Guardian* and *Times* also reported the stomach-churning details of how Dennis Nilsen had become Britain's most prolific serial killer. The headlines in these papers were less

The french doors at the Melrose Avenue flat, from which Nilsen once kept watch on his funeral pyres, now reveal a group of evidence technicians searching the garden under a makeshift canopy. Despite the passage of time—and Nilsen's best efforts to banish all traces of his victims—the police recovered more than 1,000 scraps of bone and human ash.

Officers search an alley adjacent to Melrose Avenue.
The authorities came under considerable public pressure
to identify Nilsen's many victims.

blaring, but the lurid reports they carried were just as unsettling to the public.

With the island's self-described "murderer of the century" to analyze, journalists did not confine their probing to London. As soon as the details of Nilsen's life became known, reporters headed for Scotland. They descended in droves on Strichen, the small town where Nilsen's grief-stricken mother was also searching for answers to imponderable questions.

For the police, the entire situation had turned their usual modes of investigation upside down. They knew who the killer was, and they had firm evidence that he'd committed a large number of murders. But they didn't know who many of the victims were, so they had to do their usual job backward. Their biggest asset on the case was Nilsen himself, who—though temperamental and more than a little offended by his treatment in the press—was eager to tell them everything.

Nilsen instructed police on what to look for in the Cranley Gardens flat and conducted a tour of the premises at 195 Melrose Avenue. What he told the investigators about the Melrose Avenue garden instigated an earth-sifting operation that rivaled England's major archaeological digs. Teams of police combed through every inch of soil. More forensically useful little bones had survived than Nilsen could have imagined. The care that police devoted to the evidence bespoke their need to address a tide of public anguish and anxiety provoked by the news of Nilsen's killings. Hundreds of families whose young men were missing were calling in search of information.

Nilsen's trial and conviction were relatively straightforward affairs, although the court revelations evoked tremendous public fascination and horror. Several victims who'd survived assaults by Dennis Nilsen came forward. They basically corroborated the prosecution's case, although of course they had no firsthand knowledge of the killer's postmortem barbarisms. These young men provided damaging testimony, but it was almost unnecessary because of the overwhelming mass of forensic evidence already before the court.

The only question to be resolved was whether to find Nilsen guilty of murder or of manslaughter, which in England means that guilt is mitigated by "diminished responsibility." This is tantamount to the plea of insanity in American courts. Attorneys for the prosecution and defense sparred unproductively with psychiatrists, who took both sides of the issue. The

Amid a swirl of snowflakes, undertakers bear out the portions of bodies that Nilsen left behind when he was taken to jail. The formality with which the police dealt with the bodies was a response to the general sense of shock and outrage that greeted the news of the atrocities.

barristers were seeking definitive answers; the psychiatrists were loath to give them. Their view, as usual, was that madness is not so simple to quantify, pinpoint, or define.

In the end, Dennis Nilsen was convicted of six charges of murder and two charges of attempted murder. However, it seemed that the verdict had little to do with his eventual sentencing. The judge had said that, no matter how the verdict came out, he planned to impose the same sentence—life in prison—because he believed that there was little chance of the defendant's rehabilitation.

The jury did not accept Nilsen's contention that he was too deranged to be held responsible for his acts. And the judge, after imposing the life sentence, recommended that Nilsen not be considered for parole for 25 years. Unless the convicted killer dies sooner, he is certain to remain in prison at least until November 4, 2008. It's more than likely that he will depart only as a corpse.

In the scores of letters and more than 40 journals that Dennis Nilsen has written in prison, his mental suffering is apparent. Genuine repentance and remorse remain slippery, however. In his writings Nilsen has asked whether he might not be that one-in-a-million character who is simply evil to the core. Perhaps there is no hope of ever answering that question, although it may be the case that Nilsen, highly intelligent and obsessively introspective, is the perfect candidate to make the attempt. For now, the killer can only state the bleak facts of the matter. He once wrote: "The decision to kill was never taken until a few moments before it was attempted or transacted." And also this: "I wished I could stop but I could not. I had no other thrill or happiness." ◆

I *wished I could stop but I could not. I had no other thrill or happiness.*

Soon to be reviled as one of Britain's most infamous killers, a gaunt Des Nilsen stares grimly at the camera in his booking photograph.

151

I *always had a*
fetish for murder and
death.

DAVID BERKOWITZ

4

Demons

The cream-colored 1970 Ford Galaxie was nondescript; it drew not a glance as it threaded through the Saturday shopping crowd crisscrossing high-toned Main Street. Beyond the village, the Ford slipped past short rows of catering vans whose occupants paid no notice as they carted the makings of garden parties onto privet-lined grounds. Fashionable Southampton, New York, is about two and a half hours' drive from Manhattan. It has long been one of the wealthiest summer communities on the East Coast—an enclave of rambling million-dollar homes, tennis courts, private beaches, and, in season, ceaseless traffic to New York City and back. And high season it was—August 6, 1977, a busy time when only the oddest of tourist vehicles might have drawn scrutiny.

There was nothing particularly arresting about the Ford's driver, either. He was a pudgy-faced, clean-shaven, heavyset man in his middle twenties. He had short, curly, dark hair and wore a denim jacket and jeans. Occasionally, a smile would flit across his full, oddly feminine lips. There was a Mona Lisa aspect to it, at once gentle and sly. It had a disturbing quality, that smile, but nothing else in his face commanded a second look. He was bland and ordinary almost to the point of invisibility. At least, he looked that way. There was, in fact, a peculiarity that set him most distinctly apart from the weekenders around him—only no one could see it. It was the chorus of demons who howled and chattered inside his head, the devils who swore and blasphemed, cursed and threatened. The demons lived inside him, and they were mean and vicious and thirsty for blood.

Today, the young man determined, they would drink their fill. He'd come prepared to serve them. Stuffed inside the waistband of his pants was the reassuring bulk of a .44-caliber Charter Arms Bulldog revolver. It had functioned well enough in weeks gone by, but it had its limitations. It was a cumbersome killer, requiring a trigger pull for every shot, and it could shoot only five times without a reload. For the slaughter the driver envisioned this day, the

.44 was insufficient. So, in the Ford's trunk, there was a .45-caliber Commando Mark III semiautomatic rifle, capable of expending a 30-round clip in less than 30 seconds, and two loaded clips of ammunition.

The deadly hardware, meant for mass murder, was concealed in a green U.S. Army duffel bag with a name stenciled across it: D. Berkowitz. *D* for David. On this steamy summer day, the name was as anonymous as the man who wore it. Four days later, however, it would be a name known in all the world. Four days later, David Berkowitz would at last be linked in the public mind with his deadly alter ego: Son of Sam.

David Berkowitz was still unknown that August 6, but Son of Sam was already quite famous. People talked about him night and day. He was the object of the biggest manhunt in the history of New York City. With some help from hysterical headlines, he had virtually brought that mightiest of cities to its knees in fear. He'd killed six people, blinded or paralyzed another two, and wounded an additional seven. But it was not the numbers so much as the mystery surrounding Son of Sam that inspired terror. It was the demented, semiliterate letters that he wrote to the newspapers. It was the randomness of his attacks—in the Bronx, in Brooklyn, in Queens. It was his trademark style, lumbering out of the night to approach parked cars, crouching with his heavy gun clasped in two hands, firing suddenly, spasmodically, at his victims' heads. No one knew who he was, or where he might strike next, so no one felt safe.

Southampton, however, had little cause for fear. Heretofore, Son of Sam had never hunted outside New York City. There were pretty women aplenty in the great metropolis, and pretty women were the fare that the demons preferred—especially women with long brown hair, women who parked in cars with men and kissed them. Sometimes the men were shot as well, but that was incidental. It was the women who mattered. Still, there were good-looking women in Southampton, too, and besides, it was familiar ground. David Berkowitz had been at camp there in his boyhood, and he knew a bit about the habits of the community. More to the point, Southampton was where the demons had commanded him to go.

There was no question of disobeying them. If he didn't provide blood, they'd make his life unendurable with their mad screeching and yowling. Not long ago, their caterwauling had left him so desperate that he rushed out into the street in agony. But if they hounded him, Berkowitz believed, they also protected him. They had cast an illusion around him, making him invisible to police. It must be so, he reasoned. His pursuers already knew so much about him—his choice of weapons, his taste in victims. They even knew about the demons; he'd told them in his letters. And still they couldn't catch him. The fiends were shielding him. He would give them their feast.

As the Ford cruised along, however, a summer storm blew up. Berkowitz pulled over to wait it out. Rain was bad for his mission—perhaps even a sign that he should call it off. The demons often spoke to him through the weather. He restarted the car and doubled back for home. In sleek Southampton, the summer routine remained intact, the chic, secure residents unmindful of the mayhem that had just been rained out. For David Berkowitz, it was no great matter. There would be other opportunities.

With the city in a frenzy in the wake of continued shootings, New York's tabloid *Daily News* turned its front page into a wanted poster. But readers had only a day to contemplate the police sketch before learning that a suspect was in custody and had confessed to the Son of Sam murders.

But there were none: Son of Sam had blown his one chance for mass murder. On August 10, 1977, Berkowitz, 24, was captured following a six-hour stakeout of his apartment at 35 Pine Street in Yonkers. His soft, secretive smile flashed across every front page and television screen in the country. And the world learned about the chilling contents of his army duffel bag, now swollen with even more armament than he'd lugged to Southampton. When the police retrieved the bag from Berkowitz's Galaxie, they found the Commando, a 12-gauge shotgun, a .22-caliber AR-7 semiautomatic rifle, and substantial quantities of ammunition. Once again, the killer had apparently prepared for a massive bloodletting that was averted at the last minute.

The soft-voiced Berkowitz soon enlightened his captors about his motives and mission. He was, he said, carrying out the wishes of a 6,000-year-old demon named Sam, who passed his instructions through the unlikely medium of a black Labrador retriever. Along with these muddleheaded explanations, the world also heard the single, most salient fact about the self-described monster who had wrecked so many lives, kept an army of police at bay, and terrified a tough and cynical city: There was almost nothing to know.

The monster, caught at last after one year and 12 days of terror, turned out to be a quiet, mannerly former employee of the U.S. Postal Service. Prepared to confront an evil genius or a foam-flecked maniac, the public got instead a nobody—a loner, a loser, a man who, had he not killed, would probably have passed through life leaving scarcely a trace. His fellow workers recalled him, if at all, as quiet, polite, helpful. "He was always courteous," said one. "If we had to lift anything heavy, he helped us. He was a gentleman." Even so, no one knew him very well. So isolated was he that his colleagues remembered him best for eating his lunch, alone, in a corridor outside the cafeteria. Berkowitz was capable of consideration; he'd even advised one scared coworker to wear her hair pinned up, since the .44-Caliber Killer—his first moniker in the tabloids—only shot women with long, flowing hair. But none of the post office employees had considered Berkowitz a friend.

The same held true at all his former places of employment. The terror of New York's night had been a security guard, an air-conditioner repairman, a taxi driver, an undistinguished soldier, an indifferent student. He was an unmemorable, floating speck in a teeming city. David Berkowitz had virtually no identity—no achievements, no friends, no attachments. As he summed up his predicament: "Without Sam, I'm nothing."

Many psychiatrists believe that Berkowitz's lack of identity was rooted in pathology. Based on what he said and did, they judged him to be a paranoid schizophrenic, suffering from aural hallucinations, personal grandiosity, and ideas of persecution, along with outlandish religious misconceptions. Paranoid schizophrenics often feel themselves pawns of some external force that tells them what to do and is responsible for their actions. Paranoid schizophrenia is a mental illness. The legal and the clinical definitions of insanity are altogether different, however, and in the view of the criminal justice system, Berkowitz was perfectly sane and had to answer for his deeds.

Sane or mad, Berkowitz was well aware of his own isolation; he felt it keenly. Time and again throughout his life, the slender ties he forged with the external world were torn away. He began life as an adopted child; his natural parents never married. His adoptive mother, by far his closest emotional tie, died when he was in his early teens. Bereft of firm family roots, he was further plagued throughout his life by a radical inability to communicate, especially with females. "There is a force to turn people away from me," he once wrote. "Somebody wants me destroyed, makes people dislike me and makes girls be not attracted to me in any way. If I had close friends or girl friends I would be able to resist the force."

But the leap from loneliness to murder is incomprehensibly long, and psychiatrists who questioned David Berkowitz wondered precisely what drove him. Behind his confused ramblings, one possible answer emerged: Berkowitz was consumed with unspoken rage toward women. His antipathy began with the central women in his life and eventually extended to include all his prospective victims. As he told a psychiatrist, "I blame them for everything. Everything evil that's happened in the world—somehow it goes back to them."

Berkowitz was born on June 1, 1953, and his identity problems did not take long to materialize. His name at birth was Richard David Falco. His mother, Betty Broder Falco, was born in 1914 and was raised in Brooklyn, one of nine children of a tailor. She finished grade school, then went to work in factories and offices. At 16 she became a chorus girl and performed briefly with the Ziegfeld Follies. A Jew, she married a gentile and had a daughter. The Falcos ran a fish store in the Prospect Heights section of Brooklyn until the ne'er-do-well husband deserted Betty for another woman. This was 13 years before her son was born.

Betty Falco never divorced, but for more than 20 years she carried on an affair with a Long Island businessman named Joseph Kleinman. He was also married but had managed to weave his relationship with Betty into the fabric of his family life. In keeping with his singular view of the world, he positively refused to raise a child out of wedlock: When Betty told him she was pregnant, he told her to get rid of the baby. She dutifully relinquished the infant at birth, putting him up for adoption. Thus even as Richard Falco drew his first breath, he was already profoundly an outsider.

By all rights, however, this early rejection should have passed without leaving severe emotional scars. The baby was only a few days old when he was adopted by Nathan and Pearl Berkowitz, a hardworking Jewish couple from a stable community in the Bronx. Nat Berkowitz ran a hardware store. Pearl was a warm, outgoing woman who lavished love on her new son. The couple reversed the order of the baby's given names and called him David. He would be their only child.

Nine-year-old David Berkowitz *(back row and inset)* smiles for his third-grade portrait in 1962. As a schoolboy he was a loner—as he would be all his life—and he showed early signs of abnormality. A bully and a budding pyromaniac, he also tortured animals.

Except in light of his later notoriety, nothing that's known of David Berkowitz's early childhood would seem particularly significant. He was a solitary child, but not to a worrisome extreme: His earliest memories were of cowboys and Indians, war games, and the other aggressive activities typical of many young boys. He was a chubby youngster and was teased for it. But he was not unintelligent, scoring 118—a "superior" level—on an IQ test in 1960. Young David was, however, hardly an overachiever.

Once old enough to attend school, he became a habitual truant, often feigning sickness to win permission to stay home. The dodge never failed with his doting mother, who waited on him hand and foot. Acquaintances of the family remarked that David seemed able to get anything he wanted simply by showing his temper. One of his elementary school teachers described him as a "moody child. Very easily upset." According to what he told psychiatrists after his arrest, he was also a morbid child. Time and again, he referred to his early fascination with death: "I always had a fetish for murder and death," he told one interviewer. "Sudden death and bloodshed appealed to me."

As he grew from child to adolescent, Berkowitz often pondered his own demise. "I begged to God for death," he recounted. "I used to sit on the fire escape and thought of throwing myself down, wanting to jump. When I thought about dying, I thought of being transported into a world of bliss and happiness." Sometimes he would dream about becoming a fireman, a hero, dying to save others.

He also had keen memories—painful if rather trivial—of wrongs done him by females, starting when he was very young. In prison he spoke of an incident when he was five years old: A group of girls poured sand in his hair, and his mother, unsympathetic, blamed him for the childish trouble and slapped him. There were also wrongs that he claimed to have done in return. At about the same time as the sand-throwing incident, he said, he hit a little girl with a toy gun and split her scalp.

Young David had a taste for hiding and for private fantasy. His father's nicknames for him were telling: Nat called the child variously Sneaky, Snoop, and Spy. David loved to slip through the house, doing his best to be invisible. He would steal into the kitchen for food, and before long he was eating compulsively, binging in secret.

David's first school was P.S. 77 in the Bronx, although scarcely any of his fellow pupils remember him there. A third-grade classmate recalls that he was shy and quiet, quick to weep when reprimanded. The adult Berkowitz remembered himself quite differently. He was a "wild, unruly, undisciplined child—I was the worst in the school," he recalled, probably with more drama than truth: He was not bad enough to make much of an impression on anyone else. By the time he was in the sixth grade, classmates would say, he was something of a bully and a brat, largely friendless and prone to tantrums. Unpleasant, but hardly evil. Hardly even memorable.

There was little or nothing to foreshadow a murderous obsession. But unbeknown to his schoolmates, David Berkowitz, young as he was, had long grappled with an intensely disturbing problem. When he was only three, Nat and Pearl had told him that he was adopted. They lied about the circumstances, saying that his natural mother had died at his birth. The story, Berkowitz would say, left him with a tremendous sense of guilt. He believed he'd caused his mother's death and that, consequently, his natural father had hated him.

It hardly bears noting that the vast majority of adopted children—including those in far worse circumstances than young Berkowitz—grow up to become healthy, productive adults. Perhaps he learned too young that he was adopted, or perhaps the knowledge exacerbated some inborn flaw that was the true author of his homicidal nature. Whatever the case, his childhood behavior gradually became more aberrant. By the sixth grade, he'd lost whatever thirst for learning he might have had and was often in trouble for failing to do his homework. In junior high school he engaged in petty vandalism, breaking car windows and the like. He was also on the way to becoming a pyromaniac, setting dozens of tiny fires, only to extinguish them. To psychologists, this last behavior is worrisome indeed: It signals, they say, deep-seated anger and aggression.

Berkowitz himself seemed to confirm that conclusion in his prison interviews. Even in childhood, he would say, his habits and obsessions had already taken a very dark turn. Along with setting fires, he began to torture and kill small animals, among them his mother's pet parakeet. He dispatched the bird in a typically sly way, feeding it small quantities of cleaning powder over a period of weeks. No one was ever the wiser in this episode, but a pattern was taking shape, one of hiding antisocial behavior behind a mask of innocence.

As a teenager, David Berkowitz's isolation settled on him like a second skin. Even his recreation was solitary. He favored long bike rides or retreats into the countryside for rock-climbing—always by himself. And, for the second time in his young life, he was about to lose his mother. In 1967 Pearl Berkowitz died of breast cancer. David was 14 at the time, and he was devastated by her death. Family friends recalled that he wept piteously at the funeral and returned time and again to visit her grave. Nevertheless, when he was asked years later to comment on this passage in his life, he remembered being "both happy and sad. It was freedom. She was a pest sometimes. She was nagging." Emotionally, he seemed to have become frozen.

Pearl Berkowitz's dying made David's ruinous isolation even more pronounced, and every aspect of his life suffered as a result. For all his misbehavior and truancy, he'd managed to maintain a B+ average in junior high, while his adoptive mother was alive. After the funeral his grades and his school attendance both plummeted. If Pearl's excessive attentiveness and lax discipline had brought out David's selfishness, her death called forth increasing aimlessness and resentment. The whole world, he decided, was against him. Later, under the full-blown influence of his paranoia, Berkowitz would declare that she died as "part of a master plan to break me down. It was no accident that she got cancer. Somebody put something in her food. Evil forces."

After nearly 21 months as a widower, Nat Berkowitz moved David from his familiar Bronx home to Co-op City, an agglomeration of 35 high-rise apartments in a northerly corner of the borough. The father was working long hours at his struggling business, and David, in midadolescence and more alone than ever, found a specific focus for the pain of his solitude: He didn't merely lack friends, he lacked contact with females. "The girls in Co-op City didn't find me attractive," he would tell a prison psychiatrist. "I began to hate girls and wanted to join the army." Lacking much individual identity, he found the idea of institutional identity appealing. He became an auxiliary fireman and trained as an auxiliary policeman at the local 45th Precinct.

In the spring of 1971, the 18-year-old Berkowitz suffered yet another psychological blow when his father remarried. David thus acquired a stepmother, Julia, and a 25-year-old stepsister. The teenager showed no overt disapproval of the new family arrangement, but Nat noticed that in the weeks following the ceremony David became more and more reclusive. If the marriage did not please young Berkowitz, however, apparently it did firm his resolve to seek a new life for himself: He decided to join the army. His ideas about enlistment were morbidly romantic: He wanted to "die for a cause," he said. The Vietnam War was in full swing, and Berkowitz declared himself "fanatically patriotic." He envisioned winning glory in battle as an infantryman. Instead he was stationed in Korea, where he would see no combat.

Berkowitz's gung-ho attitude quickly vanished, and it became obvious that he didn't have much of a future in the army. He was caught stealing food from the mess hall and was cited on two occasions for failing to move with his unit when ordered to do so. His dreams of valor never materialized, but he did master a skill that he would find useful in later years: the use of deadly weapons. He won the ranking of marksman, the military's basic designation for shooting proficiency.

Berkowitz's relationships with his peers in the military were typically flimsy; he had buddies, but no close friends. His barracksmates nicknamed him Wolf—a teasing reference to his abundant body hair. In later days, he would brag about liaisons with Korean prostitutes and about wide-ranging experimentation with drugs—LSD, marijuana, mescaline, amphetamines. Whether he actually acquired any of these vices is subject to doubt: His main sexual activity throughout his life appears to have been masturbation.

In January 1973 Berkowitz's unit was rotated back to the United States for assignment at Fort Knox, Kentucky, and the move apparently halted the erosion of his marginal military career. His general rating after arrival at Fort Knox declared him an "outstanding and dependable soldier." He even entered an educational program to better himself and improve his military performance. But more dramatic than his career improvement was the spiritual rebirth that Berkowitz seemed to experience in Kentucky. He took to attending services at Beth Haven Baptist Church in Louisville and soon changed from an indifferent Jew to an ardent Christian.

Not content living at home, Berkowitz enlisted in the army in 1971. Army psychological assessments described him as a normal recruit who would adjust well to infantry training.

Berkowitz's religious upbringing had been minimal: He'd avoided formal instruction and had never learned Hebrew. But this lonely, alienated northerner discovered a powerful sense of belonging in the evangelical Christianity of the Bible Belt. He found the Baptist services "really uplifting. I never felt anything like that before in my life." The sermons, he noted, were all about "demons, sin, hell, eternal damnation."

David embraced his new faith with the zeal of a convert, enrolling in every program the Beth Haven Church had to offer. He would arrive at 9 a.m. on Sundays and sometimes stay until 10 o'clock at night. He also showed up for evening services on Wednesdays, Thursdays, and Fridays. He listened to radio preachers, read religious tracts, and became almost obsessive on the subjects of the end of the world and damnation for sinners. In May 1974 he underwent the ritual of full immersion in water as he was baptized as a member of the congregation. At last, it seemed, he belonged somewhere.

Aglow with passion for his new beliefs, Berkowitz became a sidewalk proselytizer, hungry to save souls—male ones, anyway. "I just wanted to see the men get to heaven," he told a prison psychiatrist. "They're all hard-working, clean-cut patriotic men. Who the hell needed those sluts, those go-go dancers. Too many women in heaven would spoil it." In meandering letters to his father he declared that he couldn't explain his new ideas: "It's all too deep," he wrote. "I feel like a saint sometimes." Before long, however, the religious high began to fade. "I could never stay at anything too long," Berkowitz explained.

It seemed an apt analysis. He was capable of intense and single-minded fervor; he'd shown it in his avid patriotism and his wholehearted religious conversion. But the pattern of his enthusiasms was to flare hotly and die, leaving only ashes. It was as though he constantly sought some cure for his loneliness, some mooring that would tell him who he was, where he belonged, where he was going. He clutched desperately, but the anchors never held.

In June 1974 he was given an honorable discharge from the army. He traveled back to his family in Co-op City, but the reunified household didn't fare well. Reviving the traits that had earned him the nicknames of Snoop and Spy, Berkowitz became compulsively suspicious of his father's second wife. He rummaged through her personal belongings, trying, he said, "to ascertain her motive in marrying my Dad, and to make sure that there were no other men in her life. I didn't trust her one bit." Berkowitz was also leery of his stepsister, who was in every way his opposite: gregarious, motivated, friendly. The comparison was galling; the newly returned soldier began spending more and more time away from home.

By this time, he'd reverted to the secret pyromania of his earlier youth—but now on an extraordinary scale. The full details of his fire-starting escapades were not made public at the time of his capture—understandably, perhaps, since they paled beside his other crimes. But if Berkowitz's claims are to be believed, between May 13, 1974, and his arrest in 1977, he set no

fewer than 1,411 fires. He left detailed records of every episode in journals for the years 1974, 1975, and 1977. Police never found a notebook for 1976. The journals were laid out on grids that included the dates and times of the fires, the streets and boroughs in which they occurred, the numbers of the local fireboxes, and the fire department codes indicating the types of responding apparatus. Some of the fires were in empty lots, others were in cars, and at least a few resulted in major blazes that destroyed buildings. It seemed that the anger and resentment that Berkowitz could not express adequately in words were blazing anonymously all over New York City.

While his secret compulsions grew, Berkowitz was still able to hide behind his unremarkable facade. In December 1974 Nat Berkowitz announced that he was moving to Florida. His hardware store had been robbed, souring him finally on urban living. David would stay behind, losing his last sympathetic contact in the city. With his father's help, he moved into an apartment on Barnes Avenue in the Bronx. He began driving a taxi for a living, and in the spring of 1975 he enrolled at Bronx Community College.

Amid other recruits, Berkowitz dismantles an M-16 rifle during basic training at Fort Dix, New Jersey. He never won combat glory, but he would later fall back on his knowledge of weaponry.

Yet, typically, Berkowitz had no idea of what he wanted to do or become. "I wanted to go to college to specialize in something," he said, "but I didn't know what." He skipped school often, and when he did go to class he usually sat in the back of the room, abstracted and silent. He lived "in his own world, preoccupied with himself," remembers an acquaintance from those days.

Berkowitz may have lacked academic drive, but he was not without focus, one that was just as intense as his long-vanished patriotism and his religious conversion had been. He'd taken on a new project that he found all consuming: He wanted to find his natural father. After Nat Berkowitz moved to Florida, David joined an organization called ALMA, the Adoptee's Liberty Movement Association, which gives counsel and emotional support to adoptees searching for their birth parents. At an ALMA meeting he told the story of his mother's death and was flabbergasted to hear the audience laughing. Many other adoptees, he was informed, heard a similar story. His mother was more than likely alive.

David pressed Nat Berkowitz for the truth and got it. The son was jolted by what he learned: that he was "an accident," as he put it, "a mistake, never meant to be born—unwanted." The bittersweet tragedy of innocently killing his mother by being born was supplanted by a more brutal truth—that his birth mother had cast him aside. He had to find this woman, he concluded, and he set about the task with fervor, working almost around the clock. While he labored, his other compulsions were put on hold. Even his obsessive fire starting was pushed aside for a time.

The methodical care that Berkowitz devoted to his new obsession was impressive. He got a copy of his original birth certificate, discovered from it that he was born in Brooklyn to a woman named Betty Falco, and began calling every Falco in the Brooklyn telephone directory. He came up empty, but, acting on a tip from ALMA, he went to a library and began combing through out-of-date phone books. Digging back to 1965, he found a Betty Falco. Berkowitz made an inspired guess: Calling an information operator, he asked for Betty Falco at the 1965 address. She was still there; her number was absent from current phone directories because it was unlisted.

It was May 1975, almost Mother's Day. Berkowitz bought a greeting card and penned the following doggerel: "So, as once before / We've been Destined / To meet once more. / And I guess the time is now / I should say hello—but how? / Happy Mother's Day! / (You were my mother in a very special way.)"

He signed the cryptic message "R.F." for his birth name of Richard Falco and added his telephone number, then carried it to Betty Falco's Brooklyn apartment house and put it in her mailbox. Several days later, his phone rang. He had found her.

Mother and son arranged for a meeting at the apartment of Betty's daughter, David's half sister, whose name was Roslyn. The encounter must have been one of the most emotional moments in David Berkowitz's life. The shy, nervous woman he met apologized for giving him up for adoption. She spoke of the circumstances surrounding his birth and in the process revealed that even his assumptions regarding his natural father's feelings about him were a myth. The man who sired him did not blame him, or hate him, or care about him one way or another.

Cataclysmic as these revelations must have been, in later years Berkowitz never described his reunion with his mother in other than matter-of-fact terms. His initial reaction, he would say, was mainly disappointment: "I wasn't shocked. I wasn't scared," he said. "It wasn't the least bit painful. I felt pity for her." Probed more deeply on the issue, however, he would reveal a hairline crack in his normally bland demeanor. "I still, to this day, have negative feelings for my mom," he finally told a psychiatrist. "I don't have it in me to totally forgive her."

Nonetheless, mother and son struck up a continuing relationship: David visited her and his half sister regularly on weekends for the next year. But if finding his birth family was supposed to fill the void inside him, apparently it didn't, any more than patriotism or religion had. On June 6, 1975, only a few weeks after the momentous reunion, Berkowitz started lighting fires again.

During the time he was looking for his family, Berkowitz's attendance at Bronx Community College dried up entirely. He took a job as a security guard near John F. Kennedy Airport, working midnight to 8 a.m. His main company during these lonely hours were the guard dogs that went with him on rounds. His isolation from the rest of humanity was now nearly complete, and by his own account, it was sometime during this period that he first began hearing voices. Over time, they assumed identities in his mind as demons, urging him on to violence.

Aside from his mission of finding his mother, Berkowitz was barely leading a life at all. He went to work and he came home, to subsist on a diet of TV dinners, soda, and milk. Dirty dishes stacked up in the apartment, and the floor was littered with trash. In place of a shade on his window was a dull gray blanket, nailed in place to permanently block the sun. His bed was a bare mattress on the floor.

His work life was just as bleak. He quit his security job and became a duct worker for an air-conditioning company. His foreman remembers him as "quiet and a loner," so despondent on some occasions that he would break into tears. He was profoundly depressed and, increasingly, dangerously paranoid. "Dear Dad," began a November 1975 letter to his father in Florida, "it's cold and gloomy here in New York, but that's okay, because the weather fits my mood—gloomy. Dad, the world is getting dark now. I can feel it more and more. The people, they are developing a hatred for me. You wouldn't believe how much some people hate me. Many of them want to kill me. I don't even know these people, but they still hate me. Most of them are young. I walk down the street and they spit and kick at me. The girls call me ugly and they bother me the most. The guys just laugh."

After penning the message, Berkowitz vanished from his job and holed up in his apartment for 28 days. So alone had he become by then, so nearly invisible to those around him,

that no one even called to find out where he was. At about the same time, he applied for a New York State rifle permit. It was granted early the following year.

A crisis was coming to a head. In Berkowitz's alienation, the disembodied voices that had grown more insistent in recent months became his only companions. More and more, these hostile emanations took form in his mind as dogs. No one knows exactly how this fixation began. Berkowitz was bitten once by one of the guard dogs he handled on his security job, but the beasts that now haunted his psyche were entirely different. They could talk and, as he told it, "they acted human. But they weren't. They began to howl things. Yell like maniacs. They threw tantrums. Strange things. They wanted to get at children, to tear them up."

"I had come under torment," he later told investigators. "There was constant noise, howling noises. Everybody heard it. I never spoke to anyone about it." Indeed, there was no one, really, to speak to.

On March 2, 1975—in the midst of his fevered search for Betty Falco—Berkowitz

David Berkowitz kept a journal of more than 3,000 New York City fires, many of which he set himself. His meticulous record includes the type of equipment responding and the weather conditions.

DATE	BOX	Location		WORK	Time
				Q	18-24	002
				Q	92	011
		82 Ave. + 217. St.		Q	19-21	0
4/2/77	6699	61 Ave. + 262 ST.		Bx	*+2 struc vac comm	2
4/2/77	6452	Marathon Pkwy. + Thebes Ave		Bx	19-22	
4/2/77	4373 (TA)	Adee + Edson		Bx	18-23	
4/16/77	4361 (TAS)	E. Gun Hill Rd. + MACE		Bx	19-23	
5/24/77	3595	Webster bet. Gun Hill + E.233		Bx	*+2 struc vac comm	
5/26/77	2245 (ERS)	River + E. 151 ST.		Bx	19-22	
5/26/77	4373 (TA)	Adee + Edson		Q	92	
6/2/77	4027 (TAS)	Ferry Point Park		K	18-	
6/16/77	7139	40th Ave. + 11 ST.		K	18-	
7/2/77	2830	Bay shore Pkwy + Bay 13 St.		K	18	
7/3/77	3848	13th Ave + 78 ST		Bx	18	
7/3/77	2830	Bay shore Pkwy. + Bay 13 St.		Bx	*	
		+ E. 151 St				

I *wasn't going to rob her, or touch her, or rape her. I just wanted to kill her.*

slipped out after dark with a newly acquired 12-gauge shotgun. He spotted what he later described as a muzzled German shepherd, surrounded by a pack of other canines. Drawing a bead on the shepherd, he shot it. The killing somehow fit into the demonic fantasy world that was now Berkowitz's mental terrain, the prime substance of his universe. He left traces of its beginnings in his apartment on Barnes Avenue. Scrawled graffiti defaced the walls: "Kill for my Master" and "I turn children into Killers!" Around a gash in a plaster wall a message proclaimed: "In this hole lives the Wicked King."

Corrosively lonely, ill-fed, suspicious, and filled with rage, Berkowitz sought relief from his internal clamor in driving the streets of his father's old neighborhood in the Bronx. The pressure was mounting, the demon voices urging him to kill. On Christmas Eve, 1975, he tried to obey.

Early in the evening he tucked a hunting knife into the waist of his blue jeans and covered it with a jacket. Climbing into his car, he drove to Co-op City. He wound in and out along the roads around the complex's supermarket until he spied a woman leaving the store. According to Berkowitz's later account, the voices in his head told him that this was the one: "She has to be sacrificed!" the demons commanded. Berkowitz double-parked and shuffled after his prospective victim. About 30 feet from the nearest street lamp, he caught up with her and stabbed her in the back.

"She didn't do anything," he later recalled. "She just turned and looked at me." Then, as Berkowitz raised the knife again, the woman began to wail. Incredibly, the would-be killer was shocked by this: "It was terrible," he recollected. "I didn't know what the hell to do. It wasn't like the movies. She was staring at my knife and screaming."

The woman dropped her groceries and, still shrieking, began grappling with Berkowitz. He stabbed repeatedly, but to no apparent effect. Finally he panicked and bolted away from both his intended victim and his car.

There is no official record of this incident, only the assailant's own testimony. The woman either was not injured by the clumsy attack or was not cut seriously enough to bother going to the hospital. Neither did she report the assault to the authorities. For Berkowitz, everything about the incident was baffling. He seemed unable to understand why someone would struggle to live, would not complacently accept death. "I wasn't going to rob her, or touch her, or rape her," he told police in bewilderment. "I just wanted to kill her."

Minutes after this botched first attack, Berkowitz found another chance to vent his madness. His flight had taken him to the perimeter of Co-op City, within sight of his father's old apartment building, close to a pedestrian bridge over the New York State Thruway. Michelle Forman, 15 years old and a sophomore at a nearby high school, was walking across the bridge. Berkowitz pursued her and stabbed at her head from behind. He took three more thrusts at her upper body, then two more at the teenager's face. In shock, Forman flailed out, then fell to the concrete, writhing and screaming. "I never heard anyone scream like that," Berkowitz said later. "I kept stabbing and nothing would happen. I just ran off."

Bleeding profusely, Forman nonetheless tried to stop her attacker by grabbing his legs. As he vanished, she staggered toward her parents' apartment building, hit the lobby buzzer, and collapsed. She was found lying in a pool of blood: One of Berkowitz's six thrusts with the knife had collapsed one of her lungs.

Michelle Forman survived, but there was little in her account to authorities that could lead them to her assailant. Berkowitz, meantime, had fled to a diner close to the crime scene. He listened to the police sirens as he compulsively gobbled a huge meal and worried that he had failed to appease the demons.

Less than a month after the attack on Michelle Forman, his rifle permit arrived. He drove to Brooklyn and bought the Commando Mark III semiautomatic for $152.50. He also purchased four boxes of ammunition.

In February 1976 Berkowitz moved out of his drab apartment on Barnes Avenue. He left New York City entirely, renting a place over the garage of a married couple in the nearby suburb of New Rochelle. He was hoping to make a new start. That summer he'd taken the U.S. Civil Service examination and applied for a job with the post office. He'd scored 80.5 percent—fairly high, given his limited education. It was the prospect of new employment that prompted his change of apartments; he'd had word that he'd get a postal job starting March 15 at a salary of $13,000 per year—more than he'd ever earned before. He was to be a letter sorter.

Berkowitz's new landlords, Nann and Jack Cassara, accepted a $200 deposit and gave him a two-year lease. The new surroundings were far more pleasant than Berkowitz's cramped flat in the Bronx, but if the new tenant expected a move to the suburbs would still the demon voices, he was wrong. The aural hallucinations were becoming ever more intense, the devil dogs howling for blood.

The hallucinations came to focus on the Cassaras' pet, another German shepherd. According to Berkowitz, the dog's nocturnal barking made his life an utter hell: "Sometimes I couldn't come home to sleep," he said. "Sometimes I had to drive around all night." And the one canine was soon joined by others in a terrible cacophony. One Sunday morning the invisible noise became so unendurable that Berkowitz rushed screaming out onto the driveway below his apartment. An alarmed Jack Cassara came out to see what was wrong. Berkowitz shook his fists and yelled, "This place is a goddamn kennel!"

Unbeknown to the Cassaras, they too had become enmeshed in their tenant's mad fantasies. During his stay in New Rochelle, Berkowitz became convinced that some of his demons—the most important ones—lived not in the dogs, but in their owners. In his fevered imagination, Jack Cassara was really General Jack Cosmo, commander of the dog-demon army. Cosmo controlled the tormenting voices; he was the Lucifer of Berkowitz's private Hell.

Nann Cassara fared little better: "I thought they were members of the human race," Berkowitz said of his landlords. "They weren't."

In April Berkowitz tried again to flee his torment. He moved, leaving behind his $200 security deposit. His next stop would be his last before prison: 35 Pine Street, an apartment building in a quiet residential section of Yonkers. Again, the demons pursued him. General Jack Cosmo was now far away, but, Berkowitz surmised, the demon chieftan still exerted power. There was also a sort of subprince among the demons in Yonkers. He was Sam Carr, 63, the gaunt, semiretired owner of a local telephone answering service. Carr's home was at 316 Warburton Avenue, which was visible off in the distance from Berkowitz's new apartment. David had gotten acquainted with the older man when he stopped by to chat one day. Sam Carr had three children, including a daughter named Wheat who worked as a dispatcher for the Yonkers Police Department. He also had a black Labrador retriever. The dog horrified Berkowitz with hideous psychic noises. According to the killer, Sam Carr worked directly for Jack Cosmo and was a "high official of the Devil's legion."

Berkowitz had now nearly completed in his mind the set and ensemble of a grade-B horror movie. The satanic chain of command ran from Warburton Avenue to Wicker Street and a three-story frame house visible from his apartment window. At 18 Wicker Street lived Robert Neto, transformed in Berkowitz's mind into a demon known as Joquin, or the Joker. The Joker was formerly the Number Two demon, answering to General Jack Cosmo, Berkowitz believed, but now Sam Carr had usurped his power. Joquin shared a house with another prince of darkness known only as the Duke of Death. Next door, at 22 Wicker Street, was the home of evil John Wheaties, who ran a hostel of sorts for the demons who tortured Berkowitz. Devils from all around the world stopped at Wheaties's home to rest. Both these houses—plus Cosmo's home in New Rochelle—would soon have an even more nefarious purpose in Berkowitz's dream universe. When he killed, he later told investigators, the demons on the scene would snatch the souls of the victims and take them to one of the three demonic residents. "They chain the souls and have sex with them forever," he explained. "It's messy. It's brutal."

In the ether of these strange delusions, Berkowitz had fashioned a place where he finally belonged. He was Sam's

In this aerial view of Yonkers, Berkowitz's apartment complex, Pineview Towers, is in the center at the top, while neighbor Sam Carr's home is in the bottom left corner. An inset reveals the sunless squalor of the killer's bedroom.

slave, ordained to carry out the will of an entity he called a "speck of evil cosmic dust that has fallen to earth and flourished." He would later claim that Sam used him as his tool: "It was Sam that was working through me," he said. "People should take me seriously. This Sam and his demons have been responsible for a lot of killing."

On May 13, 1976, Berkowitz made a bizarre attempt to fight off the demon company crowding around him. Filling a bottle with gasoline, he made a Molotov cocktail and carried it to Sam Carr's home. Lighting the wick, he flung the bottle toward the house and ran home without waiting to observe the results. The fire burned harmlessly on the driveway; no one was injured. But Sam Carr was left to wonder who might want to persecute him in such an eccentric way.

The next month, Berkowitz was on the move again, traveling to Florida to visit his father and spend some time in Fort Lauderdale. He whiled away several days at the beach and barely spoke to anyone. After a week, he drove on to Houston to visit an old army buddy, Billy Dan Parker. The Texas trip was not entirely a social call; Berkowitz had a purpose in mind: He wanted to buy a handgun.

Parker, a construction worker, was remarkably hospitable, allowing his guest to stay for nearly a month. When the time drew near for Berkowitz to leave, he asked his host to help him get a gun—for security, he said, on the long trip home. Parker was happy to help.

In a transaction that lasted only a few minutes, the pair walked into a Houston pawnshop, where Parker filled out the gun ownership forms required of Texas residents. The purchase was a Charter Arms Bulldog revolver for which Berkowitz paid $130. He also bought three boxes of .44-caliber ammunition. He left for New York City fully prepared to satisfy the demons.

As though lying in wait, the devils overtook Berkowitz soon after he returned to his solitary existence in New York. Frantic and sleepless, he decided on July 6 that he had to act. He began what would become a grisly ritual. Stuffing his pistol into a paper bag, he got into his car to cruise the streets. He was "looking for a victim," he said, "waiting for a signal." This particular night he caught sight of two women in a car, and somehow he knew that they were the ones. He followed them, watching as they pulled into a driveway in a hilly residential neighborhood in the Bronx. He parked his car and walked back in their direction, clutching the paper bag. By the time he reached the driveway he was at a full run, but the women had disappeared. By his own account, Berkowitz spent much of July this way, driving around, waiting for a signal.

At 1 a.m. on July 29 he was cruising in the Bronx when he spotted two young women sitting in a parked blue Oldsmobile. He swung around a corner and abandoned his car, pushing the bag-covered pistol into the waistband of his trousers. With his characteristic gait, he shuffled back toward the women, Donna Lauria, 18, a medical technician, and Jody Valenti, 19, a student nurse. They were parked in front of Lauria's home; her parents had just returned from a restaurant and had spoken to their daughter before going into the house. Donna had promised to follow in a minute. At 1:10 a.m., Berkowitz walked up to the passenger side of the Oldsmobile Cutlass, pulled his revolver from the paper bag, and assumed a semicrouch. He pulled the trigger five times.

As the car windows shattered, Donna Lauria raised her hands to protect herself. One of the .44-caliber bullets struck her in the right side of the neck, killing her quickly. Another bullet hit Jody Valenti in the thigh. She screamed and fell forward, landing on the car horn. Berkowitz dashed back to his car and drove away.

He would later recall seeing "thousands of little pieces of glass," but he didn't know if he'd killed anyone until he read the newspaper the next morning. He was elated to learn of Donna Lauria's death. "It just happens to be satisfying to get the source of the blood," he said later. "I felt that Sam was relieved. I came through." The shooting had taken place a short distance from the neighborhood where he was raised.

Down in Florida, Nat Berkowitz was growing more and more concerned: His son's letters were increasingly strange and disjointed. Nat urged David to see a psychiatrist, but the son refused. Nat enlisted David's half sister to press the matter, but by then her brother's visits had all but stopped. David had a new job, he claimed, and it kept him far too busy for socializing with his family.

On August 12, the demons broke a period of relative quiet, prompting Berkowitz to place an anonymous call to the police, complaining about the noise of someone named Joquin. A dispatcher at Yonkers police headquarters took the call at 4 a.m. and sent a squad car to investigate. The officers, of course, found nothing.

Berkowitz's .44-caliber Charter Arms Bulldog—shown here actual size—supplied the distinctive signature for the Son of Sam shootings. The handgun was not the kind usually associated with street crime.

But if the police could not find the clamoring Joquin, Berkowitz nevertheless knew he was there. On October 23, after a long, sleepless night filled with harangues from Joquin and a demon called the Blood Monster, the killer struck again. At 1:45 a.m. he dressed, tucked the .44 into his belt, and drove to the borough of Queens. At the corner of 159th Street and 33rd Avenue, he glimpsed a red Volkswagen occupied by two people. Inside were Rosemary Keenan, 18, daughter of a New York City police detective, and Carl Denaro, 20, who was four days away from reporting for duty in the air force. The pair had known each other at Queens College and had met earlier that evening in a bar. Denaro escorted the policeman's daughter home, and they'd tarried in the car for a while, reluctant to say good night.

Berkowitz crept up on foot, approaching from the passenger side of the VW. He could see that one of the car's occupants had long, wavy hair. He raised the .44 and squeezed off five noisy rounds. As the echoes from his shots died away, screams rose from inside the car. But this time the shooter didn't run from the noise; he stayed behind for a minute to observe the effect of his fusillade. Rosemary Keenan was unharmed in the driver's seat, but Carl Denaro had a bullet in the back of his head. Terrified, Keenan started the car and sped away.

After two months of treatment, Denaro recovered. But the metal plate that had replaced a portion of his shattered skull ruled out any hopes of a career in the air force.

On November 25, David Berkowitz made what would be his last visit to his mother and her family, joining them for Thanksgiving dinner. At the end of the evening his kin prevailed on him to spend the night at his half sister's home. He was terribly restless, however. His sister Roslyn remembers that he seemed like a wild animal. He told her that he would never hurt her. She had no idea what he meant.

The next night, high-school student Donna DeMasi, 16, and her friend Joanne Lomino, 18, were walking toward Lomino's house in Queens after an evening in Manhattan. Shortly after midnight DeMasi noticed a strange man standing behind a nearby street lamp. She nudged her friend and the two of them walked quickly to Lomino's house, where they climbed the steps to the door. At that moment, David Berkowitz stepped into view and started to ask them a question: "Do you know where . . ."

As he spoke, he reached under his jacket and produced the .44-caliber pistol. Firing twice, he hit both women: DeMasi at the intersection of her neck and shoulder, and Lomino in the lower spine. They screamed and collapsed, falling to opposite sides of the stoop. Berkowitz watched, fascinated, then fired three shots at the Lomino house before running away. Next door, off-duty police officer Ben Taormina heard a noise and peered out of his front window. He saw the stricken women and rushed out to give artificial respiration as the first police car arrived. The bullet that hit Donna DeMasi caused no permanent damage. Joanne Lomino was not so fortunate: Her spine was crushed. She was paralyzed for life.

No howling voices beckoned David Berkowitz for the next two months. Then, on January 29, 1977, the mayhem began anew. Climbing out of bed at 10 p.m., he once again carried his loaded revolver down the street to his car. He made his way cautiously out of Yonkers to the Bronx-Whitestone Bridge and crossed into Queens. Heeding his inner demons, he proceeded to the Forest Hills section of Queens and parked at a corner in a prosperous neighborhood not far from the Long Island commuter tracks. He got out of the car and started to walk. At 12:15 a.m. a couple hurried past him, and Berkowitz caught a glimpse of a woman's long dark hair. He followed the couple to a blue

Gunned down in late July 1976, Donna Lauria was the first victim of the so-called .44-Caliber Killer. Berkowitz believed that his inner demons commanded him to kill Lauria; they also promised that she would become his "princess."

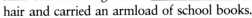

DONNA LAURIA

Pontiac Firebird and watched them get in. The driver switched on the ignition, then turned and kissed the woman as they waited for the engine to warm up. From his hiding place behind a tree, Berkowitz shuffled over to the car. Inside were John Diel, 30, a bartender, and his fiancée, a beautiful 26-year-old Austrian émigré named Christine Freund. As they broke their embrace and Diel turned to put the Pontiac in gear, the right front window shattered. Freund screamed as two bullets smashed into her right temple and neck, and a third struck the dashboard of the car. In shock and panic, Diel leaned on the horn, then scrambled out of the car and raced down the street, screaming for help. Someone who heard his shouts alerted the police, and within four minutes a squad car arrived. Not 10 minutes after the shooting, Christine Freund was at a nearby hospital, but at 4 a.m. she was pronounced dead.

Thus far in his career as a killer, David Berkowitz had been remarkably lucky. His crimes had taken place in a number of different police jurisdictions, and this meant, among other things, that a cross-referencing of reports and ballistic analyses was unlikely to happen very quickly. Moreover, the big bullets from his large-caliber gun had mostly shattered on impact, so there was little evidence for the ballistics experts to look at. As a result, the law enforcement agencies of metropolitan New York did not yet know that they were looking for a single killer in a number of scattered slayings.

This changed with the murder of Christine Freund. The following day, Bronx detectives called their counterparts in Queens and pointed out that the shooting of the previous night sounded similar to the murder of Donna Lauria in their jurisdiction. The common denominators were the mode of attack and the large caliber of the weapon. Further checking turned up another similar case, the double shooting of Joanne Lomino and Donna DeMasi. On February 2 a task force was organized under the direction of police Captain Joseph Borrelli, commander of the Queens homicide division.

But police were as yet far from homing in on David Berkowitz, and on March 8 the dogs began to howl again in the murderer's agitated mind. Although a touch of spring was in the air, he donned a heavy ski jacket and a stocking cap and set out for Forest Hills. This time he parked near the stadium that was, in those days, the site of the U.S. Open tennis tournament. It was early evening, but quite dark, and he wandered into an exclusive enclave called Forest Hills Gardens. As he strolled along a street near the edge of the community, he saw a young woman walking toward him. She had long dark hair and carried an armload of school books.

Virginia Voskerichian, 21, was the daughter of an Armenian émigré. She was a student at Columbia University, majoring in Russian language studies, and had been a naturalized United States citizen for less than two years. When the pretty young woman was nearly face-to-face with Berkowitz, he pulled the gun from his pocket. She raised her books in a vain effort to protect herself, but a single shot struck her in the mouth, hurling her backward into some bushes. She died instantly.

Berkowitz lumbered back to his car. On the way, he passed the first person ever to get a good look at him at the site of a murder, a 59-year-old civil engineer whose name has never been released by the police. "Hi, mister," Berkowitz said.

Seconds later, the killer was almost caught. A carload of police detectives spotted him from a distance, noting that he had slowed to a walk when he saw them coming. Unfortunately, the detectives were on routine street crime detail and not looking, in particular, for a murderer. They pulled alongside Berkowitz and were on the verge of questioning him when the radio announced the shooting of Virginia Voskerichian. The cops zoomed away and the slayer escaped.

As Berkowitz returned to Yonkers, he ran into a two-woman police patrol at the toll plaza of the Bronx-Whitestone Bridge. The officers had instructions to watch for a car containing a lone white male, a potential suspect in the Voskerichian murder. The Bulldog .44 was in full view on the seat beside the killer, and his Ford was just two cars away from the inspection point. At that moment, the policewomen decided to call it a day.

The next morning, the special task force met at the Queens 112th Precinct. "I think we've got a psycho here,"

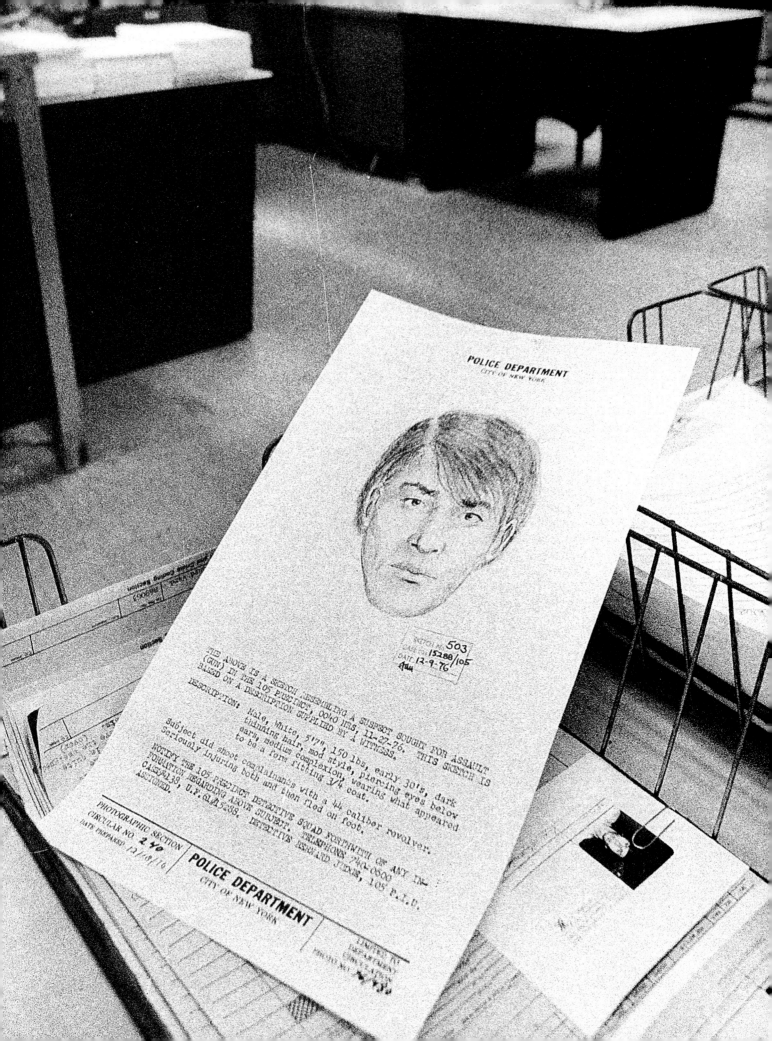

POLICE DEPARTMENT
CITY OF NEW YORK

PATROL N. 503
15288/105
DATE 12-9-76

THE ABOVE IS A SKETCH RESEMBLING A SUSPECT SOUGHT FOR ASSAULT
(GUN) IN THE 105 PRECINCT, 0040 HRS, 11-27-76. THIS SKETCH IS
BASED ON A DESCRIPTION SUPPLIED BY A WITNESS.

DESCRIPTION: Male, white, 5'7", 150 lbs, early 30's, dark
thinning hair, mod style, piercing eyes below
early, medium complexion, wearing what appeared
to be a form fitting 3/4 coat.

Subject did shoot complainants both and then fled on foot.
Seriously injuring

NOTIFY THE 105 PRECINCT DETECTIVE SQUAD FORTHWITH OF ANY IN-
FORMATION REGARDING ABOVE SUBJECT. TELEPHONE 740-0600
CASE #138, U.F.61A 5208. DETECTIVE BERNARD JENKS, 105 P.D.U.
ASSIGNED.

PHOTOGRAPHIC SECTION
CIRCULAR NO 240
DATE PREPARED 12/18/76

POLICE DEPARTMENT
CITY OF NEW YORK

The second woman Berkowitz killed was Christine Freund *(right)*, shown here in costume-party garb. Student Virginia Voskerichian *(far right)* was third to die, slain while walking home after an evening spent studying.

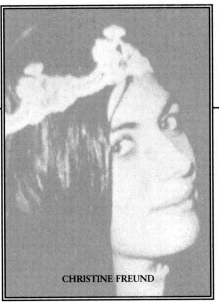

CHRISTINE FREUND

VIRGINIA VOSKERICHIAN

Captain Joseph Borrelli told his crew, speculating further that the .44-Caliber Killer probably hated women. Ballistics had matched the bullet that killed Virginia Voskerichian with the slug that had ended Donna Lauria's life. Borrelli requested 14 additional men. A day later, New York City Police Commissioner Michael Codd announced at a Manhattan press conference that there was not only a link between those two killings, but among others as well. A borough-level task force was no longer going to be enough, and Deputy Inspector Timothy Dowd, a 37-year veteran whose duties ranged throughout the city, was being given charge of an expanded investigation. Berkowitz read of these developments with great interest: "I knew that they'd get me some day," he said later. "The only question was how and when."

Caught up suddenly in a citywide drama of his own creation, Berkowitz began to crave the spotlight. As the frenetic New York tabloids ran story after story about the .44-Caliber Killer, he set to work composing a letter that would enlighten the world about the "conspiracy of evil" that was controlling his path. He worked on the letter off and on for three days, beginning on April Fools' Day. And when he was through, he penned two additional messages. Berkowitz would dole out these missives over the weeks that followed, leaving the longest of them at the site of his next major crime.

The first message was received by Sam Carr on April 10. It was an anonymous note that carped about the barking of Carr's dog. "Our lives have been torn apart because of this dog," the letter declared. It was signed "A Citizen." Nine days later Carr got a second letter, this one much more menacing in tone. "I can see that there will be no peace in my life, or my families life, until I end yours," it said. Shaken this time, Carr turned the letter over to Yonkers police, who filed a report of citizen harassment.

By then, however, Berkowitz had given New York City something much more horrifying to contemplate. On the night of April 16 he left his apartment and began cruising aimlessly through the Bronx. Less than two miles from Co-op City, he was stopped at a routine police traffic checkpoint. Asked for his license, registration, and insurance cards, he failed to produce the insurance documents. The result was a summons to appear in traffic court on July 6. Berkowitz accepted the summons and went blithely on his way, driving for hours, until he found himself back in the Bronx. He was, in fact, less than half a mile from the house where he'd killed Donna Lauria, and he spotted a couple in a car. It was 3 a.m.

Stalking victims had by now become routine for him. Parking a block away, Berkowitz walked back to the maroon Mercury he'd just seen. Approaching the passenger side of the car, he leveled his weapon, crouched, and fired four times. Inside the Mercury, Alexander Esau, 20, and Valentina Suriani, 18, both slumped down in the front seat. Suriani, a student actress, and Esau, a tow truck operator, had stopped for a moment of intimacy after a movie and dinner. Suriani had been driving; Esau, who sported shoulder-length dark hair, was in the passenger seat. Struck in the head, Suriani died almost instantly. Esau expired about two hours later at a hospital.

This time Berkowitz had deliberately killed both the woman and the man. The demons had ordered that both should die, he would claim: "General Jack Cosmo had a wife," the killer explained, and she had demanded a playmate of her own.

With the two new murders, what was already a sensational case of serial killing was about to explode into the biggest manhunt in New York's history. One of the first policemen to arrive at the scene of the Suriani-Esau murders had discovered an envelope on the ground about 10 feet from the slain couple's car. It was addressed to Joseph Borrelli and printed in slanting block letters. "Dear Captain Joseph Borrelli," the message began:

"I am deeply hurt by your calling me a wemon hater. I am not. But i am a monster. I am the 'son of Sam.' I am a little brat.

An in-basket at the 109th Precinct in Queens holds an artist's sketch of the suspect in the November 1976 shootings of Donna DeMasi and Joanne Lomino.

"When father Sam gets drunk he gets mean. He beats his family. Sometimes he ties me up to the back of the house. Other times he locks me in the garage. Sam loves to drink blood.

" 'Go out and kill,' commands father Sam.

"Behind our house some rest. Mostly young—raped and slaughtered—their blood drained—just bones now.

"Pap Sam keeps me locked in the attic too. I can't get out but I look out the attic window and watch the world go by.

"I feel like an outsider. I am on a different wavelength then everybody else—programmed too kill.

"However, to stop me you must kill me. Attention all police: Shoot me first—shoot to kill or else keep out of my way or you will die!

"Papa Sam is old now. He needs some blood to preserve his youth. He has had too many heart attacks. 'Ugh, me hoot, it hurts, sonny boy.'

"I miss my pretty princess most of all. She's resting in our ladies house. But i'll see her soon.

"I am the 'monster'—'Beelze-bub'—the chubby behemouth.

"I love to hunt. Prowling the streets looking for fair game—tasty meat. The wemon of Queens are prettyist of all. I must be the water they drink. I live for the hunt—my life. Blood for papa.

"Mr. Borelli, sir, I don't want to kill any more. No sur, no more but I must, 'honour thy father.'

"I want to make love to the world. I love people. I don't belong on earth. Return me to yahoos.

"To the people of Queens, I love you. And i want to wish all of you a happy Easter. May God bless you in this life and in the next. And for now I say goodbye and goodnight.

"POLICE: Let me haunt you with these words:

"I'll be back!

"I'll be back!

"To be interrpreted as—bang bang, bang, bank, bang—ugh!!

"Yours in murder

"Mr. Monster."

To Berkowitz, the meaning of this message may have been crystal clear. But to most readers—the bulk of the letter was speedily released to the press—it sounded like the ravings of a bona fide lunatic. It confirmed the tabloids' frenzied speculation that a demonic madman was stalking the city. The letter was frightening, as Berkowitz doubtless intended, and it personalized the previously anonymous killer in a way that must have given him great pleasure: He had an identity at last.

Overnight, more than 100 detectives were assigned to what became known as Task Force Omega, the search for Son of Sam. Police in unmarked cars beefed up patrols of residential areas in Queens and Brooklyn. But for a scared public, this was not enough: Demands for an even broader police effort began to rain down on city officials, and soon the force would grow to 200. One of those drafted for the search was detective Redmond Keenan, 51, whose 18-year-old daughter Rosemary had narrowly escaped death alongside Carl Denaro.

Despite the increased police presence, nightlife in the outlying boroughs was grinding to a halt. Discos were empty on weekends, and restaurants went hungry for customers. The Forest Hills area in particular all but shut down in the evenings. And there were other signs of the fright inspired by Son of Sam. Since several of his victims had long dark hair, women rushed to have their hair trimmed short or, in some cases, dyed blonde.

An average of 250 tips about the case flooded police hot lines daily, and every possible lead had to be checked out. Police also undertook a dogged search for the whereabouts of every one of the

Shot dead in their parked car, Valentina Suriani and Alexander Esau perished one block away from Suriani's apartment building. The female-hating Berkowitz later expressed distaste that the demons had forced him to kill a man.

VALENTINA SURIANI   ALEXANDER ESAU

28,000 Charter Bulldog revolvers ever sold by the gun's manufacturer. None of the investigative measures seemed to lead anywhere.

On April 27, in the midst of this citywide hubbub, Sam Carr heard a shot outside his home. He found his dog, Harvey, bleeding in the yard, and saw a man wearing jeans and a yellow shirt running away. Carr shouted at the man to stop, but David Berkowitz kept running. The wound was in the dog's flank and wouldn't prove fatal; the bullet was never extracted. Yonkers police investigated. They turned up nothing, but the shooting was peculiar enough to linger in their minds.

Within the next month, authorities released a psychological profile of the killer, describing him as "neurotic, schizophrenic, and paranoid." Among other things, the document speculated that the Son of Sam regarded himself as a victim of demonic possession. Police Commissioner Codd added his view—uncannily accurate—that the murderer was "probably shy and odd, a loner inept in establishing personal relationships, especially with women." The task force's motive in releasing the profile may have been to goad the killer into making a mistake.

And goad him it did. On June 3, the tabloid New York Daily News published a bombshell: Columnist Jimmy Breslin had received a letter from the Son of Sam, and the newspaper was printing selected portions of it in installments over the next two days. Like the first letter, this one was rambling, egocentric, and chilling. It harked back obsessively to the killer's first victim, Donna Lauria, and it purported to offer the police new clues for solving the case.

"Hello from the cracks in the sidewalks of New York City," the letter began, "and from the ants that dwell in these cracks and feed on the dried blood of the dead that has settled into these cracks." It rambled on at length: "Don't think that because you haven't heard from me for a while that I went to sleep. No, rather, I am still here, like a spirit roaming the night. Thirsty, hungry, seldom stopping to rest; anxious to please Sam," the killer wrote. "He won't let me stop killing until he gets his fill of blood." Berkowitz advised Breslin: "you can forget about me if you like, [but] you must not forget Donna Lauria and you cannot let the people forget her either. She was a very sweet girl."

The letter was laced with bad melodrama, including a fantasy about being "blown away by cops with smoking .38's." The police insisted that one page of the Breslin letter be kept out of the papers. It included a series of clues ("some names to help you along") that Berkowitz suggested the police run through their National Crime Information Center. Mostly, they were the names of demons—the Duke of Death, Wicked King Wicker, the 22 Disciples of Hell. But there was also one name that seemed at least possible to apply to a real human being: "John Wheaties, rapist and suffocator of young girls." Berkowitz signed the missive "'Sam's creation' .44."

Police technicians labored over the letter for weeks, but in the end they were only able to lift two partial fingerprints from it—not enough for a match. Most of the let-

Sam Carr fondly scratches his dog, Harvey, another victim of Berkowitz's gunplay. Harvey survived, but a slug remained in his flank.

Vol. 57. No. 6

DAILY NEWS

New York, Sunday, June 5, 1977

Price: 35 cents

Partly sunny, 80.
Clear tonight, 50s.
Cloudy tomorrow.
Details, page 117.

Breslin to .44 Killer:
GIVE UP! IT'S ONLY WAY OUT

NOT KNOWING WHAT THE FUTURE
HOLDS I SHALL SAY FAREWELL AND
I WILL SEE YOU AT THE NEXT JOB.
OR SHOULD I SAY YOU WILL SEE
MY HANDIWORK AT THE NEXT JOB?
REMEMBER MS. LAURIA. THANK YOU.

IN THEIR BLOOD
AND
FROM THE GUTTER

"SAM'S CREATION".44

HERE ARE SOME NAMES TO HELP YOU ALONG.
FORWARD THEM TO THE INSPECTOR FOR
USE BY N.C.I.C.:
    "THE DUKE OF DEATH"
"THE WICKED KING WICKER"
"THE TWENTY TWO DISCIPLES OF HELL"
"JOHN 'WHEATIES' - RAPIST AND SUFF-
OCATER OF YOUNG GIRLS.

PS: J.B. PLEASE INFORM ALL THE
DETECTIVES WORKING THE
SLAYINGS TO REMAIN

A Sunday edition of the *Daily News* featuring columnist Jimmy Breslin's plea to the killer to surrender sold out within an hour of hitting the newsstands. By the end of the day more than a million copies of the paper were sold—a record surpassed only on the day Berkowitz was caught. At police insistence, the paper withheld parts of the letter Berkowitz wrote to Breslin, including a list of weird names that were meaningful only to the killer.

172

ter seemed practically meaningless, so Task Force Omega was left to ponder the writer's references to Donna Lauria.

Berkowitz had developed a peculiar obsession about the first of his victims. He believed that Sam had promised him Lauria's soul after he killed her. She was the "pretty princess" of the first Son of Sam letter. But Sam's offer had proved to be a lie: In some terrible, distorted way, the slain woman had come to symbolize for Berkowitz love thwarted and love withheld. He now connected this love with murder.

The fact that Son of Sam was carrying on his macabre campaign of public letter writing was taken as a sign that, in the long run, he would probably reveal himself. Some believed it was also a sign that he actually wanted to be caught. But there would be more death and suffering before that happened.

On June 10 Berkowitz's former landlord Jack Cassara received a get-well card. On the envelope was the name "Carr" with a return address in Yonkers. The card bore a picture of a German shepherd and a truly baffling inscription. "Dear Jack," the message began, "I'm sorry to hear about that fall you took from the roof of your house. JUST WANT TO SAY 'I'M SORRY' BUT I'M SURE IT WON'T BE LONG UNTIL YOU FEEL MUCH BETTER, HEALTHY, WELL AND STRONG: Please be careful next time. Since your going to be confined for a long time, let us know if Nann needs anything." The card was signed "Sam & Francis."

Cassara was mystified. He hadn't fallen or hurt himself, and he didn't know anyone named Carr. Subsequent events would reveal that the entire episode had stemmed from Berkowitz's failing grip on reality. Once in prison he explained that he'd learned from a "demon dog" that Cassara had experienced an accident, and the news had prompted his gesture of concern.

What the card prompted was a call from Jack Cassara to the mysterious Sam Carr, at 316 Warburton Avenue. That

He won't let me stop killing until he gets his fill of blood.

same night, Jack and Nann Cassara visited Carr at his home, and they brought along the get-well card. Carr could offer no explanation, but he did say that he'd been getting some strange letters himself, letters threatening him and his dog. He went on to describe the gunshot wound to his pet, the shotgun blast that had killed a neighbor's German shepherd, and the Molotov cocktail that had landed in his driveway.

When the Cassaras returned home, they related these stories to their younger son, Stephen, and he wondered whether the strange assaults could be the work of their dog-hating former tenant, David Berkowitz. The Cassaras passed on this suspicion to Sam Carr, and his daughter Wheat relayed it to the local police. The police listened, but they heard nothing that sounded like proof that Berkowitz was causing Carr's difficulties. And nothing set off any bells that would cause them to link this harassment case with the Son of Sam murder investigation. There was, however, an interesting twist to the story: Another person in the same Yonkers neighborhood had complained of receiving bizarre letters.

This time it was Craig Glassman, a burly registered nurse and auxiliary deputy sheriff for Westchester County. In March Glassman had moved into apartment 6E, directly below Berkowitz. As a police volunteer, Glassman sometimes worked directing traffic at school crossings and special events, so he was often in and out of the building wearing his special green uniform and hat. Berkowitz found this proximity to a policeman so threatening that he'd incorporated Glassman into his private fantasy world. The part-time cop was now also a demon, a fiend named Gregunto Lacinto.

Soon Berkowitz was imagining hellish noises rising through the floor from Glassman's apartment. Gregunto Lacinto, he decided, had the power to enter his mind. Berkowitz's obsession with the new neighbor was recorded on the walls of his apartment: "As long as Craig Glassman is in the world, there will never be any peace, but there will be plenty of murders." Another inscription claimed that Glassman worshiped the devil and held power over Berkowitz.

On June 6 Glassman received a genuinely disturbing letter scrawled on blue-lined notebook paper. The writer called himself a slave and referred to Glassman as the master. "True, I am the killer," the letter said, "but Craig, the killings are at your command." The message raved on about how Glassman would burn on Judgment Day while the streets ran red with blood. Less than two weeks later, a second message arrived, and this time Glassman called the police. An ominous pattern of harassment reports was beginning to emerge in this Yonkers neighborhood.

Inside apartment 7E, Berkowitz's demonic inner choirs had once again pushed him to the brink of violence. On a muggy Saturday evening, June 25, he abandoned his garbage-strewn studio for the car—the .44, as usual, stashed in a paper bag. He drove to Queens this time, and eyeballed a disco called Elephas. The place was quiet; like most teen hangouts, it was barely surviving in the Son of Sam-depressed social climate of that summer. Berkowitz parked two blocks away and tucked the gun into his waistband. Walking back to within one block of the disco, he noticed a red Cadillac with two people talking inside. One was a girl. David came up to the passenger's window from the rear, crouched, and fired four times.

Earlier that evening 17-year-old Judy Placido had celebrated her graduation from St. Catherine's Roman Catholic Academy in the Bronx. After a party with her family she and three friends went to Elephas, where they discussed the danger posed by Son of Sam. They reassured one another

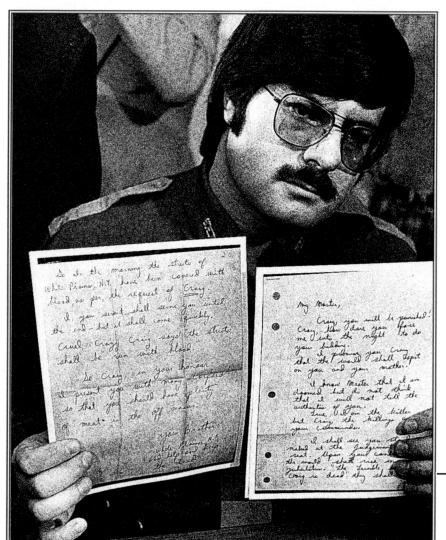

Neighbor Craig Glassman, who figured in Berkowitz's fantasies, holds threatening letters from the killer. Glassman was also mentioned on the walls of Berkowitz's apartment *(above)*.

that the killer struck only on clear nights, and this one was overcast. While at the disco Judy struck up a conversation with a young man from Queens named Salvatore Lupo. She stayed behind when her friends left, wishing to chat further with Sal. Shortly after 3 a.m. he was about to give her a ride home when the car window exploded.

Placido felt an oppressive ringing in her ears and sat helpless and dazed while her companion ran for help. After a few moments she staggered out of the car and collapsed. She'd been hit three times—in the neck, the shoulder, and the temple. Although she should have been dead, she wasn't. Sal Lupo, meanwhile, had been struck in the arm. Both of these young people would survive, but their assailant was nowhere to be found. Once again police had just missed an opportunity to capture Son of Sam. A squad car had been patrolling in the area around the nightclub until moments before the shooting.

Nearly two weeks after the Placido-Lupo shooting, police still had no idea how to find the killer. New York Mayor Abraham Beame announced that still more detectives would be assigned to the Son of Sam task force. July 29 was approaching, the first anniversary of Donna Lauria's death and the beginning of Berkowitz's shooting spree. The New York tabloids went into high gear, churning out fevered stories on the possible significance of the anniversary. But David Berkowitz would observe the big day in his own quirky fashion: He quit his job at the post office. Nothing else exceptional happened.

On July 30, however, Berkowitz was back on the prowl. After a tour of Queens and Manhattan he made his way to Brooklyn, a borough he hadn't yet visited on any of his murderous forays. Just before 2 a.m. he drove into the Jewish-Italian neighborhood of Bensonhurst, not far from where he had once worked as a security guard. He parked his car illegally next to a fire hydrant and got out to walk. As he headed up the street a police car drove by, and one of the patrolmen inside spotted the careless choice of parking places. As Berkowitz watched from a distance, an officer attached a summons to the Galaxie's windshield. Berkowitz retrieved the ticket and tossed it on the dashboard before resuming his walk.

Passing through a narrow entranceway, he wandered into a park that opened onto a stretch of water known as Gravesend Bay. This area, close by the soaring Verrazano-Narrows Bridge, was known to the killer as a lovers' lane. He spied a blue Corvette under a street lamp. In it were two people, one a woman with long brown hair. Berkowitz crept toward the back of the car.

Inside, Tommy Zaino, 19, part owner of an automobile-repair shop, and Debby Crescenco, 17, were kissing. The young woman was somewhat distracted: She knew that the style and color of her hair made her a target for Son of Sam. Beyond that, she disliked sitting in the parked car, especially under a street lamp. She asked her date to move the car, and he did—but only by about 50 feet. Minutes later, another car pulled into the spot just vacated. In it were Robert Violante, 20, a clothing salesman, and his date, Stacy Moskowitz, also 20, who worked as a secretary in the Empire State Building. This second couple had met only a few days earlier; this was their first formal date. They'd taken in a movie and gone to dinner; now they wanted to spend a few moments alone before heading back to the Moskowitz home.

By the time the Corvette's engine started up, Berkowitz had melted back into the darkness. But when Violante's Buick pulled into view, Son of Sam had no doubt that he'd found his victim for the night. It was nearly 3 a.m., and he watched as the couple got out of the car and strolled through the park. Violante pushed his date on a playground swing, then kissed her for a moment. Before long, however, Stacy Moskowitz spied Berkowitz watching from the edge of the park. When she caught him looking over a second time, she grew nervous and asked Violante to take her back to the car. To get there the couple had to walk right past Berkowitz, and Violante got a good look at his face.

Had the couple driven off right away, the night might have ended very differently. Unfortunately, they lingered a few minutes in the car—just long enough for Berkowitz to sneak up behind them and open fire.

Inside, Violante recalled later, he thought he heard a humming sound. Then nothing. He'd been shot twice in the face; his right eye was shattered and his left eye severely damaged. Suddenly, the young man was blind. His date slumped forward, struck once in the head. Violante screamed for help and pounded on the horn before staggering out of the car and collapsing.

Son of Sam had struck again, but this time there was a witness: Tommy Zaino had seen it all. When the shooting started he'd pushed his date down on the floor of the car and roared away to the nearby 62nd Precinct. Within minutes there were nearly a dozen police cars at the

The playground adjoining the lovers' lane where Stacy Moskowitz and Robert Violante were shot had shadows that hid the killer while he stalked his victims. Police recognized the work of Son of Sam when they discovered a .44-caliber bullet in Violante's car *(left)*.

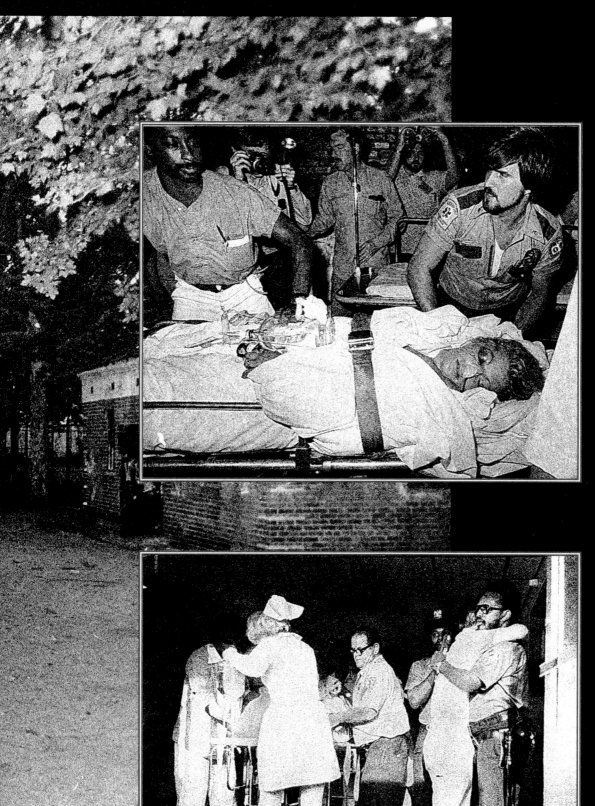

Stacy Moskowitz was still alive when she was placed on a stretcher for transport to Kings County Hospital. Struck twice in the head, she died of her injuries 38 hours later.

Doctors and nurses fight to save Robert Violante's life while his father is consoled by a police officer. David Berkowitz's bullets shattered Violante's right eye and also left him partially blind in the left eye.

Key witness Cacilia Davis walks her dog, Snowball,
in the Bensonhurst section of Brooklyn. Davis
was doing exactly this on July 30, 1977, when she
encountered David Berkowitz on the prowl. Her
recollections provided the crucial lead that helped
police crack the Son of Sam case.

scene. When officers found a large bullet embedded in the steering wheel hub of Violante's car, they knew it was the work of Son of Sam.

Berkowitz, meantime, had loped across the park, exited through a hole in the fence, and made his way back to his car. He waited for a few minutes, then drove slowly away. Instead of going home across one of the city's bridges, however, he bought a paper at an all-night newsstand and settled in a park less than a mile from the scene of the shooting. He sat on a bench and waited for the sun to rise. At 8 a.m. he returned to his car and drove back to Yonkers, passing through Manhattan on the way. By spending the night in Brooklyn, he'd avoided an intensive police watch on the bridges leaving the borough.

About 38 hours after she was shot, Stacy Moskowitz died. New York City was in pandemonium.

However, the tide of luck that had let David Berkowitz elude police had already begun to turn. Investigators had one eyewitness, and although they did not know it yet, another important witness was about to turn up. Cacilia Davis, 49, was a native of Austria and a resident of the neighborhood where Violante and Moskowitz were shot. She'd been walking her dog late on the night of the shooting and had noticed a man trying to hide behind a tree. He'd ambled in her direction, and she remembered his peculiar smile. She also remembered thinking that he may have been concealing something in his hand. Berkowitz had walked to within five feet of Davis, then turned abruptly into an opening between two buildings that led into the park. A few minutes later, Davis had heard shots, and realized with horror that she'd seen the killer. The realization filled her with dread, and she kept her knowledge to herself for three days. Finally, however, she overcame her fear and went to the police.

Detectives were fairly sure that Davis had seen Son of Sam. But

they did have some doubts, since her description of the killer's clothing did not quite match that of Tommy Zaino. Had she, in fact, been on the street at the right time? They pressed Davis for more details, and she came up with a vital scrap of information: She remembered seeing police handing out parking tickets in the neighborhood.

The detectives were dumbfounded: They'd done a routine check for summonses just after the shooting, and records showed that there'd been no tickets issued in that neighborhood that night. When the homicide detectives had a second look, they still came up empty-handed. But on August 5, five days after the shooting, they ordered an all-out search of the 62nd Precinct, home base to any patrol cars that might have wandered into the neighborhood in question. Sure enough, in a locked storage room, five more parking tickets were discovered. When they were run through a computer, the tickets revealed that a summons had been left on a Ford Galaxie sedan registered to one David Berkowitz of Yonkers.

The next day, August 6, Yonkers patrolmen Tom Chamberlain and Edward Wissner fielded a report of suspected arson at 35 Pine Street. They drove to the apartment house and met a tall, stocky man who identified himself as Craig Glassman. Someone had set a garbage fire outside Glassman's door, and when he rushed to extinguish it he discovered bullets among the smoldering refuse. He was convinced that the fire had been started by the same person who'd been sending him crazy-sounding letters. This last bit of information piqued the curiosity of Chamberlain and another cop, Peter Intervallo, who'd helped conduct interviews with Sam Carr and Jack Cassara. The two of them were already suspicious of David Berkowitz. They read Glassman's letters, and the language persuaded them that the messages had come from the same writer who'd contacted Carr and Cassara. The policemen began taking more seriously their gut feeling that the writer may also have authored the famous Son of Sam letters.

While all this was going on, David Berkowitz was making his excursion to Southampton, bent on mass murder. Sam Carr, meanwhile, was driving into New York City, hoping desperately to convince someone connected with Task Force Omega that the man who'd been harassing him was also their man.

It took the Omega detectives until Tuesday, August 9, to winnow through the mess with the lost parking tickets and come up with Berkowitz's name. Finally, with the name in hand, New York detective James Justus called the Yonkers police department. And, as fate would have it, the dispatcher who took the call was Sam Carr's daughter Wheat. At the mention of David Berkowitz's name she launched into a tirade about all her father's misadventures with the man. A few hours later, New York was in touch with the officers in Yonkers who were investigating the Carr and Glassman harassment cases. Excitement began to ripple through Task Force Omega; it seemed that a break in the case might be near.

On Wednesday, August 10, Berkowitz slept until 1 p.m. —getting plenty of rest for the long and bloody night he had planned. When he finally arose and dressed, he stashed most of his arsenal in the backseat of his car, then went back to his apartment and spent the better part of the afternoon loading and reloading his .44.

Unbeknown to him, detectives from the 10th Homicide Zone in Brooklyn by now had his car and apartment under surveillance. They'd seen the bag of weapons on the backseat of the Ford and were awaiting a search warrant to move on the apartment. A flood of New York City police headed north to Yonkers, and many officers were on the scene by early evening. While they waited, Craig Glassman walked out of 35 Pine Street and peered into Berkowitz's car. He was instantly surrounded and searched, but when he identified himself as a deputy sheriff he was invited to join in the arrest.

A little before 10 p.m. a heavyset figure walked out of the apartment building and slid into the driver's seat of the Galaxie. Detectives Bill Gardella and John Falotico were the first to approach him. Pointing his gun through the partially open passenger-side window, Gardella shouted: "Police! Don't move! Freeze!" Berkowitz slowly turned his head and smiled his Mona Lisa smile. Falotico opened the door on the driver's side. Berkowitz stepped out of the car, and Falotico handcuffed him.

"Well, you got me," said Son of Sam, and mumbled something else that was unintelligible.

Berkowitz was booked and fingerprinted at Yonkers police headquarters. Photographs of the killer were soon smiling shyly from newspapers everywhere. He looked so harmless, yet investigators had cause to believe that in catching him they'd averted a lot of bloodletting. There was, of course, the deadly array of firepower in his car. And, in the the killer's apartment, police found maps of Connecticut, New York, and New Jersey, marked and annotated in such a way that investigators took them as evidence that Berkowitz was planning to extend his killing grounds.

The day after his arrest Berkowitz was remanded to Kings County Hospital for psychiatric observation, and a deep controversy began to unfold. Based on a series of examinations, a team of three psychiatrists declared that the killer was "an incapacitated person," insane under the legal definition and therefore unable to stand trial. His lawyers mirrored this finding in their plea: not guilty, by reason of insanity. The prosecuting district attorney, however, moved immediately to have this judgment set aside, and the court appointed a special psychiatrist to act for the prosecution. Dr. David Abrahamsen conducted his own tests and found that "while the defendant shows paranoid traits, they do not interfere with his fitness to stand trial."

At a mental competency hearing before Brooklyn Supreme Court Justice Joseph Corso, Berkowitz was brought into court. His behavior certainly seemed mad. Pulling away from his guards, he assumed his familiar shooting stance and pretended to hold a pistol in his hands. Then he began to chant: "Stacy was a whore, Stacy was a whore." The family of Stacy Moskowitz, present in the courtroom, dissolved into sobs. But the mother of the slain woman was overcome with rage and shouted out: "You're an animal."

Yet, in the end, Berkowitz was declared sane, and his lawyers immediately changed his plea to guilty. On June 12, 1978, he was sentenced to six consecutive terms of 25 years to life—one for each of the six murders. He began serving this sentence at New York's grim Attica Prison.

In February 1979 Berkowitz called a press conference at Attica. He said that he wanted to let people know that his stories about demons were all a fabrication. He described

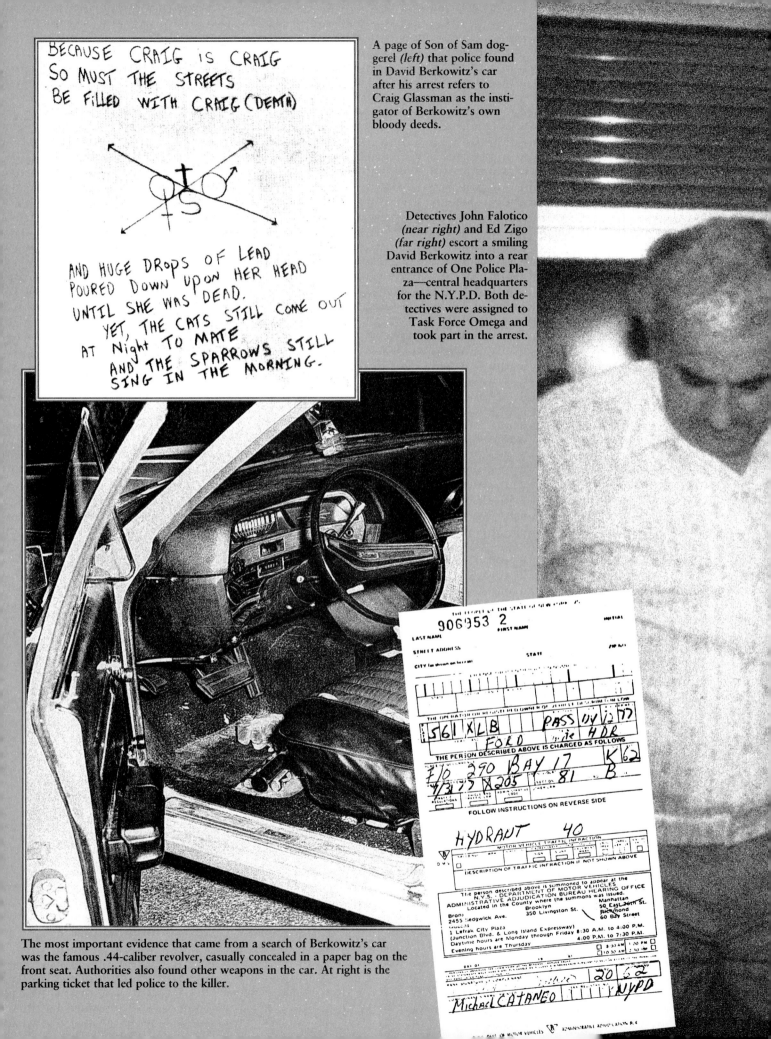

BECAUSE CRAIG IS CRAIG
SO MUST THE STREETS
BE FILLED WITH CRAIG (DEATH)

AND HUGE DROPS OF LEAD
POURED DOWN UPON HER HEAD
UNTIL SHE WAS DEAD.
YET, THE CATS STILL COME OUT
AT NIGHT TO MATE
AND THE SPARROWS STILL
SING IN THE MORNING.

A page of Son of Sam dog-gerel *(left)* that police found in David Berkowitz's car after his arrest refers to Craig Glassman as the insti-gator of Berkowitz's own bloody deeds.

Detectives John Falotico *(near right)* and Ed Zigo *(far right)* escort a smiling David Berkowitz into a rear entrance of One Police Pla-za—central headquarters for the N.Y.P.D. Both de-tectives were assigned to Task Force Omega and took part in the arrest.

The most important evidence that came from a search of Berkowitz's car was the famous .44-caliber revolver, casually concealed in a paper bag on the front seat. Authorities also found other weapons in the car. At right is the parking ticket that led police to the killer.

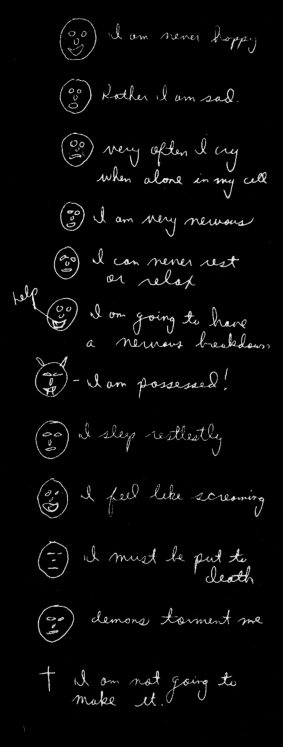

I am never happy

Rather I am sad.

very often I cry
when alone in my cell

I am very nervous

I can never rest
or relax

help

I am going to have
a nervous breakdown

- I am possessed!

I sleep restlessly

I feel like screaming

I must be put to
death

demons torment me

† I am not going to
make it.

Berkowitz doodled these faces and their accompanying notes of sad self-reflection after wounding Judy Placido and Sal Lupo in late June 1977. He later explained that the "cell" mentioned in the third note referred to the prison of his own mind.

them as lies "invented by me in my own mind to condone what I was doing." He was trying, he said, to forestall publication of a book on his life and murders, and a possible movie on the same subject. His fear was that the revelations would inspire someone to "get even with me and try to hurt one of my family."

Reporters present at the press conference described him as lucid and calm. The urge to kill, Berkowitz claimed, had left him entirely. "Whatever it was has just worked out of me — I've mellowed," he told the press. "I don't know what it is that started it and I don't know what it is that caused me to lose interest. I don't know."

Son of Sam went on to say that he fully expected to die in prison and that he was still very much a loner. He ate alone, had little to say to other prisoners, and received very few visitors. He missed his family, he said. And he missed driving his car.

Not many psychiatrists place a lot of stock in the prisoner's contention that he didn't really suffer from delusions. They point, for one thing, to the elaborate drawings and graffiti scrawled on the walls of his apartment, which would seem to indicate that the demons were — for him — more than just a convenient ruse. Psychiatrists also hark back to an apparent suicide attempt as evidence of a profoundly unstable mental condition. During a competency hearing, Berkowitz had to be physically restrained from flinging himself out an upstairs window. He said at the time that angels would catch him if God meant for him to be saved.

Among the psychiatrists who observed the prisoner in the days leading up to his trial were Daniel Schwartz and Richard Weidenbacher. They suggest other factors that may have led to his denial of the demons. They recall, for instance, that Berkowitz came for a time under the influence of a Baptist lay minister who was allowed to spend considerable time with him in the hopes of drawing him out of a severe depression. The minister, Schwartz and Weidenbacher contend, convinced Berkowitz that the only way to attain divine forgiveness was to accept full responsibility for his crimes. They think that the killer, for the sake of his soul, renounced his demonic world, even though it still may have been quite real for him.

Since the time of the Attica press conference Berkowitz has been moved to the Sullivan Correctional Facility in Fallsburg, New York. Throughout his incarceration he has been a model prisoner. ◆

I am so glad I've been apprehended but I
wish that someone would help me.

final desperation

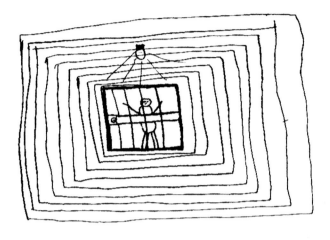

I am not well Not at all

During evaluation at Kings County Hospital after his arrest Berkowitz drew
himself in a real cell of sorts. He believed the walls were closing in on him.

Acknowledgments

The editors thank the following individuals and institutions for their valuable assistance in the preparation of this volume:

Joe Aloi, Tallahassee, Florida; Craig Bowley, New York, New York; Louise Bundy, Tacoma, Washington; Professor James Coleman, Duke University School of Law, Durham, North Carolina; Sergeant Ray Crew, Tallahassee Police Department, Tallahassee, Florida; Steve Frances, Lisle, Illinois; John Wayne Gacy, Jr., Menard, Illinois; Elizabeth Hager, Taylorville, Illinois; Special Agent William Hagmaier, Federal Bureau of Investigation, Behavorial Science Unit, Quantico, Virginia; Eric Helgesen, Photography Supervisor, Des Plaines Police Department, Des Plaines, Illinois; Lawrence Klausner, Roslyn, New York; Joseph Kozenczak, Director, International Group Investigative Services, Oak Brook, Illinois; Richard Larsen, Seattle, Washington; Polly Nelson, Washington, D.C.; Dr. Art Norman, Portland, Oregon; Lynn Pulford, *Glenwood Springs Post,* Glenwood Springs, Colorado; Robert K. Ressler, Spotsylvania, Virginia; Ann Rule, Seattle, Washington; Dr. Daniel Schwartz, Director of Forensic Psychiatry, Kings County Hospital, Brooklyn, New York; Jerry Thompson, Sandy, Utah; Dennis Webb, *Glenwood Springs Post,* Glenwood Springs, Colorado; Dr. Richard Weidenbacher, Department of Forensic Psychiatry, Kings County Hospital, Brooklyn, New York.

Bibliography

Books:

Abrahamsen, David, *Confessions of Son of Sam.* New York: Columbia University Press, 1985.

Bataille, Georges, *The Trial of Gilles de Rais.* Transl. by Richard Robinson. Los Angeles: AMOK, 1991.

Begg, Paul, Martin Fido, and Keith Skinner, *The Jack the Ripper A to Z.* London: Headline Book, 1991.

Benedetti, Jean, *Gilles de Rais.* New York: Stein and Day, 1972.

Bullock, Elizabeth, et al., *Chicago Murders.* Ed. by Sewell Peaslee Wright. New York: Duell, Sloan and Pearce, 1945.

Cahill, Tim, *Buried Dreams: Inside the Mind of a Serial Killer.* New York: Bantam Books, 1989.

Cameron, Deborah, and Elizabeth Frazer, *The Lust to Kill.* New York: New York University Press, 1987.

Crimes and Punishments, by the Editors of Time-Life Books (Library of Curious and Unusual Facts). Alexandria, Virginia: Time-Life Books, 1991.

Crockett, Art, ed., *Serial Murderers.* New York: Windsor, 1991.

DeFord, Miriam Allen, *Murderers Sane & Mad: Case Histories in the Motivation and Rationale of Murder.* London: Abelard-Schuman, 1965.

Dickson, Grierson, *Murder by Numbers.* London: Robert Hale, 1958.

Di Maio, Dominick J., and Vincent J. M. Di Maio, *Forensic Pathology.* New York: Elsevier, 1989.

Frank, Gerold, *The Boston Strangler.* New York: New American Library, 1966.

Franke, David, *The Torture Doctor.* New York: Hawthorn Books, 1975.

Freeman, Lucy, *"Before I Kill More . . . ."* New York: Crown, 1955.

Gacy, John Wayne:
A Question of Doubt: The John Wayne Gacy Story. New York: Craig Bowley Consultants, 1991. Unpublished manuscript.
They Call Him Mr. Gacy: Selected Correspondence of John Wayne Gacy. Brighton, Colorado: McClelland Associates, 1989.

Gaute, J. H. H., and Robin Odell, *The New Murderers' Who's Who.* New York: International Polygonics, 1989.

Gollmar, Robert H., *Edward Gein.* New York: Windsor, 1990.

Gribble, Leonard, *They Had a Way with Women.* New York: Roy, 1967.

Holmes, Ronald M., and James De Burger, *Serial Murder.* Newbury Park, California: Sage, 1988.

Honeycombe, Gordon, *The Murders of the Black Museum: 1870-1970.* London: Hutchinson, 1982.

Jaffe, Frederick A., *A Guide to Pathological Evidence: For Lawyers and Police Officers.* Toronto: Carswell, 1983.

Kendall, Elizabeth, *The Phantom Prince: My Life with Ted Bundy.* Seattle, Washington: Madrona, 1981.

Klausner, Lawrence D., *Son of Sam: Based on the Authorized Transcription of the Tapes, Official Documents and Diaries of David Berkowitz.* New York: McGraw-Hill, 1981.

Kolarik, Gera-Lind, with Wayne Klatt, *Freed to Kill: The True Story of Serial Murderer Larry Eyler.* New York: Avon Books, 1992.

Kozenczak, Joseph, and Karen Henrikson, *A Passing Acquaintance.* New York: Carlton Press, 1992.

Larsen, Richard W., *Bundy: The Deliberate Stranger.* Englewood Cliffs, New Jersey: Prentice-Hall, 1980.

Levin, Jack, and James Alan Fox, *Mass Murder: America's Growing Menace.* New York: Plenum, 1988.

Leyton, Elliott, *Hunting Humans: Inside the Minds of Mass Murderers.* New York: Pocket Books, 1986.

Linedecker, Clifford L.:
The Man Who Killed Boys. New York: St. Martin's Press, 1980.
Night Stalker: A Shocking Story of Satanism, Sex and Serial Murders. New York: St. Martin's Press, 1991.

Lisners, John, *House of Horrors.* London: Corgi Books, 1983.

McConnell, Brian, and Douglas Bence, *The Nilsen File.* London: Futura, 1983.

Mant, A. Keith, ed., *Taylor's Principles and Practice of Medical Jurisprudence.* London: Churchill Livingstone, 1984.

Martinez, Lionel, *Murder in North America*. Secaucus, New Jersey: Wellfleet Press, 1991.

Masters, Brian, *Killing for Company: The Case of Dennis Nilsen*. London: Hodder and Stoughton, 1991.

Michaud, Stephen G., and Hugh Aynesworth:

The Only Living Witness. New York: Penguin Books, 1989.

Ted Bundy: Conversations with a Killer. New York: New American Library, 1989.

Olsen, Jack, *The Man with the Candy: The Story of the Houston Mass Murders*. New York: Simon and Schuster, 1974.

Rignall, Jeff, and Ron Wilder, *29 Below*. Chicago: Wellington Press, 1979.

Rule, Ann, *The Stranger beside Me*. New York: Penguin Books, 1989.

Rule, Ann (writing as Andy Stack), *Lust Killer*. New York: New American Library, 1988.

Rumbelow, Donald, *Jack the Ripper: The Complete Casebook*. Chicago: Contemporary Books, 1975.

Schechter, Harold, *Deranged: The Shocking True Story of America's Most Fiendish Killer!* New York: Pocket Books, 1990.

Sullivan, Terry, and Peter T. Maiken, *Killer Clown*. New York: Grosset & Dunlap, 1983.

Terry, Maury, *The Ultimate Evil: An Investigation into a Dangerous Satanic Cult*. New York: Bantam Books, 1989.

Winn, Steven, and David Merrill, *Ted Bundy: The Killer Next Door*. New York: Bantam Books, 1980.

Periodicals:

Ackland, Len, "Suspect Was 'Likeable, Charming,' Ex-Wife Says." *Chicago Tribune*, December 23, 1978.

Axthelm, Pete, and Michael Ryan, "A Condemned Man's Last Request." *People*, February 6, 1989.

"Bill and George." *Time*, July 29, 1946.

Bishop, Katherine, "Corona Convicted Again in 25 Farm Worker Slayings."

The New York Times, September 24, 1982.

"Boston Strangler Slain in Jail." *New York Post*, November 26, 1973.

"Budd Girl's Body Found; Killed by Painter in 1928." *The New York Times*, December 14, 1934.

Buder, Leonard, "Suspected .44 Killer's Father Terms Himself a Victim, Too." *The New York Times*, August 14, 1977.

"Bundy's Final Warning: Interview Became a Condemnation of Pornography." *The Seattle Times*, January 25, 1989.

"The Case against Corona." *Newsweek*, September 25, 1972.

"The Case of William Heirens." *Life*, July 29, 1946.

Chambers, Marcia, "Berkowitz Charged in Queens Murders." *The New York Times*, August 24, 1977.

"Claim That Bundy Committed Philadelphia Murders Is Disputed." *Philadelphia Inquirer*, January 27, 1989.

"Corona in Court." *Newsweek*, June 14, 1971.

"Death in the Orchards." *Time*, June 14, 1971.

Duncan, Don, "Bundy." *The Seattle Times*, January 25, 1989.

Duncliffe, Bill, "Boston Strangler: 'I Want to Know Why I Did It.'" *New York World Journal Tribune*, January 11, 1967.

Elmer-DeWitt, Philip, "Taking a Byte Out of Crime." *Time*, October 14, 1985.

Elson, Mary, "Suspect's Former Employes Tell of Sexual Advances." *Chicago Tribune*, December 23, 1978.

"Ex-Worker at Children's Home Is a Suspect in 24 Slayings." New York *Daily News*, August 26, 1984.

Fenton, John H.:

"'Boston Strangler' Flees Mental Institution." *The New York Times*, February 25, 1967.

"'Strangler' Is Seized Near Boston." *The New York Times*, February 26, 1967.

Fitzpatrick, Tom:

"Backyard Parties and 'Rotten

Things.'" *Chicago Sun-Times*, December 31, 1978.

"'I Feel This Is All a Bad Dream': Neighbor." *Chicago Sun-Times*, December 28, 1978.

"A Five-Time Murderer Prowls New York By Night, and Vows He Will Kill Again." *People*, June 20, 1977.

Garelik, Glenn, and Gina Maranto, "Multiple Murderers." *Discover*, July 1984.

Gerberth, Vernon J., "The Serial Killer and the Revelations of Ted Bundy." *Law and Order*, May 1990.

Givens, Ron, and Kristen Christopher, "The Night Stalker of L.A." *Newsweek*, August 26, 1985.

Gorman, John, "Gacy Seized Year Ago but Freed, Records Show." *Chicago Tribune*, January 7, 1979.

Gorman, John, and Jean Zyda, "Murder Suspect's '2 Faces' Revealed." *Chicago Tribune*, December 23, 1978.

"Grand Jury Gets Budd Kidnap Case." *The New York Times*, December 18, 1934.

"Grim Search for London Murder Victims." *The New York Times*, February 12, 1983.

"Guilty Times 25." *Time*, January 29, 1973.

"Heirens Confesses in No-Chair Deal." *The New York Times*, August 7, 1946.

"Heirens Gets Life for Three Killings." *The New York Times*, September 6, 1946.

"Heirens Lawyers Urge Statement." *The New York Times*, July 27, 1946.

"Holmes and His Victims." *The New York Times*, July 27, 1895.

"Holmes Cool to the End." *The New York Times*, May 8, 1896.

"Holmes His Own Lawyer." *The New York Times*, October 29, 1895.

"Holmes in a Ton of Cement." *The New York Times*, May 9, 1896.

"Holmes Is Found Guilty." *The New York Times*, November 3, 1895.

"It's God's Will." *Time*, March 24, 1980.

Jaediker, Kermit, "His Hobby Was

Murder." *The New York Sunday News,* June 28, 1970.

"Joe D. Ball Kills Self While He Is Quizzed This Morning." *San Antonio Light,* September 25, 1938.

Katz, Leonard, "Boston Strangler Escapes." *New York Post,* February 24, 1967.

Kelly, Susan, "The Untold Story behind the Boston Strangler." *Boston,* April 1992.

Kneeland, Douglas E.:
"For Yuba City Suspect, Early Prosperity Ended in an Unsuccessful Plea for Welfare." *The New York Times,* June 16, 1971.
"Parents of Missing Youths Hope, Fear—and Wait." *The New York Times,* December 31, 1978.
"Suspect in Mass Deaths Is Puzzle to All." *The New York Times,* January 10, 1979.

Kotulak, Ronald, and William Juneau, "Plan Special Search Technique for Victims' Bones." *Chicago Tribune,* December 24, 1978.

Kozenczak, Joseph R., and Karen M. Henrikson, "Still Beyond Belief." *Policing,* summer 1989.

Larsen, Richard, "Bob Keppel: Quiet, Restrained, Matter-of-Fact and Smart." *The Seattle Times,* January 29, 1989.

McCall, Cheryl:
"The Enigma of Ted Bundy: Did He Kill 18 Women? Or Has He Been Framed?" *People,* January 7, 1980.
"Ted Bundy's Crime and Punishment." *The Seattle Times,* January 29, 1989.

Macdonald, Katharine, "Citizens Clobber 'Stalker' Suspect." *The Washington Post,* September 1, 1985.

McFadden, Robert D., "Profiles of Psychopath's Victims and Circumstances of Shootings." *The New York Times,* June 28, 1977.

MacPherson, Myra:
"Bundy and the Unexpiated Horror." *The Washington Post,* January 23, 1989.
"The Roots of Evil." *Vanity Fair,* May 1989.

"Man Linked to Deaths of 19 in Middle West." *The New York Times,* October 31, 1983.

Marja, Fern, "Lacked an Honest Sex Education." *New York Post,* September 9, 1946.

"Massacre at Yuba City." *Newsweek,* June 7, 1971.

Masters, Brian, "Dahmer's Inferno: What Are the Secret Torments of Jeffrey Dahmer?" *Vanity Fair,* November 1991.

Meislin, Richard J., "Berkowitz Says That He Faked Tales of Demons." *The New York Times,* February 23, 1979.

"Merola Says Berkowitz's Diaries May Link Slayer to 2,000 Fires." *The New York Times,* May 9, 1978.

Montgomery, Paul:
"Henley Sits Unmoved as Texas Outlines Its Case." *The New York Times,* July 10, 1974.
"Houston Suspect Heard on Killing." *The New York Times,* January 25, 1974.
"Trial in Torture-Murder Ring Is Lagging." *The New York Times,* January 28, 1974.

Mount, Charles, and Ronald Koziol, "Contractor Is Charged in Murder." *Chicago Tribune,* December 23, 1978.

"A Murderer's Deadly Deal." *Newsweek,* January 14, 1991.

Mustain, Gene, "Neighborhood Bar—and Gay Haunts." *Chicago Sun-Times,* December 31, 1978.

"The Muswell Hill Murders." *Murder Casebook* (London), Vol. 1, Part 2.

"Nilsen on Nilsen: The Tortured Words and Thoughts of a Mass Murderer." *The Sunday Times* (London), November 6, 1983.

"The Night Stalker." *Murder Casebook* (London), Vol. 7, Part 101.

Ogintz, Eileen, and David Axelrod, "John Gacy's Neighborhood: 'It Will Never Be the Same.' " *Chicago Sun-Times,* January 7, 1979.

"Orgy of Killings." *Murder Casebook* (London), Vol. 4, Part 54.

Petacque, Art, and Hugh Hough, "Rignall Convinced Gacy Had a Partner."

Chicago Sun-Times, December 31, 1978.

"The Phantom Strangler." *Time,* March 22, 1963.

"Pitezel Probably Alive." *The New York Times,* November 22, 1894.

"The Plainfield Butcher." *Murder Casebook* (London), Vol. 2, Part 24.

Plummer, William, "Night Stalker." *People,* September 16, 1985.

"Police Get a 2d Note Signed By 'Son of Sam' in .44-Caliber Killings." *The New York Times,* June 5, 1977.

Racktenwald, William, and Eileen Ogintz, "Youth, 19, Reveals That Gacy Twice Tried to Seduce Him." *Chicago Tribune,* December 27, 1979.

Seigel, Max H.:
"Berkowitz Asserts Demons Ruled Him." *The New York Times,* October 21, 1977.
"Berkowitz Given 25 Years to Life in Each of 6 'Son of Sam' Slayings." *The New York Times,* June 13, 1978.
"Berkowitz Is Ruled Fit for Trial; Declares He'll Have 'a Lot to Say.' " *The New York Times,* October 22, 1977.
"Upstate Judge Orders Berkowitz Committed to Psychiatric Center." *The New York Times,* April 7, 1978.

Smothers, Ronald:
"Neighbor Who Got Threat Letters Was at Arrest." *The New York Times,* August 12, 1977.
"Notoriety Haunts Real-Life 'Sam.' " *The New York Times,* September 21, 1977.

"The Son of Sam Killings." *Murder Casebook* (London), Vol. 1, Part 12.

Stengel, Richard, "Stalking the Serial Killer." *Time,* September 9, 1985.

Sterba, James P., "Murder Charges Are Filed against Two Teen-age Boys in Houston Case." *The New York Times,* August 12, 1973.

"Suicide of Elmendorf Man Uncovers Murder in Mass Death Inquiry." *San Antonio Light,* September 25, 1938.

"Suspect in 'Son of Sam' Murders Arrested in Yonkers; Police Say .44-Caliber Weapon Is Recovered." *The New York Times,* August 11, 1977.

"Texan Said to Admit Role in 25 Killings." *The New York Times,* August 10, 1973.

Turner, Wallace:
"Corona, Mass Murderer, Is Stabbed 32 Times in California Prison." *The New York Times,* December 3, 1973.
"Corona Facing Retrial in Farmworker Deaths." *The New York Times,* February 21, 1982.
"250 Policemen Volunteer to Hunt in Spare Time for 'Son of Sam.' " *The New York Times,* August 4, 1977.
"Typical Northwest Home Conceals 'House of Horrors.' " *Chicago Tribune,* December 24, 1978.

Underwood, Nora, with Suzanne Goldenberg, "A Grisly Allure." *Maclean's,* September 19, 1988.

Van Gelder, Lawrence, "Notes on People." *The New York Times,* February 8, 1972.

"Victim in California Case Sobs in Recalling Ordeal." *The New York Times,* April 15, 1986.
"When Did the Trail of Death Start?" *The Seattle Times,* January 24, 1989.

White, David F.:
"Ex-Landlady Asserts She Knew It Was He." *The New York Times,* August 13, 1977.
" 'Gut Feeling' Confirmed for Real-Life Sam." *The New York Times,* August 12, 1977.

Win, Steven, and David Merrill, "Ted Bundy: The Whole Story." Parts 1-5. *The Weekly* (Seattle), September 6-October 10, 1978.

Other Sources:

Carol DaRonch interview (transcript), *Geraldo,* September 9, 1988.
"Chronicle" (television program), February 27, 1992, WCVB TV, Boston, Massachusetts.

Cases argued and determined in the Supreme Court of Illinois. No. 53212. The People of the State of Illinois, Appellee, v. John Wayne Gacy, Appellant. June 6, 1984, September 28, 1984.

Dorothy Lewis, psychiatrist, New York University School of Medicine (testimony), United States District Court for the Middle District of Florida, Orlando Division, Theodore Bundy v. Louie L. Wainwright, Case #86-968-Civ-Or1-18, December 15, 1987.

Interviews with Ted Bundy, January 20-22, 1989 (transcript), Robert Keppel, Chief Investigator, Criminal Division, Office of Attorney General, Washington, D.C.

Index

188

Picture Credits

vate collection. **65:** Associated Press/Topham, Edenbridge, Kent, England. **67:** *The Chicago Tribune,* Chicago, Illinois. **68, 69:** Background, *The Chicago Tribune,* Chicago, Illinois, inset, © Craig Bowley Incorporated. **70, 71:** UPI/Bettmann, New York. **72:** Gamma/Frank Spooner Pictures, London. **73:** AP/Wide World Photos, New York. **74:** Background, Des Plaines Police Department, Des Plaines, Illinois, inset, AP/Wide World Photos, New York. **76:** Private collection. **78, 79:** UPI/Bettmann, New York. **80, 81:** © Craig Bowley Incorporated; private collection (3). **82, 83:** Private collection (2)—Joseph Kozenczak (2). **84:** UPI/Bettmann, New York. **87:** © Craig Bowley Incorporated. **88-91:** AP/Wide World Photos, New York. **92:** Giraudon, Paris. **93:** London Borough of Tower Hamlets Local History Library and Archives, London. **94, 95:** UPI/Bettmann, New York. **96:** Ullstein Bilderdienst, Berlin. **97:** Suddeutscher Verlag Bilderdienst, Munich. **98, 99:** UPI/Bettmann Newsphotos, New York. **100, 101:** The Institute of Texan Cultures, The San Antonio Light Collection, San Antonio, Texas, retouched by Time-Life Books. **102:** Background, AP/Wide World Photos, New York, insets, The Bettmann Archive, New York (2). **103:** AP/Wide World Photos, New York. **104, 105:** Frank Scherschel for LIFE (2)—AP/Wide World Photos, New York. **106:** Francis Miller for LIFE. **107:** UPI/Bettmann Newsphotos, New York. **108:** AP/Wide World Photos, New York. **109:** Gerry Lewin, Salem, Oregon; private collection. **110:** AP/Wide World Photos, New York. **111:** Houston *Chronicle,* Houston, Texas—UPI/Bettmann, New York. **112:** UPI/Bettmann, New York. **113:** AP/Wide World Photos, New York. **114, 115:** AP/Wide World Photos, New York. **116:** Express Newspapers, London. **118:** Express Newspapers, London—Syndication International, London. **120, 121:** Topham Picture Source, Edenbridge, Kent. **122:** © Mrs. Elizabeth Scott. **123:** Press Association, London. **124, 125:** Background, Ronnie Sinclair/Marshall Cavendish, London, insets, Marshall Cavendish (2). **127:** © Mrs. Elizabeth Scott. **128:** Syndication International, London (2)—© Mrs. Elizabeth Scott. **129:** © Mrs. Elizabeth Scott. **131:** Press Association, London. **133:** Rex USA, New York—London News Service, London. **134, 135:** Press Association, London. **139:** Syndication International, London—Express Newspapers, London (2). **140, 141:** Black (Crime) Museum, London. **143:** Rex Features, London. **145:** Mail Newspapers/Solo Syndication, London. **146, 147:** Black (Crime) Museum, London, except bottom left, Press Association, London. **148, 149:** Press Association, London. **150:** Syndication International, London. **151:** Black (Crime) Museum, London. **152:** UPI/Bettmann, New York. **154:** From *Son of Sam* by Lawrence D. Klausner, McGraw-Hill Book Company, New York, 1981. **156-159:** Courtesy Time Inc. Magazines Picture Collection. **161:** UPI/Bettmann, New York. **164:** From *The Ultimate Evil* by Maury Terry, Bantam Books, New York, 1987—copied by Henry Groskinsky for Time-Life Books. **166:** Copied by Henry Groskinsky for Time-Life Books. **167:** From *Son of Sam* by Lawrence D. Klausner, McGraw-Hill Book Company, New York, 1981. **168:** AP/Wide World Photos, New York. **169, 170:** The *New York Post,* New York. **171:** Pomerantz/The *New York Post,* courtesy Time Inc. Magazines Picture Collection. **172:** The *Daily News,* New York. **174:** UPI/Bettmann, New York; copied by Henry Groskinsky for Time-Life Books. **176, 177:** Background and bottom left, copied by Henry Groskinsky for Time-Life Books; AP/Wide World Photos, New York—The *New York Post,* New York. **178:** AP/Wide World Photos, New York. **180, 181:** UPI/Bettmann, New York—copied by Henry Groskinsky for Time-Life Books; AP/Wide World Photos, New York; UPI/Bettmann, New York. **182, 183:** From *Son of Sam* by Lawrence D. Klausner, McGraw-Hill Book Company, New York, 1981.

Time-Life Books is a division of Time Life Inc.,
a wholly owned subsidiary of
THE TIME INC. BOOK COMPANY

TIME-LIFE BOOKS

PRESIDENT: Mary N. Davis

MANAGING EDITOR: Thomas H. Flaherty
Director of Editorial Resources: Elise D. Ritter-
Clough
Executive Art Director: Ellen Robling
Director of Photography and Research: John Con-
rad Weiser
Editorial Board: Dale M. Brown, Janet Cave, Ro-
berta Conlan, Laura Foreman, Jim Hicks, Blaine
Marshall, Rita Thievon Mullin, Henry Woodhead
*Assistant Director of Editorial Resources/Training
Manager:* Norma E. Shaw

PUBLISHER: Robert H. Smith

Associate Publisher: Sandra Lafe Smith
Editorial Director: Russell B. Adams, Jr.
Marketing Director: Anne C. Everhart
Director of Production Services: Robert N. Carr
Production Manager: Prudence G. Harris
Supervisor of Quality Control: James King

Editorial Operations
Production: Celia Beattie
Library: Louise D. Forstall
Computer Composition: Deborah G. Tait
(Manager), Monika D. Thayer, Janet Barnes
Syring, Lillian Daniels
Interactive Media Specialist: Patti H. Cass

Library of Congress Cataloging in Publication Data
Serial Killers/by the editors of Time-Life Books.
p.   cm. — (True Crime)
Includes bibliographical references and index.
ISBN 0-7835-0000-9
1. Serial murders--Case studies.
I. Time-Life Books.   II. Series.
HV6515.S47 1992
364.1'523—dc20   92-26522
                                        CIP
ISBN 0-7835-0001-7 (lib. bdg.)

TRUE CRIME

SERIES EDITOR: Laura Foreman
Series Administrator: Jane A. Martin
Art Director: Christopher Register
Picture Editor: Jane Jordan

Editorial Staff for *Serial Killers*
Text Editors: Robert A. Doyle (principal), Janet Cave
Associate Editors/Research: Susan Arritt, Vicki War-
ren, Robert H. Wooldridge, Jr.
Assistant Editor/Research: Jennifer L. Pearce
Assistant Art Director: Brook Mowrey
Copy Coordinator: Elizabeth Graham
Picture Coordinator: Jennifer Iker
Editorial Assistant: Donna Fountain

Special Contributors: Jim Halpin, Patricia A. Pa-
terno, Robert Speziale (research); Kenneth C. Dan-
forth, Margery A. duMond, Juli Duncan, Anthony
K. Pordes, Duncan Spencer, George Russell, Daniel
Stashower (text); John Drummond (design); Mel
Ingber (index).

Correspondents: Elisabeth Kraemer-Singh (Bonn);
Christine Hinze (London); Christina Lieberman
(New York); Maria Vincenza Aloisi (Paris); Ann
Natanson (Rome). Valuable assistance was also pro-
vided by Sarah Moule (London); Elizabeth Brown,
Katheryn White (New York).

Consultants:
James Alan Fox, Ph.D., is professor and interim
dean of the College of Criminal Justice at North-
eastern University in Boston. A nationally recognized authority on multiple homicide, Dr. Fox has
written eight books, including *Mass Murder: America's Growing Menace; The Gainesville Student Murders;* and *Overkill.* He has also authored dozens of
articles, primarily on crime statistics and on mass
and serial murder. Dr. Fox consults frequently with
police investigators and attorneys on cases of multiple homicide.

Robert R. "Roy" Hazelwood of the Federal Bureau
of Investigation is a supervisory special agent assigned to the Behavioral Science Unit at the FBI
Academy, Quantico, Virginia. A veteran of 21 years
with the unit, Mr. Hazelwood holds a masters degree in counseling psychology and has completed
advance study in forensic medicine. He has co-
authored two books, *Practical Aspects of Rape Investigation* and *Autoerotic Fatalities,* and has published more than 30 articles dealing with violent
sexual crimes. Mr. Hazelwood has lectured to more
than 100,000 members of the law enforcement,
mental health, correctional, and academic communities in the United States, Canada, Europe, Asia, the
Caribbean, and Australia. He has consulted on more
than 3,000 criminal cases. Frequently called as an
expert witness in local, state, and federal courts,
Mr. Hazelwood has also testified before presidential
commissions and subcommittees of Congress.

Brian Masters is a distinguished British critic, jour-
nalist, and author. He has written 16 books, including the definitive study of London serial killer Dennis Nilsen, *Killing for Company,* from which
Chapter 3 of this book was adapted. Denoting
wide-ranging interests, Mr. Masters' other works
include the nonfiction book *The Swinging Sixties*
and several biographies, among them accounts of
the lives of 17th-century French dramatist Molière
and modern existentialists Jean-Paul Sartre and Albert Camus. Mr. Masters recently completed a book
about American serial slayer Jeffrey Dahmer.

Craig Bowley is a New York-based television pro-
ducer, theater consultant, and book editor. An expert on the John Wayne Gacy case, Mr. Bowley
produced in 1992 the first filmed interview with
Gacy, an interview conducted by retired FBI Special
Agent Robert K. Ressler. Mr. Bowley has published
two books on Gacy: *They Call Him Mr. Gacy* and
They Call Him Mr. Gacy II, both compilations of
John Gacy's correspondence from prison.

**TIME ®
LIFE
BOOKS**

*For information on and a full description of any of
the Time-Life Books series listed above, please call
1-800-621-7026 or write:*
Reader Information
Time-Life Customer Service
P.O. Box C-32068
Richmond, Virginia 23261-2068

This volume is one of a series that examines the
phenomenon of crime.